I0816843

INTERCULTURAL STUDIES
Schriftenreihe des Zentrums
für Interkulturelle Studien (ZIS)

Volume 8

Edited by
DILEK DIZDAR · ANTON ESCHER
ALFRED HORNUNG · DIETER LAMPING
Zentrum für Interkulturelle Studien (ZIS)
Interdisziplinäre Forschungsplattform
der Johannes Gutenberg-Universität Mainz

Developing Transnational American Studies

Edited by

NADJA GERNALZICK
HEIKE C. SPICKERMANN

For ALFRED HORNUNG
on his seventieth birthday

Universitätsverlag
WINTER
Heidelberg

Bibliografische Information der Deutschen Nationalbibliothek
Die Deutsche Nationalbibliothek verzeichnet diese Publikation in der Deutschen Nationalbibliografie; detaillierte bibliografische Daten sind im Internet über *http://dnb.d-nb.de* abrufbar.

UMSCHLAGBILD
© Siona Benjamin: *Finding Home No. 9* (1998)

ISBN 978-3-8253-6950-7

Imprimé en Allemagne · Printed in Germany
Umschlaggestaltung: Klaus Brecht GmbH, Heidelberg
Druck: Memminger MedienCentrum, 87700 Memmingen

Gedruckt auf umweltfreundlichem, chlorfrei gebleichtem und alterungsbeständigem Papier

Den Verlag erreichen Sie im Internet unter:
www.winter-verlag.de

It's important for us to pause for a moment
and make sure that we are talking with each other
in a way that heals, not a way that wounds.
Barack Obama

Dilek Dizdar, Anton Escher, and Dieter Lamping

Contents

Preface and Acknowledgements

Nadja Gernalzick and Heike C. Spickermann

In a world determined by global environmental phenomena and economic networks as well as by political interests and movements of continental or planetary scale, affecting the lives of people everywhere, Transnational American Studies have been developed by international and internationally minded scholars to address the need for knowledge and awareness across borders and across the limits of national politics and institutions. In a decisive change from the comparativist pattern of investigation between two or more assumed units, the transnational approach intends a further integration of cultural systems.

In response to the end of the Cold War and the fast pace of globalization since the 1990s as well as to a vision and critique of transatlanticism, transnationality and transnationalization have gained increased attention as topics within American Studies, propelled significantly by the discussion on transnational attentiveness rather than isolationist thinking after 9/11. Drawing on the paradigm shift produced by the work in Postcolonial Studies after World War II alongside that of decolonization, and marking the modifications made to the world system after the end of the Cold War, Transnational American Studies address hybridities, borderlands, contact zones and planetary thinking in ways that negotiate the change from a nineteenth-century, national-philological or regional-studies approach to a future of Transnational Studies in the United States, Transnational Studies in France, Transnational Studies in India, Transnational Studies in Polynesia, or Transnational Studies in China. Like the fluidities, relations, and processes considered to determine its agenda, Transnational American Studies itself is an evolving field, mobilized by its seemingly oxymoronic name. Conceptualizations of transition, for example by address to relationality as developed in Caribbean Studies or to world literature, are in dialogue with the vocabularies of transnationality. Transnational American Studies develop as much by creating agencies as by responding to determining forces.

In her 2004 Presidential Address to the American Studies Association, Shelley Fisher Fishkin influentially summarized and reviewed the agenda for the disciplinary emergence of Transnational American Studies. Alfred Hornung, together with colleagues from Europe and the United States, since its inception has supported the initiative by the American Studies Association to "extend[...] American Studies activities to the whole world, while, at the same time, inviting Americanists from all over to share in a transnational academic enterprise, seeing non-American colleagues as equal partners in the common research project" (Hornung 2011). With the exact intention of opening nationally bound perspectives, *The Journal of Transnational American Studies* was founded in 2008. Discussions of cosmopolitanism and its political and academic traditions in diverse languages, of citizenship and planetarity, of cultural and economic hegemony, of distribution of wealth worldwide and of the future role of comparative literature as well as of studies of world literature all were and are integral to the work undertaken in Transnational American Studies. With their transnational turn, the focus of American Studies has become resituated in increasingly international, global constellations of knowledge production and cultural transfer as well as in multi- and transnational discourses. With their productive, cooperative, and conciliatory program, transnational studies invite and require support.

This volume combines Transnational American Studies from diverse angles in the four general areas “Repositioning the American South”, “Life, Literature, Ecocriticism”, “Life Writing and Medicine” and “Critical Studies of the Nation”. Written by American Studies and Comparative Literature scholars, the contributions are not restricted to American Studies as a nationally bound field, but extend and pertain to transnational and global discourses. Such topics as cross-border cultural movements, interdisciplinarity, the critical study of racism in popular culture, or the international reception and translation of literature and film indicate transnational interests. Transnational studies also involve historiography and the critical discussion of theories of nation states since their inception.

With renowned expertise on the life and works of Mark Twain, SHELLEY FISHER FISHKIN continues to pertinently reveal the international impact of Twain’s writings in past and contemporary literary life, by way of their reception, translation, and worldwide distribution. Twain spent a third of his life outside the United States and held a transnational, almost universal perspective on the world. A unique phenomenon, despite attending difficulties of translation, his humorous writings gained success worldwide and in many different languages. Fishkin follows Twain between the United States and the regions and continents he visited during his travels. In detail, she addresses Twain’s remarkable knowledge of languages other than English, his sparkling play with words, and humorous reflections on linguistic specificity with respect to *The Innocents Abroad* (1869) and *The Adventures of Huckleberry Finn* (1884–1885), to demonstrate that in his time Twain could hardly find an equal within the realm of transnationality.

As scholar of American Studies and acclaimed singer-songwriter, MANFRED SIEBALD selects a theme related to literature, music and history. Richard Rodgers and Oscar Hammerstein’s musical *Oklahoma!* was first performed in 1943 at the St. James Theatre on Broadway in New York. Siebald analyzes the success of the musical and how its creators transformed its source, the theatrical play *Green Grow the Lilacs* by Lynn Riggs (1931). The adaptation across media into the plurimediality of the musical effects an increase of antagonism of cultures depicted. Stylistics of songs in the play are compared to the musical and explicated with regard to the expectations of the receiving public. The characters and their constellation as well as distinctions between settlement, unsettled existence, landownership, and nation building reveal unresolved questions in U.S. American history and its communities.

CHARLES R. WILSON chooses the autobiography of Katharine Du Pre Lumpkin, *The Making of a Southerner* (1947), to describe the former Southern culture through the eyes of Lumpkin as first an ingenuous child and then eventually as a more and more critical activist. In detail, the passages regarding her Southern family background and its involvement in what are considered race relations illustrate the cultural constitution of the ‘Southern way of life’ as well as the cultural construction of race, which is increasingly challenged by the life-writing author’s personal experience and thought. In discussing *The Making of a Southerner* from a transnational perspective, Wilson treats one of the most harrowing aspects of U.S. American history in a way that critically invokes how structures and elements like those employed in Southern raciology of the United States continue to find resurgence in countries across the globe.

ZHANG LONGXI, addressing world literature, treats the lives and works of two autobiographers, Tao Qian (365–427) from China and Henry David Thoreau (1817–1862) from the United States, in respect of their common relation to both nature and solitude. He investigates how proximity to the natural environment can be sensed through the works of the authors across medial, temporal, and cultural differences, and shows how their writing links the experience of nature to a spiritual aspect. The authors lived at different times and places as well as in different cultures and nations that, in many respects, even appear oppositional. However, by addressing aesthetics and human faculties of perception, Zhang uncovers connections of a shared concept of nature and its transfer through and across languages. Including further authors of world literature like Michel de Montaigne and Rainer Maria Rilke, he shows that the experience of nature can only be transferred through an art of suggestion by which the authors render imagination that is beyond descriptive language and invite the readers' cocreation of imaginative spaces beyond limitations of culture.

NADJA GERNALZICK shows how the relational discourse supporting transnationality is figured also in the text, translation, and reception of Álvar Núñez Cabeza de Vaca's *La Relación* (1542). She reads the incommensurabilities in the semiotization of first contact in the colonial travel narrative that is chronologically pre-nationalist and proto-humanist as examples of posthumanism. The negotiation of group association and human communality by the reader, which the narrator of the sixteenth century challenges and provides an opportunity for, becomes an exercise not only in transnationality but also in transtemporality.

Before an extensive background in research on sustainability in the sciences and the arts, HUBERT ZAPF discusses sustainability in and by literature, including the investigation of dynamic ambiguities resulting from the imaginative connection of past and future. Literature becomes a transhistorical medium of sustainability for the cultural ecosystem as well as for cultural evolution from a perspective that ranges across the disciplinary and institutional divide between the life sciences and the humanities.

RÜDIGER KUNOW investigates the storylines of narratives of persons with Alzheimer's disease, in order to address questions how living without memory and writing across semantic gaps may be adequately analyzed. He interprets Alzheimer's as a "figure of interruption" and shows its impact in analyses of narratives in blog entries and autobiographical projects as well as in biographical life writing about Alzheimer patients by their close relatives, such as Jonathan Franzen's memoir "My Father's Brain: What Alzheimer's Takes Away" (2001).

Through the autobiography of Elizabeth Blackwell (1821–1910), CARMEN BIRKLE inquires into the circumstances of becoming a female doctor in the nineteenth century. In detail, she investigates the obstacles and contingencies of a gendered education system for physicians. Birkle reveals what was specially demanded of female health practitioners who wanted to acquire a doctorate so as to officially practice as medical professionals and also demonstrates the difficulties for female patients in receiving adequate treatment, for historically it had been the professional midwife only who was permitted to follow a vocation in medicine as a woman. The investigation provides insights into the restrictions on female efforts to become academics, and it links to the history of women's rights in the United States and Europe while explaining the historical developments specifically in respect of the medical discipline and its paradoxical (un)concern for the materiality of bodies.

Discussing surveillance practices, BIRGIT DÄWES enters a contemporary discussion on the relation of mediality and everyday experience of observation practices by means of contemporary U.S. American TV series and adaptations. She critically shows the problematics of how a series like *Homeland* (2011), adapted from an Israeli series, operates through technologies that transgress national borders as well as through transnational patterns of relationship. The contribution is grounded in early theoretical models of surveillance, such as the panopticon as prison architecture by Jeremy Bentham in the late eighteenth century, later taken up by Michel Foucault for development of critiques of governance and governability in modernity that have become influential worldwide.

NICOLE WALLER reveals linkages between the local and the national in a discussion of Spike Lee's documentary film *When the Levees Broke* (2006) that examines the situation in New Orleans after hurricane Katrina, one of the deadliest hurricanes in the history of the United States. She inquires into the relation of regional and federal liability in case of administrative failure of compliance and thereby tests the limits of institutional entities, with particular regard to raciological delineations and their racist entrenchments. Her considerably textured critical discussion pertains to global humanism in the circumscriptions of the nation state.

MITA BANERJEE discusses Barack Obama's auto/biography *Dreams from My Father* (1995) as a "kaleidoscope of difference" beyond stereotyping. She shows how the narrator tells stories of and with different people from his environment, individually acknowledging each person's situation. By Obama's example, Banerjee explicates that differences do not have to be treated as restrictive opposites, but rather that there is a possibility of differentiation of differences, up to the magnitude of the metaphor of the "kaleidoscopic". At the same time, Mita Banerjee's writing is a tribute to Alfred Hornung's latest efforts in co-founding the Institute für Transnational American Studies at Johannes-Gutenberg University Mainz. The initiators of the founding of the research institute had envisioned it to be named in honor of Barack Obama, former president of the United States, which was accomplished in 2017.

This collection was initiated by the Center for Intercultural Studies at the Johannes-Gutenberg University Mainz on the occasion of Alfred Hornung's seventieth birthday. The contributions to *Developing Transnational American Studies* are by authors from different generations who are international colleagues as well as former students of Alfred Hornung. Transnational thinking is continued and shared in their articles across a variety of critical approaches. The transnational turn of American Studies methodologically addresses a concern for humanity beyond nationalism and racism and is diversely marked in Alfred Hornung's research and fields of specialization, in particular in his work on life writing and auto/biography.

Alfred Hornung joined the faculty of Johannes-Gutenberg University as Professor of English and American Studies in 1988 and directed the transdisciplinary Center for Intercultural Studies at Johannes-Gutenberg University from 2000 to 2005. He was appointed Honorary Director of the Center in 2010. Founded in 1997, the Center for Intercultural Studies (Zentrum für Interkulturelle Studien, ZIS) aims at generating interdisciplinary synergy between the diverse humanities and cultural-studies institutes at Johannes-Gutenberg University Mainz through initiating concerted research projects, lecture series and symposia which mediate between academic departments and disciplines. Under the direction of Alfred Hornung, the Center for Intercultural Studies through a variety of programs and funding developed into a vital basis for international cooperation, inviting and involving scholars and guest lecturers either from or having migrated to the United States, China, Canada, the Caribbean, Australia, North Africa and Europe. Alfred Hornung's longtime commitment to the ZIS indicates his professional goals as an American Studies scholar who actively and passionately participates in the multiple efforts to create a transnational network of intercultural relations and to pursue research on transnational and cross-cultural history and change.

Alfred Hornung's service on behalf of the Center for Intercultural Studies is one of his many contributions to the advancement of transnationality and American Studies worldwide. For many years and through his prolific creativity as a scholar, he has promoted American Studies as a principally comparativist field in the academic community, with publications in all areas of life writing and ecocriticism as well as regarding the fields of modernism, postmodernism, and intercultural studies. Over the years he has cooperated with colleagues, institutions, and organizations in Europe, the Americas, Africa, Australia, and China. With colleagues at Johannes-Gutenberg University Mainz, he co-founded the Obama Institute for Transnational American Studies that was inaugurated in early 2017 and where he currently works as a Research Professor and serves as the Speaker. The Obama Institute for Transnational American Studies at Mainz University was established as a forum of exchange with international partner universities. Before the foundation of the Obama Institute, Alfred Hornung was longtime Chair of the then Institute for American Studies at Mainz University.

Next to his functions at Johannes-Gutenberg University on behalf of transnational American Studies, Alfred Hornung held a number of important positions nationally and internationally. He was President of The Society for the Study of Multi-Ethnic Studies: Europe and the Americas (MESEA) from 2000 to 2004 and President of the German Association for American Studies from 2000 to 2005. He has been Member at Large of the Executive Committee of the International American Studies Association (IASA) since 2003 and was a Member of the International Committee of the American Studies Association (ASA) from 2004 to 2008. From 2008 to 2016 he was Elected Member of the Review Board of the German Research Foundation (DFG) for European and North American Literatures. He is a Founding Member of the International Auto/Biography Association (IABA) and of IABA-Europe. In 2009 he became Founding Member and Vice President of the World Ecological Organization (WEO), Beijing. He was Chair of the National Review Board of the German Council of Science and Humanities for the Evaluation of English and American Studies at German Universities from 2009 to 2012, and since 2012 has participated on the Scientific Advisory Board of the Ludwig Boltzmann Institute in Vienna, Austria.

His activities in the service of transnational academic cooperation and diplomacy include various guest professorships and fellowships at European, American, Canadian and Chinese universities, among others at Harvard, Yale, the National Humanities Center in North Carolina, the Center for American Culture Studies at Columbia University in New

York, and the John D. Rockefeller Center in Bellagio, Italy. He is a Member of the Center for Cross-Cultural Studies at Beijing University. His commitment to transnational cooperation and understanding has been recognized and honored since the very start of his academic career when he was appointed Honorary Citizen of the State of Texas in 1979. For his endeavours towards transnationalizing science, he received a number of international awards, including the 2013 Carl Bode-Norman Holmes Pearson Award for Outstanding Contributions to American Studies by the American Studies Association, Washington. In 2014 he was elected a Member of Academia Europaea, and in 2017 a Member of the Advisory Board of the Institute of World Literature at Harvard University. In addition to his dedication to transnationalizing American Studies that has included a formidable amount of worldwide traveling, Alfred Hornung has contributed to and supported various scholarly journals. From 1991 to 2002 he was general editor of the journal *Amerikastudien/American Studies* and is an editor of the American Studies Monograph Series on behalf of the German Association for American Studies. He is also an editor of *The Journal of Transnational American Studies* and on the editorial board of several journals, including *Atlantic Studies*, *Contemporary Foreign Literature* (Nanjing), *a/b: Auto/Biography Studies* and *The European Journal of Life Writing*. With the former and current directors of the Center for Intercultural Studies, he has co-edited the series Intercultural Studies on behalf of the Center since 2014.

Alfred Hornung's research and publications from the late 1970s until today attest to his commitment to political and social change against injustice and suffering through critique and mediation by academics and intellectuals across borders, such as his doctoral dissertation on the Muckraking Movement in the United States of the 1910s and his postdoctoral thesis on autobiography as transformative means of meeting challenges in cultural history of the United States from Puritanism to postmodernity. From an interest in relations between autobiography, democracy, and literary anthropology; their problematization by the avant-garde and by postmodern writers; comparative studies of ethics, aesthetics and moral codes in literature; and to extensive research and publication on postcolonialism, interculturality, multiculturalism, transculturality, globality and planetarity, Alfred Hornung's academic work over four decades has continually expanded in scope from a transatlantic to a transoceanic worldview while remaining anchored in a concern for the changes in individual lives and experiences in specific times and places. His continuing critique of nationalisms and segregations eventually met with the emergence of Transnational American Studies. Phenomena of border crossing and transformation, developments in cultural studies and world politics as well as citizenship and rights discourses are topical in his lifelong contributions to American Studies from many places of the world, and, coherently, in the opening of American Studies, also in respect of academic disciplinary and institutional politics, towards Transnational American Studies.

Among Alfred Hornung's latest publications in American Studies that underline the transnational orientation of his research are "ChinAmerica: Global Affairs and Planetary Consciousness" in *American Studies as Transnational Practice: Turning Towards the Transpacific*, edited by Yuan Shu and Donald E. Pease (2016); the Chinese translation under the title 生态学与生命写作 of the collection *Ecology and Life Writing* he co-edited with Zhao Baisheng, and its publication in Beijing (2016); and the collection *Obama and Transnational American Studies*, edited in 2016. Alfred Hornung's newest published interventions in Transnational American Studies concern the further transnationalization of auto/biography studies: the biography *Jack London: Abenteuer des Lebens* (2016), the programmatic "Life Writing in and beyond the Anglophone World" (2017) and a tribute to eminent life-writing scholar Philippe Lejeune from France, "Le pacte Philippe" (2018).

We thank Alfred Hornung for his inspiration and example, the contributors for their critical writing and research, Beate Neumeier for her support in designing and coordinating the symposium *Transnational American Studies* at the Center for Intercultural Studies in 2016 and Anton Escher, Director of the Center since 2006, for his generous gesture of initiating and realizing the symposium in honor of Alfred Hornung. For proofreading and stylistic advice we thank Sabine Kim, Roberto Luis Ellis and Jamie Karnik, and for formatting and editorial support Camilla Blei and Teresa Cordero Villar.

Mainz, October 2018

Nadja Gernalzick and Heike C. Spickermann

Repositioning the American South

Originally of Missouri, Now of the Universe[1]

Mark Twain and the World

Shelley Fisher Fishkin

If we set out to look for an American author most likely to achieve a world readership, we would be hard-pressed to find a *less* promising candidate than Mark Twain at the start of his career. Twain's first national fame came with a sketch about a storyteller in a California mining camp and the uptight easterner whom this storyteller regaled with a tale about an inveterate gambler and all the animals he bet on ("The Celebrated Jumping Frog of Calaveras County" in TWAIN [1867] 1996). That story was the lead piece of Twain's first book, *The Celebrated Jumping Frog of Calaveras County and Other Sketches*. While his countrymen delighted in what one American reviewer called the book's "quaint humor" and "pithy wisdom", an early French reader, Thérèse Bentzon, wrote that the humor – particularly "what the Americans call *slang*" – was "quite difficult for us to understand" (BENTZON 1872 [trans., Greg Robinson] in FISHKIN 2010*c*: 28; 25).

If European readers found the dialect and slang of Twain's first book hard to penetrate, the insults he hurled at them in his second book were downright insufferable (TWAIN [1869] 1996). The idea that the author of *The Innocents Abroad* would one day be the toast of Europe probably seemed even more preposterous than the idea that the author of "The Jumping Frog" would one day get an honorary degree from Oxford.

In 1907, Twain's close friend William Dean Howells referred to "Mark Twain, originally of Missouri, but then provisionally of Hartford, and now ultimately of the Solar System, not to say the Universe" (HOWELLS 1907: 601). How did the "wild humorist of the Pacific slope" (as he was known in his early career) become a writer embraced with affection on six continents? How did he become an author whose work would be translated into scores of languages and published in virtually every country with a publishing industry? How did a child reared in a provincial town in Missouri come to think of himself – and come to be thought of by others – not as a citizen of Missouri, or Connecticut or even of the United States, but of the world? These are some questions this essay will address.

The *Innocents Abroad*, the record of a trip Twain took to Europe in the company of a group of middle-class, middle-brow fellow Americans, was, in the opinion of the German novelist, critic, and philologist Eduard Engel "a thoroughly irritating book" (ENGEL 1880 [trans., Valerie Bopp] in FISHKIN 2010*c*: 33). It was not written for readers like him. It was written for readers back home, designed to help armchair travelers see Europe and the Holy Land as they might have seen it with their own eyes. It was designed to let his countrymen see Europe at his side, learning something along the way, but not in a manner that constantly reminded them of how new their own country was and how lacking in all the conventional trappings of civilization. *The Innocents Abroad* was designed to let

[1] Title quotation after William Dean Howells (HOWELLS 1907: 601). Portions of this essay draw on FISHKIN, "American Literature in Transnational Perspective" (2015), and FISHKIN, "Transnational Mark Twain" (2016).

Twain's fellow Americans learn something about the Old World while keeping their self-respect. Eduard Engel was not amused. Writing in 1880, he found the book crude and "unforgiveable", and opined that "[i]f the muses are in favor of Mark Twain, they will not allow him to cross the Atlantic again" (ENGEL 1880 [trans., V.B.] in FISHKIN 2010*c*: 34; 31). Twain expected readers in Europe to hate it. In late 1870, Twain read in the *Boston Advertiser* that "a solemn, serious critique" of the English edition of his book had just appeared in the *London Saturday Review* (TWAIN 1871). Before he even set eyes on that review, Twain could not resist writing a parody of what a humorless, literal-minded review of his book might look like, nor could he resist publishing it in the December 1870 issue of Galaxy in the "Memoranda" section that he edited – supposedly reprinted from the London journal. Twain's review of his own book included this passage:

> That we have shown this to be a remarkable book, we think no one will deny. That it is a pernicious book to place in the hands of the confiding and uninformed, we think we have also shown. That the book is a deliberate and wicked creation of a diseased mind, is apparent upon every page. (TWAIN 1870)

Twain confessed to the hoax in the next issue of *Galaxy*, writing that

> the idea of such a literary breakfast by a stolid, ponderous British ogre of the quill was too much for a naturally weak virtue, and I went home and burlesqued it – revelled in it, I may say. I never saw a copy of the real "Saturday Review" criticism until after my burlesque was written and mailed to the printer. (TWAIN 1871)

The real review must have been a bit of a letdown. It contained no exasperated fulminations about "the insolence, the impertinence" or the "majestic ignorance of this author" (TWAIN 1870). Although the English critic did acknowledge that the reader of the review might be persuaded that "Mr. Twain is a very offensive specimen of the vulgarest kind of Yankee", he added:

> And yet, to say the truth, we have a kind of liking for him. There is a frankness and originality about his remarks which is pleasanter than the mere repetition of stale raptures; and his fun, if not very refined, is often tolerable in its way. In short, his pages may be turned over with amusement, as exhibiting more or less consciously a very lively portrait of the uncultivated American tourist, who may be more obtrusive and misjudging, but is not quite so stupidly unobservant as our native product. We should not choose either of them for our companions on a visit to a church or a picture-gallery, but we should expect most amusement from the Yankee as long as we could stand him. (*Saturday Review* 1870: 468)

"[T]he mere repetition of stale raptures", as the English reviewer put it, was *de rigeur* in travel books of the day, but Twain's book was different. In *Innocents Abroad*, and in later works, Twain broke out of the mold with such original freshness that many Europeans who justly could have been offended were intrigued instead. Thérèse Bentzon, who found his slang so impossible to translate, found that she could not deny the "unquenchable verve" of his prose (BENTZON 1872 [trans., G.R.] in FISHKIN 2010*c*: 26). A little over a decade later, one of her countrymen, Henry Gauthier-Villars, would be so taken with Twain's refreshing style and the humor that infused it that he would claim Twain as a new model for the kind of writing his fellow Frenchmen should strive to produce.

Gauthier-Villars had little use for the "refined stylists" then in vogue in France who "compose a sentence with the minute labor of a mosaicist", with results that are "tangled-up" and "precious", as he put it (GAUTHIER-VILLARS 1884: 94; [trans., S.F.F.] qtd. in FISHKIN 2010*a*: 56). He bemoans their disdain for the "gaiety, spontaneity", and "literary good health" so abundant in the work of Mark Twain (GAUTHIER-VILLARS 1884: 94; [trans., S.F.F.] qtd. in FISHKIN 2010*a*: 56). The first book on Mark Twain published *anywhere* turns out to be the one Gauthier-Villars published in French, in Paris in 1884, where he wrote: "Hello then, charming writer with no model or imitator! I bid you welcome among us, newcomer with endless verve; the sound of the hurrahs you have raised has already crossed the ocean. We have been waiting for you [...]" (GAUTHIER-VILLARS 1884: 12; [trans., G.R.] in FISHKIN 2010*a*: 58).

Even Engel, who found Twain's first European travel book "thoroughly irritating" had to admit that Twain's comments on German that appeared in his second European travel book were remarkably sound. Engel wrote that "the best Mark Twain has ever accomplished is his appendix to [*A Tramp Abroad*] titled 'The Awful German Language'. Here ignorance, good humor, and wit form such a strange mixture that when reading it one really does not know if one should get angry or laugh. I preferred the latter and advise any reader of this appendix to do the same" (ENGEL 1880; [trans., V.B.] in FISHKIN 2010*c*: 37). Engel, the great turn-of-the-century authority on German, credits Twain with having somehow aptly hit upon many a "a sad truth" about the language, such as when he is deploring the "parenthesis disease" that allows a "sort of luminous intellectual fog" to substitute for "clearness", or when he considers the frequently convoluted, interminable quality of German sentences (ENGEL 1880; [trans., V.B.] in FISHKIN 2010*c*: 38). This is the piece, after all, in which Twain refers to German as a language in which a man can "travel all day in one sentence without changing cars" [TWAIN 1907: 2–3]). Engel claimed in 1880, concerning one point Twain raised, that it was "well-known" that a reform "is on its way", one which he wagered Mark Twain could witness if he visited Germany again in another ten years (ENGEL 1880; [trans., V.B.] in FISHKIN 2010*c*: 38) and which eventually was decreed by the German Orthographic Conference of 1901. While in 1880 Engel had called Twain's first travel book "crude and unforgiveable", by the time he published his *History of American Literature* in 1897, he had changed his mind: He called Twain's "eye for the ridiculous" in *Innocents Abroad* "wonderful" (ENGEL 1897; [trans., V.B.] in FISHKIN 2010*c*: 40). German students, by the way, seem to have been fans of Twain before their elders came around. Thomas Wentworth Higginson recalled a breakfast he had with two German students in 1878: "As for Mark Twain, they all quote him before they have spoken with you fifteen minutes and always give him a place so much higher in literature than we do. I don't think any English prose writer is so universally read" (HIGGINSON 1921: 300).

Charles Darwin kept *Innocents Abroad* on his bedside table, within easy reach when he wanted to clear his mind and relax at bedtime (TWAIN [1907–1909] 2015: 79). Chancellor Otto von Bismarck committed favorite parts of that book to memory to share with his grandchildren (FISHER 1922: 16). Friedrich Nietzsche offered to send *Tom Sawyer* to some good friends as a gift (NIETZSCHE [1879] 1988: 73). Joseph Conrad often thought of *Life on the Mississippi* when he "was in command of a steamer in the Congo and stood straining in the night looking for snags" (Conrad qtd. in *Mentor* 1924: 45), while Jorge

Luis Borges used it as a source for the book in which he made his debut as a storyteller (SARLO 1993: 28). Nobel Laureate Kenzaburo Ōe cites *Huckleberry Finn* as the book that spoke so deeply to his condition in war-torn Japan that it inspired him to write his first novel (Ōe, comment in 1996).

Writers the world over marveled at the art Twain wrought from the speech of ordinary people – speech whose previous appearance in literature had most often been treated with ridicule. Borges observed that, in *Huckleberry Finn*, "for the first time an American writer used the language of America without affectation"; the book, Borges believed, "taught the whole American novel to talk" (BORGES [1967] 1971: 37). Twain's dazzling experiments with the vernacular helped inspire writers around the world to create art out of the language spoken by their countrymen – writers like Johannes V. Jensen, considered the father of modern Danish literature, the first great modern Danish author (JENSEN 1910; [trans., Jan Nordby Gretlund] in FISHKIN 2010*c*: 119).

From the breezy slang and deadpan humor that peppered his earliest comic sketches to the unmistakably American characters who populated his fiction, Twain's writings introduced readers around the world to American personalities speaking in distinctively American cadences. H. L. Mencken wrote in the *New York Evening Mail* in 1917:

> His humor was American. His incurable Philistinism was American. His very English was American. Above all, he was an American in his curious mixture of sentimentality and cynicism, his mingling of romanticist and iconoclast. [Emerson's] *English Traits* might have been written by any one of half a dozen Germans. The tales of Poe, printed as translations from the French, would have deceived even Frenchmen. [...] But in *Huckleberry Finn*, in *A Connecticut Yankee*, and in most of the short sketches there is a quality that is unmistakably and overwhelmingly national. They belong to our country and our time quite as obviously as the skyscraper or the quick lunch counter. (MENCKEN 1917: 9)

Writers around the world endeavored to place Twain in their own national literary traditions, alongside the titans of world literature who were more familiar to them and their readers. In 1924, in a Yiddish paper in Vilna, the Yiddish critic Maks Eric, for example, wrote an extended comparison of Twain with Sholem Aleichem; the Spanish novelist Angel Guerra and Cuban writer José Martí compared Twain with Cervantes (ERIC [1924] [trans., Zachary Baker]: 151–157; GUERRA [1903] [trans., Edward M. Test]: 105–109; MARTÍ 1890 [trans., Rubén Builes and Cintia Santana]: 53–54; all qtd. in FISHKIN 2010*c*).

Howells found it hard to account for Twain's worldwide popularity. Referring to Twain's humor, he wrote: "When I think how purely and wholly American it is, I am a little puzzled at its universal acceptance" (HOWELLS 1910: 139). It is all the more remarkable that Twain won such a fervent international following when we realize that many readers around the world were often encountering Twain in translations of very mixed quality. For example, as Birgit Wetzel-Sahm has shown, August Schacht, a nineteenth-century German translator of one of Twain's best-known sketches, took the liberty of changing the tone, the characters, and the plot of the sketch, making it scarcely recognizable as the piece Twain wrote (WETZEL-SAHM 1986). As Henry Gauthier-Villars reminds us: "Be aware that the old Italian saying *traduttore, traditore* is especially true when applied to Mark Twain – to translate him is to betray him" (GAUTHIER-VILLARS 1884; [trans., G.R.] in FISHKIN 2010*c*: 59). He cautions that translations may not capture "the joyous temerity of the American prose, or the joyous eccentricity of the expressions Twain creates from whole cloth, or the sharp edges of the humor to which the original use of slang adds irresistible comedy" (GAUTHIER-VILLARS 1884; [trans., G.R.] in FISHKIN 2010*c*: 60). His observation resonates with that of the Japanese writer Kakuzo Okakura, who wrote that "[t]ranslation is always a treason, and as a Ming author observes, can at its best be only the reverse side of a brocade, – all the threads are there, but not the subtlety of colour or design" (OKAKURA [1906] 1912: 48).

Tsuyoshi Ishihara notes that Kuni Sasaki's translation of *Huckleberry Finn* so sentimentalized Huck and made him so respectable that the Huck that Japanese readers first encountered would be hard for an English reader to even recognize. Sasaki's version of Jim is even more removed from Twain's. Sasaki simply omits two of Jim's most important scenes in the novel – the scene where he rebukes Huck for fooling with him after they are separated in the fog, after which Huck forces himself to apologize, and the scene where Jim recalls, with deep shame, the time he beat his little daughter 'Lizbeth for not doing as she was told before he realized that she was deaf (ISHIHARA 2005: 24–26). In addition, Sasaki also misreads or deletes exchanges central to the book's satirical look at racism – such as the famous exchange between Huck and Aunt Sally about the steamboat explosion. Ishihara notes that Sasaki frequently seems to misunderstand Twain's irony and clearly does not understand Twain's efforts to satirize racism in the novel (ISHIHARA 2005: 26–27). It is fortunate that a much more accurate Japanese translation of *Huckleberry Finn* by Tameji Nakamura appeared in 1941. It was this inexpensive paperback edition from a prestigious Japanese publisher that a young boy in the remote mountain village of Shikoku read (ISHIHARA 2005: 58–59). This child's name was Kenzaburo Ōe, and he would go on to win the Nobel Prize in literature. His mother managed to barter some rice for a copy of this book in war-torn Japan. Since Japan was then at war with the United States, Ōe was warned that "if your teacher asks you who is the author, you must answer that Mark Twain is the pseudonym of a German writer" (ISHIHARA 2005: 59). After the war, when Ōe read the book again – this time in English – he called it "a work that 'opened the door to the world of literature'" for him (ISHIHARA 2005: 59). Ōe's translator John Nathan notes that

> [i]t was Huck's moral courage, literally Hell-bent, that ignited his imagination. For Ōe the single most important moment in the book was always Huck's agonized decision not to send Miss Watson a note informing her of Jim's whereabouts and to go instead to Hell. With that fearsome resolution to turn his back on his times, his society, and even his god, Huckleberry Finn became the model for Ōe's existential hero. (NATHAN 1977: xii)

When I met Ōe in Austin, Texas and asked him whether his first book, *Prize Stock*, or *The Catch*, was responding directly to Twain's most famous novel, Ōe wrote in my copy of his latest book that I had brought for him to sign: "Yes, I agree with your opinion about Huck, the narrative of my first novel is under the shadow of Huck." The Japanese scholar Shoji Goto "has suggested that since Ōe's works have had a tremendous impact on postmodern Japanese literature", *Huckleberry Finn*, through Ōe, has played an important role in the development of that literature as well (ISHIHARA 2005: 59–60).

Looking at statistics only through 1976, Twain's books have been published in some fifty-five countries and translated into seventy-two foreign languages (RODNEY 1982:

xxii). According to Robert Rodney, there were over 600 German-language editions of Twain's works by 1976, over 500 Spanish-language editions, well over 200 editions each in French and Italian, almost 200 in Swedish, and more than 100 in Dutch, Danish, Portuguese, and Serbo-Croatian. In addition to enjoying a tremendous readership in English-speaking countries – Great Britain, Canada, Australia, New Zealand, and South Africa – Twain was particularly popular, as well, in Spain, Italy, Russia, Yugoslavia, Japan, France, Hungary, Norway, Sweden, Brazil, and India. He also had "sustained popularity during various periods in Mexico, Czechoslovakia, the Netherlands, Belgium, Denmark, Turkey, Romania and Israel", and substantial audiences in countries including Iceland, Chile, Colombia, Uruguay, and China. After World War II, multiple editions of his work were published in Cuba, Albania, Greece, Iran, Egypt, Pakistan, Indonesia, Malaysia, Taiwan, and Korea. He has been translated into Arabic, Bengali, Bulgarian, Burmese, Estonian, Farsi, Finnish, Greek, Hebrew, Hindi, Indonesian, Japanese, Korean, Latvian, Lithuanian, Magyar, Malay, Marathi, Polish, Tagalog, Tamil, Turkish, Thai, Ukrainian, and Yiddish, among other languages. Twain's "literary legacy" eventually included "every nationality with a publishing enterprise large enough to support the translation and publication of his writings" (RODNEY 1982: xxiv; xxiii).

From the start, Twain's international fans appeared in every class of society. Twain was stunned, during a trip to Berlin, to find the *Portier* of his lodging house claim *Life on the Mississippi* as his favorite book on the same day that the Emperor Wilhelm II had told Twain that it was his favorite book (HENDERSON 1912: 142). The work that spoke to Cuban revolutionary and national hero José Martí was *Connecticut Yankee*. Martí wrote in *La Nación* in 1890, just a little over a month after the *Yankee* was published, that the book was "fueled by indignation" (MARTÍ 1890; [trans., R.B. and C.S.] in FISHKIN 2010*c*: 54). He recognized that Twain was committed as a writer and as a citizen of a democracy to values that Martí shared: both men rejected the claims of aristocracy to deference and legitimacy; both abhorred injustice; both sympathized with the downtrodden and disempowered; both disdained writing that was pretentious and affected. Martí read *Connecticut Yankee* as much more than a satire of medieval chivalry: He recognized it as compelling criticism of *contemporary* injustice. He wrote that Twain "makes evident – with an anger that sometimes borders on the sublime – the vileness of those who would climb atop their fellow man, feed upon his misery, and drink from his misfortune"; "[t]here are paragraphs in Twain's book", Martí writes, "that make me want to set off for Hartford to shake his hand" (MARTÍ 1890; [trans., R.B. and C.S.] in FISHKIN 2010*c*: 53–54). I love that comment: Martí doesn't say anything quite like that about any other writer he admires. Martí clearly saw the author of *A Connecticut Yankee in King Arthor's Court* as one Yankee who dissented, as Martí himself did, from some of the conventional pieties of the exploitative society in which he lived. Martí saw Twain as a writer whose social critique of modern society paralleled Martí's own in important ways. These issues at the core of *Connecticut Yankee* were most often sidestepped by reviewers who preferred to focus on the book's less controversial mockery of a long-dead age of chivalry. Twain seems to have modeled for Martí how a writer could prompt readers to think about social justice in fresh ways. Both of these areas would inform Martí's own writing in the years that followed. Is it not intriguing that a Martí who would entitle his most widely reprinted essay "Nuestra América", or "Our America", referred to the author of *Connecticut Yankee* with affection, one year earlier, as "Nuestro Mark Twain", or "Our Mark Twain" (MARTÍ 1890, qtd. in FISHKIN 2010*b*: 48)?

Until relatively recently, readers in the United States were likely to be largely unfamiliar with the Mark Twain that writers in China and the Soviet Union had been praising for much of the twentieth century. As Maxwell Geismar put it in *Scanlan's* in 1970:

> During the Cold War era of our culture, mainly in the 1950s although extending back into the '40s and forward far into the '60s, Mark Twain was both revived and castrated. The entire arena of Twain's radical social criticism of the United States – its racism, imperialism, and finance capitalism – has been repressed or conveniently avoided by the so-called Twain scholars precisely because it is so bold, so brilliant, so satirical. And so prophetic. (GEISMAR 1970: 33)

But while most Americans in the twentieth century had been encountering a "castrated" tame Twain, to borrow Geismar's word, readers in China and the Soviet Union were encountering a Twain unafraid to launch salvos at the hypocrisy and failings of the country that he loved. I have only relatively recently begun to understand the extent to which Mark Twain's achievement as a writer, and his role as a social and cultural critic may have been distorted by imperatives of the Cold War. In part *because* Chinese and Soviet writers and critics lauded the Twain who was a searing critic of his country, American writers and critics largely dismissed that Twain as a figment of the Communist propaganda machine and valorized *America's* Twain as a writer to be celebrated primarily as a humorist rather than as a satirist and social critic. The propaganda functions to which Twain's writing was put are obvious, but Americans threw out the baby with the bathwater when they downplayed the validity of Twain's criticisms of his country – which were also criticisms of *their* country – and, unfortunately, in some ways, of America today, as well.

In 1960, as president of the National Association of Writers in China, Lao She, one of the leading Chinese authors of the twentieth century, delivered a speech in Beijing to commemorate the fiftieth anniversary of Mark Twain's death. Although it served China's ruling interests at the time, and contains some of the expected Cold War jargon, it also contains some insightful readings of pieces by Twain with which American readers were then largely unfamiliar. With a few exceptions (most notably work by Philip Foner and Geismar), Twain's trenchant critiques of the country he loved tended to be as ignored in the United States at midcentury as they were celebrated in China. Only in the nineties with the publication of Jim Zwick's book *Mark Twain's Weapons of Satire: Anti-Imperialist Writings on the Philippine-American War* in 1992 would American scholars generally decide that this aspect of Twain deserved their attention.

Lao She wrote in 1960:

> In the fall of 1900, Mark Twain returned to the United States after being absent nine years. He told the press, "And so I am an anti-imperialist. I am opposed to having the eagle put its talons on any land." He also gave strong support to the Chinese people's fierce struggle against imperialist aggression. As early as 1868, in his essay entitled "Treaty with China," he berated the shameless invaders for their forceful setting up of concessions. (LAO 1995; [trans., Zhao Yuming et al.] in FISHKIN 2010*c*: 284)

Lao also applauded Twain's exposé in "Treaty with China" of injustices inflicted on the Chinese in California. To this day relatively few Americans have even heard of "Treaty with China", an article Twain published in the *New York Tribune* in 1868. Indeed, this article is so obscure that its first reprinting since its initial publication was in 2010 in *Journal of Transnational American Studies*, which also features an analysis of it by Martin Zehr.

The Twain that Lao She celebrated was the anti-racist Twain, the Twain who was "[p]eace loving, democracy loving, anti-imperialist and anti-colonialist" (LAO 1995; [trans., Z.Y. et al.] in FISKIN 2010*c*: 287). This is the Twain that was also valued by Soviet critic Yan Bereznitsky. But both Bereznitsky and Lao She complained that this was the Twain that Americans preferred to bury or ignore (BEREZNITSKY 1959*a*; [trans., R.B.] in FISHKIN 2010*c*: 278; LAO 1995; [trans., Z.Y. et al.] in FISHKIN 2010*c*: 287). While the "part of [Twain's] literary heritage we should value most", according to Lao She was his searing social critique, American critics by and large maintained that what was most important about Twain was his humor. Indeed, this view of what mattered most about Twain dominated writing on Twain throughout the twentieth century, and continues in the twenty-first. Personally I find Lao She's view of what matters most about Mark Twain compelling – there is humor, to be sure, but it is the social criticism beneath it that makes it lasting. As Twain himself once said: "Humor must not professedly teach, it must not *professedly* preach; but it must do both if it would live forever" (TWAIN [1907] 2013: 153).

Mark Twain traveled throughout the world more than any other American writer of his era. His travels helped him take global perspectives on issues such as racism, imperialism, and anti-Semitism. It was often when he was abroad that he gained the clearest understanding of his own country. For example, while travelling in India, when he saw a German abuse a native servant, the abuses of slaves that he had witnessed in his childhood flooded his memory (TWAIN [1897] 1996: 351–352). The anti-Semitism he observed in the Reichsrath of the Austro-Hungarian Empire and the Dreyfus affair resonated for Twain with the anti-Black racism that fueled lynchings in the United States, and with the racist assumptions that underlay Western powers' imperialism in Asia and Africa (FISHKIN 2005). Prejudice, racism, the exercise of unjust authority – these qualities crossed borders, and as Twain had the chance to see them in a range of contexts, his insights into the dynamics of these phenomena were sharpened profoundly.

Twain interacted with people of all nations whenever he travelled abroad. In a notebook, Twain wrote: "During 8 years now I have filled the position – with some credit, I trust, of self-appointed ambassador-at-large of the United States of America – without salary" (PAINE 1912: 1072). Although he claimed to have been offered various posts over the years, he held no official title, but he was, in fact, seen as representing his country wherever he was.

Travel, Twain wrote, is "fatal to prejudice, bigotry and narrow-mindedness, and many of our people need it sorely on these accounts" (TWAIN [1869] 1996: 658). Twain's travels had a profound impact on the development of his understanding of world affairs, on his sensibilities as a writer, and on his compassion towards his fellow human beings. One of his most important stories, "The War-Prayer", which was not published until after his death, is rooted, as the critic Hua Hsu tells us, "in the lessons one learns looking beyond borders, studying the dynamics of international power and politics and noting the hypocrisy of spreading ideas like freedom, liberty and salvation by force" (HSU 2009: 78–79). Hsu goes on to suggest that "The War-Prayer" "isn't merely the creation of a great humorist or social critic; it is the creation of one of American culture's great travelers. Roughing it on the road, Twain achieved insights into the human condition and the tenuousness of national affiliations that were unavailable to his more provincial peers" (HSU 2009: 79). Hsu believes that "the success of 'The War-Prayer' as a cogent and prescient piece of criticism calls for a reappraisal of Twain as a trans-Pacific traveler, an American with a consciously *global* viewpoint" (HSU 2009: 79).

Twain had a working knowledge of several languages besides his native tongue. He knew enough German to write about its peculiarities and flaws in a piece that is still read and taught more than a century after he wrote it (TWAIN [1880] 1996). He knew enough French to write a parody of what his most famous story might sound like if translated directly into that language; and he knew enough Italian to write a memorable piece about learning it (TWAIN [1874] 1996; TWAIN [1906] 1996). And truth be told, he spent about a third of his life living outside the United States. But he was never charged with having abandoned his country, as others in his position might have been. George Ade observed in 1910 that "[p]robably no other American could have lived abroad for so many years without being editorially branded as an expatriate. In some sections of our country it is safer to be an accomplice in homicide […], than it is to be an 'expatriate.'" (ADE 1910; in FISHKIN 2010*c*: 122). In fact, Ade suggests that the regard in which Twain was held on the world scene probably bolstered his credit at home rather than jeopardizing it. Ade asked: "[I]s it not possible that much of the tremendous liking for Mark Twain grew out of his success in establishing our credit abroad? Any American who can invade Europe and command respectful attention is entitled to triumphal arches when he arrives home" (ADE 1910; in FISHKIN 2010*c*: 124). Ade goes on to observe that

> Mark Twain was probably the best of our emissaries […]. He had been in all parts of the world and had made a calm and unbiased estimate of the relative values of men and institutions. Probably he came to know that all had been cut from one piece and then trimmed variously. He carried with him the same placid habits of life that sufficed him in Connecticut and because he was what he pretended to be, the hypercritical foreigners doted upon him and the Americans at home, glad to flatter themselves, said, "Why, certainly, he's one of us". (ADE 1910; in FISHKIN 2010*c*: 125–126)

During the last few years, a play that Twain wrote in Vienna in 1898 called "Is He Dead?" debuted on Broadway in 2007 and has since been produced in Australia, Canada, China, Romania, Russia, Sri Lanka and the UK – but not yet in Germany.[2] I hope to see a German production of it some day. Major conferences devoted to Twain were held during the last

[2] For the play as Twain wrote it in Vienna in 1898 see TWAIN 2003. The version produced on Broadway in 2007 was adapted by David Ives and produced in association with Fishkin. For the production history of the 411 productions since 2007 see "Production History" at the link to *Is He Dead*? by TWAIN and IVES, which may be accessed at *https://www.playscripts.com /play/1365* [24 July 2016]. The script (TWAIN and IVES) is available at this link and future productions may also be licensed at this link.

few years in Lisbon and in Yokohama, a mammoth Mark Twain encyclopedia was published in Tokyo in Japanese, and the ninety extant Chinese translations of *Huckleberry Finn* alone were analyzed in a new book by Selina Lai-Henderson, *Mark Twain in China*. Over a century after his reported death – much exaggerated, I might add – Mark Twain continues to be an ambassador-at-large for his country – without a salary.

List of Works Cited

ADE, GEORGE [1910]: Mark Twain as Our Emissary. *The Century Illustrated Magazine* 81.2 (December): 205–206. In SHELLEY FISHER FISHKIN (Ed.): *The Mark Twain Anthology: Great Writers on His Life and Works*. New York: Library of America, 2010, 121–126.

BENTZON, THÉRÈSE [1872]: Les Humoristes Américains: Mark Twain. [The American Humorists: Mark Twain] *Revue de Deux Mondes* 100 (15 July 1872): 313–315 [trans. by Greg Robinson]. In FISHKIN (Ed.): *The Mark Twain Anthology*, 24–29.

BEREZNITSKY, YAN [1959*a*]: Mark Twain on the Bed of Procrustes. *Literaturnaya Gazeta* (Moscow) 18 August: 4 [trans. by Robert Belknap]. In CHARLES NEIDER (Ed.): *Mark Twain and the Russians: An Exchange of Views*. New York: Hill and Wang, 1960, 13–15. Repr. in FISHKIN (Ed.): *The Mark Twain Anthology*, 278–279.

BEREZNITSKY, YAN [1959*b*]: The Question is Significantly More Profound: A Letter to Charles Neider. *Literaturnaya Gazeta* (Moscow) 12 December: 5 [trans. by Robert Belknap]. In CHARLES NEIDER (Ed.): *Mark Twain and the Russians: An Exchange of Views*. New York: Hill and Wang, 1960, 19–24. Repr. in FISHKIN (Ed.): *The Mark Twain Anthology*, 280–282.

BORGES, JORGE LUIS, in collaboration with ESTHER ZEMBORAIN DE TORRES [1967]: *An Introduction to American Literature* [Introducción a la literature norteamericana]. Trans. and ed. by L. CLARK KEATING and ROBERT O. EVANS. Lexington: University Press of Kentucky, repr. edition 1971.

CASTELLANOS, JESÚS [1910]: Mark Twain. In *Los Optimistas*. Madrid: Editorial América, 115–120 [trans. by Edward M. Test]. In FISHKIN (Ed.): *The Mark Twain Anthology*, 133–136.

ENGEL, EDUARD [1880]: Mark Twain: Ein Amerikanischer 'Humorist'. [Mark Twain: an American Humorist] *Magazin für die Literatur des Auslandes* 98: 575–579 [trans. by Valerie Bopp]. Excerpt repr. in FISHKIN (Ed.): *The Mark Twain Anthology*, 30–39.

ENGEL, EDUARD [1897]: "Mark Twain". Excerpt from *Geschichte der englischen Litteratur von den Anfängen bis zur Gegenwart*, mit einem Anhang: Die nordamerikanische Litteratur [*A History of English Literature from the Beginning to the Present*, with an Appendix: North American Literature] 2nd ed. (Leipzig: Verlag von J. Baedeker), 65–68 [trans. by Valerie Bopp]. In FISHKIN (Ed.): *The Mark Twain Anthology*, 39–41.

ERIK, MAKS [1924]: Sholem Aleichem and Mark Twain. *Tog* (Vilna) 23 May, and 30 May [trans. by Zachary M. Baker]. In FISHKIN (Ed.): *The Mark Twain Anthology*, 151–157.

FISHER, HENRY W. (1922): *Abroad with Mark Twain and Eugene Field: Tales They Told a Fellow Correspondent*. New York: Nicholas L. Brown.

FISHKIN, SHELLEY FISHER (2005): Mark Twain and the Jews. *Arizona Quarterly* (Spring) 61.1: 137–166.

FISHKIN, SHELLEY FISHER (2010*a*): Henry Gauthier-Villars. In FISHKIN (Ed.): *The Mark Twain Anthology*, 56.

FISHKIN, SHELLEY FISHER (2010*b*): José Martí. In FISHKIN (Ed.): *The Mark Twain Anthology*.

FISHKIN, SHELLEY FISHER (Ed.) (2010*c*): *The Mark Twain Anthology: Great Writers on His Life and Works*. New York: Library of America.

FISHKIN, SHELLEY FISHER (2015): American Literature in Transnational Perspective: The Case of Mark Twain. In CAROLINE F. LEVANDER and ROBERT S. LEVINE (Eds.): *Companion to American Literary Studies*. Malden, MA: Wiley-Blackwell, 279–293.

FISHKIN, SHELLEY FISHER (2016): Transnational Mark Twain. In YUAN SHU and DONALD PEASE (Eds.): *American Studies as Transnational Practice: Turning Toward the Transpacific*. Lebanon, New Hampshire: University Press of New England (Re-Mapping the Transnational: A Dartmouth Series in American Studies), 109–137.

GAUTHIER-VILLARS, HENRY [1884]: Mark Twain. Paris: Imprimeur-Libraire [trans. by Greg Robinson]. In FISHKIN (Ed.): *The Mark Twain Anthology*, 57–60.

GEISMAR, MAXWELL (1970): Mark Twain and the Robber Barons. *Scanlan's Monthly*, March, 33–39.

GUERRA, ÁNGEL [1903]: Prólogo. In MARK TWAIN: *Cuentos Escogidos*, ed. by ÁNGEL GUERRA (Prologue to MARK TWAIN: *Selected Tales*). Madrid: Libreria Moderna, 1903 [trans. by Edward M. Test]. In FISHKIN (Ed.): *The Mark Twain Anthology*, 105–107.

HENDERSON, ARCHIBALD. (1912): *Mark Twain*. New York: F.A. Stokes.

HIGGINSON, MARY THACHER (Ed.) (1921): *The Letters and Journals of Thomas Wentworth Higginson, 1846–1906*. New York: Houghton Mifflin.

HOWELLS, WILLIAM DEAN (1907): Recollections of an Atlantic Editorship. *Atlantic Monthly* 100 (November): 594–606.

HOWELLS, WILLIAM DEAN (1910): *My Mark Twain: Reminiscences and Criticisms*. New York/London: Harper and Brothers.

HSU, HUA (2009): The Trans-Pacific Lesson of Mark Twain's "War-Prayer". *Mark Twain Studies* (Japan) 2; repr. in the "Reprise" section of *Journal of Transnational American Studies* 1.1: 78–80, web [24 July 2016].

ISHIHARA, TSUYOSHI (2005): *Mark Twain in Japan: The Cultural Reception of an American Icon*. Columbia, Missouri: University of Missouri Press (Mark Twain and His Circle).

JENSEN, JOHANNES V. [1910]: Mark Twain. *Politiken* (Copenhagen), 23 April: 5 [trans. by Jan Nordby Gretlund]. In FISHKIN (Ed.): *The Mark Twain Anthology*, 117–120.

LAI-HENDERSON, SELINA (2015): *Mark Twain in China*. Stanford, CA: Stanford University Press.

LAO, SHE ([1960] 1995): Mark Twain: Exposer of the "Dollar Empire". A Speech by Lao She Commemorating the Fiftieth Anniversary of the Death of Mark Twain [trans. by Zhao Yuming, Sui Gang, and J. R. LeMaster]. *US-China Review* 19 (Summer): 11–15. In FISHKIN (Ed.): *The Mark Twain Anthology*, 283–288.

MARTÍ, JOSÉ [1890]: Escenas Norteamericanas [North American scenes]. *La Nación*, Buenos Aires (sent 9 January 1890, and published 20 February 1890). Repr. in *Obras Completas de Martí*. Havana: Editorial Trópico, 1941, 1575–1579 [trans. by Rubén Builes and Cintia Santana]. In FISHKIN (Ed.): *The Mark Twain Anthology*, 53–55.

MENCKEN, H. L. (1917): Mark Twain's Americanism. *New York Evening Mail* (1 November): 9.

Mentor (1924): Conrad Pays Tribute to Mark Twain. 12.4 (May): 45.

NATHAN, JOHN (1977). Introduction to KENZABURO ŌE: *Teach Us to Outgrow Our Madness: Four Short Novels*. New York: Grove Press.

NIETZSCHE, FRIEDRICH [1879]: Letter to Franz and Ida Overbeck, 14 November 1879 [trans. by Walter Kaufman]. In WALTER KAUFMAN (Ed.): *The Portable Nietzsche*. New York: Penguin Books, 73. (Repr. edition 1988, first published 1954).

ŌE, KENZABURO: Comment inscribed by Ōe to Shelley Fisher Fishkin on the title page of his book *Nip the Buds and Shoot the Kids* in Austin, Texas in 1996 (book in private collection of the author).

OKAKURA, KAKUZŌ ([1906] 1912): *The Book of Tea*. New York: Duffield.

PAINE, ALBERT BIGELOW (1912): *Mark Twain, a Biography*. Vol. IV. New York: Harper and Brothers.

RODNEY, ROBERT M. (1982): *Mark Twain International: A Bibliography and Interpretation of his Worldwide Popularity*. Westport, CT: Greenwood Press.

SARLO, BEATRIZ (1993): *Jorge Luis Borges: A Writer on the Edge*. London: Verso.

Saturday Review of Politics, Literature, Science and Art (1870): The Innocents Abroad (8 October 1870, 30): 467–468.

TWAIN, MARK [1867]: The Celebrated Jumping Frog of Calaveras County. In MARK TWAIN: *The Celebrated Jumping Frog of Calaveras County and Other Sketches*. New York: Oxford University Press, 1996 (The Oxford Mark Twain, ed. by SHELLEY FISHER FISHKIN), 7–19.

TWAIN, MARK (1868): Treaty with China. *New York Tribune* (4 August): 1–2. Repr. *Journal of Transnational American Studies*. Vol. II, no. 1 (2010). Web [24 July 2016].

TWAIN, MARK [1869]: *The Innocents Abroad*. New York: Oxford University Press, 1996 (The Oxford Mark Twain, ed. by SHELLEY FISHER FISHKIN).

TWAIN, MARK [1870]: Memoranda. *The Galaxy* (December). Web [24 July 2016].

TWAIN, MARK [1871]: Memoranda. *The Galaxy* (January). Web [24 July 2016].

TWAIN, MARK [1874]: The "Jumping Frog." In English. Then in French. Then clawed back into a Civilized Language Once More by Patient, Unremunerated Toil. In: *Sketches, New and Old*. New York: Oxford University Press, 1996 (The Oxford Mark Twain, ed. by SHELLEY FISHER FISHKIN), 28–43.

TWAIN, MARK [1880]: "The Awful German Language". Appendix D from *A Tramp Abroad*. New York: Oxford University Press, 1996 (The Oxford Mark Twain, ed. by SHELLEY FISHER FISHKIN), 601–619.

TWAIN, MARK [1885]: *Adventures of Huckleberry Finn*. New York: Oxford University Press, 1996 (The Oxford Mark Twain, ed. by SHELLEY FISHER FISHKIN).

TWAIN, MARK [1897]: *Following the Equator*. Repr. in MARK TWAIN: *Following the Equator and Anti-Imperalist Essays*. New York: Oxford University Press, 1996 (The Oxford Mark Twain, ed. by SHELLEY FISHER FISHKIN).

TWAIN, MARK [1898]: *Is He Dead? A Comedy in Three Acts*. Ed. by SHELLEY FISHER FISHKIN (with Foreword, Afterword and Notes), text established by the Mark Twain Project. Illustrations by Barry Moser. Berkeley: University of California Press, 2003.

TWAIN, MARK [1898] and DAVID IVES (2007): *Is He Dead? A New Comedy by Mark Twain as Adapted by David Ives*. New York: *Playscripts.com*.

TWAIN, MARK [1906]: Italian Without a Master. In MARK TWAIN: *The $30,000 Bequest and Other Stories*. New York: Oxford University Press, 1996 (The Oxford Mark Twain, ed. by SHELLEY FISHER FISHKIN), 171–185.

TWAIN, MARK [1907]: *Christian Science*. New York: Oxford University Press, 1996 (The Oxford Mark Twain, ed. by SHELLEY FISHER FISHKIN).

TWAIN, MARK [1907]: Autobiographical dictation, 31 July 1906. In *Autobiography of Mark Twain*. Vol. II, ed. by BENJAMIN GRIFFIN, HARRIET E. SMITH, VICTOR FISCHER, MICHAEL FRANK, SHARON K. GOETZ, LESLIE DIANE MYRICK and ROBERT H. HIRST. Berkeley: University of California Press, 2013, 151–157.

TWAIN, MARK [1907–1909]: *Autobiography of Mark Twain*. Vol. III. Ed. by HARRIET E. SMITH, BENJAMIN GRIFFIN, VICTOR FISCHER, MICHAEL B. FRANK, AMANDA GAGEL, SHARON K. GOETZ, LESLIE DIANE MYRICK, and CHRISTOPHER M. OHGE. Mark Twain Papers. Berkeley: University of California Press, 2015.

WETZEL-SAHM, BIRGIT (1986): Deadpan Emotionalized: American Humor in a German Translation of Mark Twain's "Journalism in Tennessee". *Studies in American Humor*, New Series 2, 5.1 (Spring): 3–16

ZEHR, MARTIN (2010): The "Treaty with China," and the Chinese Connection. *Journal of Transnational American Studies* 2.1. Web [24 July 2016].

ZWICK, JIM (Ed.) (1992): *Mark Twain's Weapons of Satire: Anti-Imperialist Writings on the Philippine-American War*. Syracuse: Syracuse University Press (Syracuse Studies on Piece and Conflict Resolution).

Cultural Range Wars in R. Lynn Riggs's *Green Grow the Lilacs* and Rodgers and Hammerstein's *Oklahoma!*

Manfred Siebald

When the musical *Oklahoma!* opened at the St. James Theatre, New York, on 31 March 1943, it was understood that author Oscar Hammerstein II and composer Richard Rodgers had created a new version of a play that had been successful in some measure, but then not profitable enough to make it a lasting success: Lynn Riggs's *Green Grow the Lilacs* (1931). Hammerstein and Rodgers had, in fact, not just revised some elements of a nostalgic play with interspersed folk songs – they had crafted a complex plurimedial treatment of a historical period in which diverging economic and political interests led to physical range wars that can be seen as clashes of distinct cultures.

While neither the play nor the musical present actual fighting over land claims or grazing rights – physical conflicts are only hinted at in passing – the constellation of characters and the action in general suggest an antagonism between farmers and cowboys that is left somewhat unresolved in the play and is solved temporarily in the musical as the Indian Territory gradually approaches membership in the Union as the State of Oklahoma.

I have commented elsewhere (SIEBALD 2006, 2007, 2008) on the fact that the plots of quite a few American musicals in the wake of *Show Boat* (1927) feed on ethnic, social, political, and cultural conflicts, and my claim has always been that the plurimediality of this genre seems especially suited to making the complexity of such conflicts visual and audible and to negotiating between the opposing forces by employing a greater number of semiotic codes than novels, poetry or plays can muster. In addition to the linguistic signs of written texts, theatre uses paralinguistic signs, nonverbal acoustic signs like noises and music; kinesic signs like mimics, gestures, proxemics, dance; signs involving the appearance of actors (makeup, hairstyle, costume); and signs of the performance space like architecture, stage decoration, props, and lighting (according to FISCHER-LICHTE 1994: 25–179). But even more than the theatrical play, the musical appears to be the generic site for the employment of the greatest number of semiotic codes. Though *Green Grow the Lilacs* is somewhat plurimedial in that it uses more songs than are usual in a play, *Oklahoma!* easily outdoes it when it comes to the integration of various codes that together reflect the complex conflict of the plot. I intend to deal with several questions in this article: How are the Oklahoma range conflicts represented in the play and the musical, and to what purpose? Specifically, how do the various semiotic codes outline two distinct cultures at war and how do they fabricate a thematic and dramatic coherence?

Range Wars in the Old West

Range wars have long served as fictional settings of novels and movies about the American West, Owen Wister's *The Virginian* being a prominent example. In the second half of the nineteenth century, the diverging interests of ranchers, on the one hand, and farmers, on the other, led to conflicts that were not to be solved by the voluntary or involuntary removal of one of the adversaries to any open land in the West. In the Old West, the conflicts usually were of a mainly economic nature – they were fought over water resources, over grazing rights of cattle and sheep, and the fencing-in of farmland. Today, this tradition continues but, as Paul Lindholdt has recently observed, "stakes in the New West have changed, and range wars now rage over issues like the preservation of native wildlife habitats and biological diversity [...]" (LINDHOLDT 2015: 39).[1]

The historical development toward statehood of the Indian Territory later known as Oklahoma was a complex affair. It not only involved the transformation of a region with a notorious past – the use of the land to accommodate Native tribes unwanted in the East – into a recognized state of the Union; it also revealed the plights of homesteaders who tried to make a living in the face of natural vicissitudes and of ranchers and cattle drivers who had to adapt to the modern times of the railroad; and there were also conflicts among Native tribes, and ethnic conflicts involving African Americans held as slaves by Native Americans that had to be solved (SMITH 2007).

To many people, the Trail of Tears of the 1830s – the forced removal of the Five Civilized Tribes to what was to be called the Indian Territory – was a thing of the past at the end of the century, but the policies of the majority of tribes during the Civil War were still remembered: Most of the Natives had aligned with the South and had been punished by the federal government, which gave parts of the Territory to such tribes as the Cheyenne and the Arapaho. A further act of punishment was the allotment of almost two million acres to white settlers (BOYER et al. 2000: 496).

The Homestead Act of 1862 had promised settlers a maximum of 160 acres – later doubled in the Enlarged Homestead Act of 1909 (ABBOTT 1994: 472) – for farming and living on the land for five years. The lot could also be bought after six months. When on 22 April 1889, at the shot of a pistol, some 60,000 potential settlers, the so-called "boomers", stormed into those parts of the Indian Territory which had been opened by Congress for land-seeking would-be residents (STILL [1961] 1975: 238–239), they had to face the fact that many "sooners" had squatted on the land before the official beginning of the race for the best sites. Events like the founding of the town of Guthrie (which grew from zero to 10,000 inhabitants within a single day) were called "magical beyond belief" in the media (HOWARD 1889, qtd. in STILL [1961] 1975: 239), but the competition among the homesteaders was so great and the claim disputes so intense that it would take a long time before something like a collective identity, let alone a common culture, emerged.

A further complication was the fact that "[c]attle raising was becoming an increasingly specialized business by the 1880s", and the fight over "[free] grass" pitched cattle corporations and their poorly paid cowboys against farmers and against each other (WHITE 1994: 262–263). When cattle prices fell in the 1880s, conditions got even worse. The attainment of a collective identity of "territory people" thus seemed almost impossible.

[1] This phenomenon can be observed from the nineteenth century until today, beginning with the Johnson County War in 1889–1893 (see DAVIS 2010), to the present (see the video of Farnham on *ABC News* 2014; the articles "Oregon Ranchers" [*CBS News* 2016], and "Bundy Brothers" [*The New York Times* 2016]).

What was, on the surface, an economic conflict about grazing grounds and arable land was, of course, also a clash of myths (cowboy vs. homesteader). It was, in fact, a sort of cultural range war. If we define culture as a life view expressible and expressed through religious, artistic, and social means, then the years around the turn of the century saw not just a haggling about properties or material values. They saw a clash of different attitudes toward the environment, different images of humanity, different lifestyles, and different sets of moral values. Or, as Lynn Riggs phrased it in the preface to his play, they saw two ways in which people "relate themselves to the earth and to other people" (RIGGS [1931] 2003: 4).

That also pertains to *Oklahoma!*. While Andrea Most, in her study of the dynamics of Jewish assimilation, has claimed that the musical presents "a set of characters with individual problems that demand resolution" (MOST 1998: 79), I claim that these characters and their problems are representative of different cultures – lifestyles and ways of thinking – that seem to be incompatible but have to be reconciled in some way or other.

R. Lynn Riggs, Green Grow the Lilacs *(1931)*

Lynn Riggs (1899–1954), of the Cherokee Nation, has been called "the greatest of western dramatists" (MAGUIRE 1987: 211), and his play *Green Grow the Lilacs*, although he did not write it somewhere on the Prairies but in France, is a tribute to the West as the site of human endurance.

In the play, the political and economic interests clashing before the Territory's attainment of statehood intertwine with a love triangle (around farmer Laurey Williams) which ends in a deadly fight between a cowboy (Curly McClain) and a farmhand (Jeeter Fry) that leaves the farmhand dead. The play ends with the court trial still pending and thus the question of legal responsibility still unresolved. Apart from various references to the historical process,[2] Riggs's play does little to take sides or to suggest solutions – probably because of a totally different agenda. According to the playwright's preface, it might have been subtitled *An Old Song*:

> The intent has been solely to recapture in a kind of nostalgic glow (but in dramatic dialogue more than in song) the great range of mood which characterized the old folk songs and ballads I used to hear in my Oklahoma childhood – their quaintness, their sadness, their robustness, their simplicity, their hearty or bawdy humors, their sentimentalities, their melodrama, their touching sweetness. (RIGGS [1931] 2003: 4)

Thus, Riggs deliberately left the "conventions of ordinary theatricality – a complex plot, swift actions, etc. –" and tried to "exhibit luminously, in the simplest of stories, a wide area of mood and feeling" (RIGGS [1931] 2003: 4). It does not become quite clear what was more important to him: the characters and the simple story, or the fourteen songs that he interspersed in the action. If we look for any tight correspondence between the songs and the action, we will be somewhat disappointed. But at least they do help to delineate the types of cowboy and farmer.

[2] There are, for example, references that foreshadow the situation in Oklahoma in the 1930s, such as Laurey's dream of going to California, where the oranges grow (RIGGS [1931] 2003: 24).

The opening song, "As I walked out one bright sunny morning" with its chorus about the cattle, the "little dogies", whose future "bright home" will be Wyoming (RIGGS [1931] 2003: 7), serves to identify Curly McClain as a cowboy.[3] The dogies turn up again in the next song, "A-ridin' ole Paint" (Riggs [1931] 2003: 11–12) – at a point in time when bow-legged Curly boasts about being the state's best "bronc buster" (Riggs [1931] 2003: 10). If these songs accomplish anything, it is the evocation of the open range, which Curly later misses when he has fallen in love with Laurey and in spite of his initial ignorance of agriculture[4] is planning to be a farmer who, despite the hostile weather conditions, loves the land:

> If I'd ever a-thought –! Oh, I'd orta been a farmer, and worked hard at it, and saved, and kep' buyin' more land, and plowed and planted, like somebody – 'stid of doin' the way I've done! Now the cattle business'll soon be over with. The ranches are breakin' up fast. They're puttin' in barbed w'ar, and plowin' up the sod fer wheat and corn. Purty soon they won't be no grazin' – thousands of acres – no place fer the cowboy to lay his head. (RIGGS [1931] 2003: 70–71)[5]

On their wedding night, Curly tells Laurey:

> Look at the way the hay field lays out purty in the moonlight. Next it's the pasture, and over yander's the wheat and the corn, and the cane patch next, nen the truck garden and the timber. Everthing laid out fine and jim dandy! The country all around it – all Indian Territory – plumb to the Rio Grande, and north to Kansas, and 'way over east to Arkansaw, the same way, with the moon onto it. (RIGGS [1931] 2003: 76–77)

Apart from the general function of establishing the cowboy identity and thus preparing its demise, most of the other songs show little connection to the action. The play's title song, "Green Grow the Lilacs", is sung for the first time when Curly has heard that his adored Laurey Williams will go to the party with another man. The stanzas tell the story of an abandoned young lover who is going into the army, "to change the green lilacs to the red, white, and blue" (RIGGS [1931] 2003: 20). When he has sung the song with its "absurd yet plaintive charm" and its "sentimental periods", he appears to be "miraculously healed" (RIGGS [1931] 2003: 20).

In scene 4, Old Man Peck suggests "a little singin' to give us a rest" during the party (RIGGS [1931] 2003: 62), and what follows is a kind of hootenanny with songs whose lyrics have only the faintest connection to the action. Peck, since he knows only sad songs, proposes the highly distressing story about Custer's Last Stand with its ending about the "blue-eyed boy" being dead and leaving his praying mother and his girlfriend behind. The next song consists of four stanzas of Tom Ford's poem "There Is a Lady, Sweet and Kind", the seventeenth-century language of which is spectacularly incompatible with the

[3] Hammerstein found the lyrical stage direction at the beginning of Riggs's play ("[…] giving off a visible golden emanation that is partly true and partly a trick of imagination, focusing to keep alive a loveliness that may pass away") so impressive that he decided to put it into song (HAMMERSTEIN [1949] 1985: 9).

[4] Curly admits to Jeeter that he does not "know a peach tree from a cornstalk" (RIGGS [1931] 2003: 41).

[5] There are other negative mentionings of barbed wire, e.g., by Aunt Eller (RIGGS [1931] 2003: 55).

Oklahoma dialect of the dialogue: "Cupid is wingèd and doth range / Her country so my love doth change [...]" (RIGGS [1931] 2003: 65–66) and, from the mouth of an American cowboy, rings somewhat peculiar. The conspicuous absence of songs from the last dramatic scene shows how little, in fact, music corresponds, or adds, to the storyline in this play. Here the song pool on which Riggs could draw proves to have been just too small.

Richard Rodgers and Oscar Hammerstein II, Oklahoma! *(1943)*

Oscar Hammerstein liked Riggs's play nonetheless and publicly paid his due to the dramatist: "Mr. Riggs' play is the wellspring of almost all that is good in Oklahoma!. I kept many of the lines of the original play without making any changes in them at all for the simple reason that they could not be improved on – at any rate, not by me. Lynn Riggs and Green Grow the Lilacs are the very soul of Oklahoma!."[6] However, in his "Notes on Lyrics", Hammerstein seems to comment unfavorably on Riggs when he says that he does not believe in musical comedies which "cannot sustain a story interest when it is interrupted continually by songs that are of little value to the plot" (HAMMERSTEIN [1949] 1985: 15). He believes in a "well-integrated musical play" instead (HAMMERSTEIN [1949] 1985: 15).

Thus, *Oklahoma!* avoids presenting any of the traditional folk songs used in the earlier play but offers songs that tightly fit into the action, comment on past and current events, and foreshadow future developments, respectively. Riggs sorely missed in the musical the folk songs of *Green Grow the Lilacs* and privately dismissed the new original songs as "show tunes" (WEAVER 2003: xii). And Dwight McDonald accused *Oklahoma!* of containing "folk-fakery" and of being an example of "midcult", i.e., "a saccharine corruption of 'high culture' for the middlebrow American audience" (qtd. in LAWSON-PEEBLES 1996: 5). In spite of all that, it was tremendously successful in commercial terms. Indeed, Hammerstein, by using dialect in the dialogue and lyrics, and Rodgers, by the simplicity of his melodies, produced one of the most successful musicals of all times.

In 1943, their concept still ran counter to the expectations of the standard "musical comedy audience" that primarily expected "the sight of pretty girls in pretty clothes moving about the stage, the sound of their vital young voices supporting the principals in their songs" (HAMMERSTEIN [1949] 1985: 8). When writer and composer embarked on their long cooperation, they were aware of their limitations and their fortes, as Hammerstein observed: "I don't believe that either Dick or I would be very successful essentially as popular songwriters – writers of songs detached from plays. We can write words and music best when they are required by a situation or a characterization in a story" (HAMMERSTEIN [1949] 1985: 14).

Both had individual records of successfully reworking literary pieces when they decided to transform Riggs's play into a musical. Most scholars agree that the first musical to transcend the vaudeville tradition of more or less unrelated "numbers" was Hammerstein's *Show Boat* (1927), which can be considered the first "book musical".

[6] *The New York Times*, 4 September 1943, qtd. in Liner Notes, RIGGS [1931] 2003.

Range Wars in Oklahoma! *Songs*

According to Joseph Roach, *Oklahoma!* forms an "interlocking system of performance skills – not solely singing, dancing, and acting (or writing, directing, and designing) – but all of those together, not subordinated to music as in opera, but coordinated as an integrated ensemble of autonomous elements" (ROACH 2007: 179). The most conspicuous specimen of such an integration of diverse elements – or semiotic codes – in *Oklahoma!* is the combination of the poetic and musical codes in the form of songs.

From the beginning, Hammerstein indicated through text, subtext, and song the features of the ranges that farmers and cowboys fought over. In the very first stage direction we find a telling juxtaposition: "[...] cattle in a meadow, blades of the young corn" – elements that are then taken up in the first song, which talks of "corn as high [ ] as a elephant's eye" and of cattle which "are standin' like statues". (RODGERS/HAMMERSTEIN [1842] 1959: 7) Since the first characters to be seen and heard are a farm woman and a cowboy, we get a sense of the dominant thematic constellation early on.

The antagonism between farmers and cowboys is also reflected in the two camps of suitors who have set their minds on winning Laurey Williams's favor: farmer Jace Hutchins and the hired farmhand Jud Fry (Riggs's Jeeter), on the one side, and cowboy Curly McClain, on the other. Jud, although he "[j]ist about runs the farm by hisself", is so occupied with winning Laurey, however, that "he don't know a plow from a thrashin' machine" (RODGERS/HAMMERSTEIN [1942] 1959: 17) and spends his time stalking her. The opposition between the cowboy's and the farmer's lives is not just an occupational but a cultural contrast, as Curly tells Jud before they have a shooting competition (which the cowboy wins) in Jud's dismal smokehouse: "In this country, they's two things you c'n do if you're a man: Live out of doors is one. Live in a hole is the other" (RODGERS/HAMMERSTEIN [1942] 1959: 44). Jud resists this cultural claim made by "[...] that Smart Aleck cowhand / Who thinks he is better'n me!" (RODGERS/HAMMERSTEIN [1942] 1959: 47)

After the antagonism of the two lifestyles and cultures has thus been firmly established, the song in 2.1 not only sums the situation up, but tries to propose a deceptively simple solution:

> The farmer and the cowman should be friends.
> Oh, the farmer and the cowman should be friends.
> One man likes to push a plow,
> The other likes to chase a cow,
> But that's no reason why they cain't be friends.
> (RODGERS/HAMMERSTEIN [1942] 1959: 51)

The solution – friendship between the adversaries – which the song suggests is, of course, not the result of an elaborate political or economic analysis. In fact, the conflict is downsized and played out as a difference between subjective likes and dislikes. A non-political character is also suggested by Jud's singing the song "like a Negro at a revivalist meeting" (RODGERS/HAMMERSTEIN [1942] 1959: 42).

One last example of reconciliation through song is the duet "People Will Say We're in Love" (RODGERS/HAMMERSTEIN [1942] 1959: 36–38). After the lovers' "violent antagonism" (HAMMERSTEIN [1949] 1985: 14) in 2.2 has subsided and Laurey has accepted Curly's proposal, he turns the doubtful "People will say we're in love!" into a triumphant "Let people say we're in love!" (RODGERS/HAMMERSTEIN [1942] 1959: 72). In the context of the historical narrative, the love-and-marriage trope serves to affirm a mounting self-confidence of soon-to-be Oklahomans and comprises the overcoming of misgivings and doubts within a few stanzas.

The following propagandistic appeal that "Territory folks should stick together, / Territory folks should all be pals" (RODGERS/HAMMERSTEIN [1942] 1959: 52) tries to establish a collective identity – but still in the context of the old Indian Territory. The time, as indicated at the beginning of the musical, being "*Just after the turn of the century*" (RODGERS/HAMMERSTEIN [1942] 1959: 4), the idea of statehood is still one step away, and unification is called for only in terms of socializing: "Cowboys, dance with the farmers' daughters! / Farmers, dance with the ranchers' gals!" (RODGERS/HAMMERSTEIN [1942] 1959: 52) Whether the proposed "dance" is a prelude to, or an early stage of, human reproduction, ultimately leading to future generations that do not know the differences between farmer and cowboy any more, is left to the audience's imagination.

After this, the song turns into a kind of playful court case, foreshadowing the mock trial in the last scene. At this point, one of the main complaints about the changing times – the fencing in of land by the farmers – is mentioned, but it is overruled by the call for an intercultural understanding between the two parties. The chorus pulls things together and points to a more harmonious future: It is the vision of the territory turning into a state within the Union:

> And when this territory is a state,
> And jines the union jist like all the others,
> The farmer and the cowman and the merchant
> Must all behave theirsel's and act like brothers.
> (RODGERS/HAMMERSTEIN [1942] 1959: 54)

This is taken up by the musical's title song. "Oklahoma" freely mixes elements of farm and ranch: barley, carrots and "pertaters", "[p]asture for the cattle", "[s]pinach and termayters", "[f]lowers on the prairie where the June bugs zoom", "[p]len'y of air and plen'y of room", "[p]len'y of room to swing a rope!" (RODGERS/HAMMERSTEIN [1942] 1959: 76).

Curly and Laurey, on the occasion of their wedding, thematize the overarching parallel of marriage and intercultural reconciliation, both implying a fresh start:

> CURLY
> Startin' as a farmer with a brand-new wife –
> LAUREY
> Soon be livin' in a brand-new state!
> (RODGERS/HAMMERSTEIN [1942] 1959: 75)

As Carey Wall argues, "Laurie's [*sic*] leap from autonomous girl into no-longer-autonomous wife parallels and interprets her community's leap into the society-making of a 'brand-new state'" (WALL 1996: 27). It is the combination of the two conflicting realms that forms a collective identity out of warring factions, and an identification of people with the land itself:

> We know we belong to the land,
> And the land we belong to is grand!
> (RODGERS/HAMMERSTEIN [1942] 1959: 76)

There are many more instances of songs that are highly effective in epitomizing issues, outlining reasons or solutions, or propelling the action forward.

Why is *Oklahoma!* so successful in semioticizing conflict and solution through song – more so than *Green Grow the Lilacs*? Hammerstein's belief in the effectiveness of the combined linguistic and musical codes is clear enough: "No dialogue could do this dramatic job as vividly and quickly as does the song" (HAMMERSTEIN [1949] 1985: 19). Riggs employs songs in order to conjure up the feelings of a bygone time, and it is mostly their iconic character that is of value for the action. Hammerstein and Rodgers, on the other hand, use songs as distinct carriers of meanings – as building blocks, not as wall-paper.

Range Wars in Oklahoma!*: Proxemics and Dance*

As may be expected, the effects of the musical and linguistic codes are supplemented and augmented in *Oklahoma!* by those of the proxemic code, which is employed ubiquitously – for instance, when Laurey and Gertie "*step toward each other menacingly*" – signaling their rivalry over Curly (RODGERS/HAMMERSTEIN [1942] 1959: 35). And when the men complain about the way in which the institution of marriage threatens their freedom (calling it a scandal and an outrage) and announce: "We gotta start a revolution!", the girls ironically take them up on this, telling them to "[r]evolve" – which is realized in a physical way: "*The boys swing around, see the girls and are immediately cowed*" (RODGERS/HAMMERSTEIN [1942] 1959: 35).

But ultimately it is the repeated employment of dance proper – the combined effects of proxemics and music – that makes substantial contributions to the evolution of the action. From Will's reverie about the progress and the unlimited opportunities and possibilities of Kansas (RODGERS/HAMMERSTEIN [1942] 1959: 15), which he sings about but also visualizes in a two-step, to the waltzing chorus of girls on the way to the Box Social (RODGERS/HAMMERSTEIN [1942] 1959: 28–29), the rhythmic movements of solo dancers, ensembles, and the entire cast help to express the sentiments that propel the action along. It is partly through the interaction of individual dancers and the community that anything like a sense of community or even a collective identity evolves (see MOST 1998: 79).

The most memorable example, however, of dance as a signifier can be found in Laurey's drug-infused dream (1.3). There, Laurey, Curly, and Jud are represented by "dream figures" (RODGERS/HAMMERSTEIN [1942] 1959: 50) who dance "ecstatically" and "gaily" before enacting a surrogate courtship and wedding. When the dream counterpart of Jud appears and usurps Curly's place, the scene turns into a menacing representation of his sinister desires – with women doing an "amusing, satirically bawdy dance" (RODGERS/HAMMERSTEIN [1942] 1959: 50). The ensuing fight between Curly and Jud results in Curly's death, reciprocally foreshadowing the musical's final scene in which the farmhand attacks the cowboy but is accidentally killed himself. Thus the element of dance structurally sets the stage for "the plot twist that drives the entire second act" (MOST 1998: 85). All in all, dance – in traditional and new styles, in individual performances and ballet scenes – is used by Rodgers and Hammerstein not only to enhance the messages of dialogue and song, but to carry meanings and evoke sentiments that otherwise would not be recognizable in the plot.

The Historical Moment at the Time of the Play's and the Musical's Genesis

The political and economic situation in which Riggs's play and the musical were created was no less complex than the time depicted in these works, and it has received a spate of critical comments. Hundreds of thousands of "Okies" were fleeing from the man- and nature-made Dust Bowl catastrophe of the mid-1930s (see KENNEDY 1998: 195), which for many people had aggravated the disastrous effects of the stock market crash of October 1929 and the ensuing Depression. Roosevelt tried to deal with that in his New Deal measures. In 1941, America entered World War II. Can these developments explain the creation and publication of a play and a musical about the beginning of the century?

Theories about the political strategies behind the creation of *Oklahoma!* in 1943 abound. Raymond Knapp sees surprising parallels between "a series of treaties and forced migrations of American Indians" and land thefts in Indian Territory in the late nineteenth century, on the one hand, and Germany's "series of provocative land grabs" in the 1930s, in which neighboring regions and countries were occupied or annexed (KNAPP 2005: 124–125), on the other. He goes so far as to hypothetically compare Riggs to a Polish dramatist who looks back on the past:

> [...] we might imagine, in a fully Germanized Europe some thirty years later, a Pole born around mid-century on a "reservation" somewhere in the former Poland writes a play that re-creates nostalgically a past era, which is then converted into a musical that celebrates the emergent German community overcoming its petty internal conflicts and assuming its place as a full-fledged "state" of the German Reich – to be performed in Berlin or Leipzig for an audience who had managed to forget that Poland had once belonged to someone else and that its very name announced that fact. (KNAPP 2005: 125–126)

Other critics have suspected the play of being undercover propaganda for various Roosevelt policies of the 1940s. Bruce Kirle, for instance, claims that the political impact of Rodgers and Hammerstein's musical was carefully planned: Hammerstein supported Roosevelt's policies by resolving not only the conflict between interventionists and isolationists, but also the one between New Dealers and conservatives. Moreover, Kirle claims that the play helped defuse the rampant wartime anti-Semitism in the United States by making the liminal figure of the peddler Ali Hakim a representative of Jewishness and having him "assimilated into the community almost against his will" (KIRLE 2003: 263).[7] To me, such pointed claims, which turn play and musical into thinly disguised allegories, seem a little far-fetched. However, there are broader views that one can certainly subscribe to:

> American nationalist mythologies [...] exhibit a specifically American strain of inclusiveness and reconciliation; not surprisingly, mythologizing musicals frequently use the marriage trope to represent the merger of supposed incompatibilities. Such mergers, and America's capacity to nurture them, provide the implicit foundation of America's peculiar strength as a nation. (KNAPP 2005: 122)

Conclusion

Thus, *Oklahoma!*'s insistence on the possibility of reconciliation between the rivaling parties in the cultural range wars can at least be seen as a contribution to the formation and strengthening of centripetal mythologies. Riggs's play has been said to have a "dark side more ominous than the treatment of evil in *Oklahoma!*" (MAGUIRE 1987: 212) and, indeed, the musical mostly ignores negative elements like, for instance, ethnic discrimination or racially motivated violence that might support centrifugal tendencies. Racial conflicts, according to Knapp, are generally absent in musicals of this sort since these are meant "to reassure a nation of its own essential goodness" (KNAPP 2005: 122).

Just like Riggs's play, *Oklahoma!* focuses on the economic anxieties of homesteaders and ranchers and on the questions of jurisdiction in the Territory before statehood, but it produces a more positive outlook than the play. Its ending – an *ad hoc* court (considered illegal by the federal marshall) acquits the cowboy on his wedding night – wraps up all the proposed solutions in optimistic singing: "Oh, What a Beautiful Mornin'" (RODGERS/ HAMMERSTEIN [1942] 1959: 84).

But *Oklahoma!* is much more sophisticated than that. What seems like a victory of ranch over farm – the cowboy involuntarily killing the farmhand – is counterbalanced by the cowboy himself giving up his free life on the prairies and turning into a farmer, which makes the farmers' side prevail. There seem to be only losers in this cultural range war – or, seen from another angle – only winners. As the range wars gradually abate in *Green Grow the Lilacs* – even more so in *Oklahoma!* – and as hegemonic attempts at obtaining dominance over another culture are abandoned in favor of an intercultural understanding, the vanishing of clear binary structures reveals something like an early transcultural perspective.

Green Grow the Lilacs may be a bit more detailed when treating the Territory's difficulties in transforming itself into a State of the Union, but it falls short of making the best of all the available theatrical means. The poetic and musical codes of the interspersed songs do not point in the same direction as the plot. *Oklahoma!*, on the other hand, can

[7] Andrea Most makes a similar point (MOST 1998: 87) and additionally maintains that Rodgers and Hammerstein were influenced by 1940s Zionism with its "utopian socialist vision of a homeland where Jews could return to the soil, become farmers, and claim the land as their own. The show's poignant and nostalgic rendering of the Oklahoma land mirrored a long-sustained Jewish dream of homecoming" (MOST 1998: 81).

be said to harmonize the jarring discords between farmer and rancher a little too easily, but it certainly is more successful in employing mutually supportive semiotic codes of the theatre.

List of Works Cited

ABBOTT, CARL (1994): The Federal Presence. In CLYDE A. MILNER II, CAROL A. O'CONNOR, and MARTHA A. SANDWEISS (Eds.): *The Oxford History of the American West*. New York: Oxford University Press, 469–500.

AUGHTRY, CHARLES EDWARD (1959): Lynn Riggs at the University of Oklahoma. *Chronicles of Oklahoma* 37.3: 280–284. *http://digital.library.okstate.edu/Chronicles/v037/v037p280.pdf.*

AUGHTRY, CHARLES EDWARD (1959): *Lynn Riggs, Dramatist. A Critical Biography*. Diss. Brown University.

BENTON, JOSEPH (1956): Some Personal Remembrances about Lynn Riggs. *Chronicles of Oklahoma* 34.3: 296–301. *http://digital.library.okstate.edu/Chronicles/v034/v034p296.pdf*

BOYER, PAUL, CLIFFORD E. CLARK, JOSEPH F. KETT, NEAL SALISBURY, HARVARD SITKOFF, and NANCY WOLOCH ([4]2000): *The Enduring Vision. A History of the American People*. Boston: Houghton Mifflin.

BRAUNLICH, PHYLLIS COLE (1988): *The Cherokee Night* of R. Lynn Riggs. *Midwest Quarterly* 30.1: 45–59.

BRAUNLICH, PHYLLIS COLE (1990): The Oklahoma Plays of R. Lynn Riggs. *World Literature Today* 64.3: 390–394.

COX, JAMES H. (2011): Tribal Nations and the Other Territories of American Indian Literary History. In CAROLINE F. LEVANDER and ROBERT S. LEVINE (Eds.): *A Companion to American Literary Studies*. Chichester: Wiley-Blackwell, 356–372.

DAVIS, JOHN W. (2010): *Wyoming Range War. The Infamous Invasion of Johnson County*. Norman: University of Oklahoma Press.

FISCHER-LICHTE, ERIKA ([3]1994): *Das System der theatralischen Zeichen*. Vol. I of *Semiotik des Theaters: Eine Einführung*. 3 vols. Tübingen: Narr.

HAMMERSTEIN, OSCAR II ([1949] 1985): Notes on Lyrics. *Lyrics*. Milwaukee, WI: Hal Leonard Books, 3–48.

HOWARD, WILLIAM W. (1889): The Rush to Oklahoma. *Harper's Weekly* 33, 18 May, 391–394.

KENNEDY, DAVID M. (1999): *Freedom from Fear. The American People in Depression and War, 1929–1945*. New York: Oxford University Press.

KIRLE, BRUCE (2003): Reconciliation, Resolution and the Political Role of *Oklahoma!* in American Consciousness. *Theatre Journal* 55.2: 251–274.

KNAPP, RAYMOND (2005). *The American Musical and the Formation of National Identity*. Princeton: Princeton University Press.

LAWSON-PEEBLES, ROBERT (1996): Introduction. In ROBERT LAWSON-PEEBLES (Ed.): *Approaches to the American Musical*. Exeter: University of Exeter Press, 1–18.

LINDHOLDT, PAUL (2015). *Explorations in Ecocriticism. Advocacy, Bioregionalism, and Visual Design*. Lanham, MD: Lexington Books.

MAGUIRE, JAMES H. (1987): Western American Drama to 1960. In J. GOLDEN TAYLOR (Ed.): *A Literary History of the American West*. Fort Worth: Texas Christian University Press, 204–220.

MILNER, CLYDE A. II, CAROL A. O'CONNOR, and MARTHA A. SANDWEISS (Eds.) (1994): *The Oxford History of the American West*. New York: Oxford University Press.

MORDDEN, ETHAN (1983): *Broadway Babies. The People Who Made the American Musical*. New York: Oxford University Press.

MOST, ANDREA (1998): *"We Know We Belong to the Land." The Theatricality of Assimilation in Rodgers and Hammerstein's* Oklahoma! *PMLA* 113.1: 77–89.

RIGGS, LYNN ([1931] 2003): *Green Grow the Lilacs*. In *The Cherokee Night and Other Plays*. Norman: University of Oklahoma Press, 2–105.

ROACH, JOSEPH (2007): World Bank Drama. In WAI CHEE DIMOCK and LAWRENCE BUELL (Eds.): *Shades of the Planet: American Literature as World Literature*. Princeton: Princeton University Press, 171–183.

RODGERS, RICHARD, and OSCAR HAMMERSTEIN II ([1942] 1959): *Oklahoma!*. In *Six Plays by Rodgers and Hammerstein*. New York: Modern Library, 1–84.

SIEBALD, MANFRED (2006): Carmen am Broadway. Oscar Hammersteins *Carmen Jones*. In KLAUS LEY (Ed.): *Caecilia – Tosca – Carmen: Brüche und Kontinuitäten im Verhältnis von Musik und Welterleben*. Tübingen: Francke, 225–234.

SIEBALD, MANFRED (2007): Intercultural War and Peace in American Literary Musicals. *Show Boat, West Side Story, The Capeman*. In ALFRED HORNUNG (Ed.): *Intercultural America*. Heidelberg: Universitätsverlag Winter, 309–322.

SIEBALD, MANFRED (2008): "The party in Berlin is over." *Cabaret* und die politischen Kulturen eines amerikanischen literarischen Musicals. In WERNER KREMP und DAVID SIRAKOV (Eds.): *Globaler Gesang vom Garten der Freiheit: Anglo-amerikanische Populärmusik und ihre Bedeutung für die US-Außenpolitik*. Trier: Wissenschaftlicher Verlag Trier (Atlantische Texte 28), 59–69.

SMITH, CHRIS (2007): Going to the Nation. The Idea of Oklahoma in Early Blues Recordings. *Popular Music* 26.1: 83–96.

STILL, BAYRD (Ed.) ([1961] 1975): *The West: Contemporary Records of America's Expansion across the Continent, 1607–1890*. New York: Capricorn, 238–239.

WALL, CAREY (1996): There's No Business like Show Business. A Speculative Reading of the Broadway Musical. In ROBERT LAWSON-PEEBLES (Ed.): *Approaches to the American Musical*. Exeter: University of Exeter Press, 24–43.

WEAVER, JACE (2003): Foreword. In LYNN RIGGS: *The Cherokee Night and Other Plays*. Norman: University of Oklahoma Press, ix–xv.

WHITE, RICHARD (1994): Animals and Enterprise. In CLYDE A. MILNER II, CAROL A. O'CONNOR, and MARTHA A. SANDWEISS (Eds.): *The Oxford History of the American West*. New York: Oxford University Press, 237–276.

WILSON, ELOISE: "Lynn Riggs. Oklahoma Dramatist." Ph.D. diss., University of Pennsylvania, 1957.

News, Videos

ABC News (2014): Nevada Rancher Threatens "Range War" Against Feds. Video by Alan Farnham, (7 April). *http://abcnews.go.com/US/video/nevada-rancher-threatens-range-war-feds-23234265* [14 October 2016].

CBS News (2016): Oregon Ranchers Reject Cliven Bundy Family Occupation. (3 January). *http://www.cbsnews.com/news/oregon-ranchers-reject-cliven-bundy-family-occupation/* [14 October 2016].

The New York Times (2016): Bundy Brothers Acquitted in Takeover of Oregon Wildlife Refuge. (27 October 2016). *http://www.nytimes.com/2016/10/28/us/bundy-brothers-acquitted-in-take over-of-oregon-wildlife-refuge.html* [28 October 2016].

Contesting the Southern Way of Life
Katharine Du Pre Lumpkin's Autobiography and the Progressive American South during the Interwar Years

Charles Reagan Wilson

The term 'way of life' can be a powerful evocation of an ideology. During the Great Depression, commentators coined the term 'American way of life' to describe the collective identity and culture of the besieged people of the United States. It was a cultural construct that was popular in the New Deal as shorthand for 'democracy', in that era that promoted democratic participation and social reform. During the Cold War it continued to have that meaning, but businessmen and industrialists defined the 'American way' as free enterprise, as distinct from the Soviet Union's collectivist economic system. More recently, after 9/11, Americans once more began using the term in response to terrorism's threat to fundamental religious, democratic, and nationalistic values. In the aftermath of the terrorist attacks in Paris in December of 2015, French commentators and others noted that the attacks were on the 'French way of life', noting that the violence at Parisian restaurants, an important music venue, and at a soccer field all reflected fundamental aspects of French lifestyle, or more generally, the nation's way of life.

Reflections on the society, worldviews, and cultures of the American South have also generated a construct called the 'Southern way of life'. Nineteenth-century white Southerners before the Civil War had outlined a defense of slavery that they saw as the essence of a 'Southern civilization'. Defeat in the Civil War and the experience of Reconstruction, which white Southerners identified with corrupt and incompetent African American rule, led white Southerners to define a memory of the Confederate experience and the Old South as the essence now of a white supremacist Southern way. By the early twentieth century, white Southerners had put into place an extraordinary degree of political, economic, religious, social, and cultural orthodoxy that made challenging the conventional understandings of a Southern way a life-threatening affair. To be sure, there were reformers, but many of them were ineffective and others had to leave the region under the threat of what W. J. Cash called the region's "Savage Ideal" of violently enforced orthodoxy (Cash [1941] 1956: 135).

The South in the early and mid-twentieth century produced many autobiographies and memoirs that charted the personal experiences of living under the Southern way of life. One of the richest of these is *The Making of a Southerner*, which appeared in 1947, at the end of several generations of people living under the sway of white-dominated institutions, but it was also at the end of World War II, which had helped to unleash forces of change in the South and nation that would lead to a new activist stage of the Civil Rights Movement. The author, Katharine Du Pre Lumpkin, tells the story of the rise in the post-Civil War years of Southern orthodoxy around the memory of the Civil War and the codification of white supremacy, both of which were at the heart of the dominant construct of the Southern way of life. The book is significant in showing how this dominant ideology came to be embodied in cultural attitudes and institutions. It is remarkable also in probing analysis of how she escaped from the rigid ideological orthodoxy she grew up in, from the white supremacist version of the Southern way of life, and came to promote a more egalitarian biracial version of the Southern way.

Katharine Du Pre Lumpkin was born in Georgia in 1897, the youngest child in a large family that had struggled with the loss of antebellum wealth because of the effects of the Civil War. Her father, William, was a Confederate officer, and in Reconstruction he was a member of the Ku Klux Klan, which helped reestablish white dominance from the brief effort to empower African American freedmen and women immediately after the war. Although the family name, Lumpkin, still commanded social prestige after the Civil War, her father lost great wealth as a result of the war, and he had to work for the railroad to make a living, moving to South Carolina, where he only lived a few months before dying and leaving his wife and children to try to live off the proceeds of a farm on poor land. Her father had been sustained after the war by romanticized memories of the Old South and his commitment to the Lost Cause. In her autobiography, Lumpkin shows how a Southern child in the turn-of-the-twentieth-century South learned the Southern identity, including the belief there was a distinctive Southern way of life whose preservation was of life and death importance. She was a child at a particularly turbulent time in the South, as the 1890s saw agricultural crisis, the revolt of farmers in the Populist movement, and the creation of a rigorous legal structure for a segregated society that enforced white power.

The Lost Cause movement had gained unprecedented social and political authority by then, linking white supremacy to a sacralized memory of Southern white history. The Civil War experience and Confederate defeat gave intensified meaning to the Southern regional consciousness that had emerged during the sectional crisis before the war. White Southerners nurtured their identity as a separate people within the American nation. Out of defeat came the myth of the Lost Cause, the sentimentalization of the Confederate experience after the war ended. Robert E. Lee was turned into/iconized as a virtual saint and Stonewall Jackson became a Christian martyr. Their images and those of other Confederate heroes were found in schools and on stained glass windows in churches. White Southerners had their sacred relics like the Confederate battle flag, the song "Dixie", and the Confederate monuments that still anchor Southern towns and cities. White Southerners celebrated distinctively regional rituals such as Confederate Memorial Day, the funerals of Confederate veterans, and the reunions of living veterans.

The 1890s saw the emergence of several powerful organizations that worked relentlessly to control the public memory of the South around idealized images of the Confederacy and antebellum Southern slave society. Katharine Du Pre Lumpkin's mother was a leader in the Lost Cause effort; her sister, Elizabeth, was a popular speaker at Confederate memorial activities, and Katharine herself was a member of the Children of the Confederacy. As Jacquelyn Dowd Hall notes, in the hands of such elite women, "the performance of Southern identity secured the identification of Southernness with whiteness" (Dowd Hall 1998: 111), as well as carving out a new public space in which Southern women could be leaders.

Every spring, Southerners enacted the rituals of what became the public memory of the region, gathering around the Confederate monument and sending their prayers, sermons, and speeches up to what had become a tribal God of the Protestant evangelical religion that overwhelmingly dominated the region. Lumpkin recalls in her memoir the physical landscape of the celebration of the Lost Cause: "May was the perfect time, for refreshing breezes could almost certainly be counted on", she writes; "trees and shrubs were at their deepest green, the great elms and oaks casting cool shade [...]" (115). Memory of the Southern way, based on the celebration of the Confederacy, rested on sensual images that evoked Southern places. "And when would flowers ever be so bountiful or varied again as in May, letting us literally strew them on the path of the old men and smother our carriages and floats with them in the parade?" (115). This celebration in the springtime of new life represented a cultural renewal, as the memory of the Lost Cause was revitalized each year.

The home was another setting that reminded white Southerners of their way of life centered on the memory of the war. Storytelling was the crucial occasion for keeping memory alive. Lumpkin writes of hearing stories as a child from her mother's friends about the past: "How many times I would sit at their feet and ask for the old tales of the plantation but more especially of the war" (123). The books she read were in the "same nostalgic vein" (123). She mentions several novels by Thomas Nelson Page, the literary romanticizer of the antebellum Southern plantation, and others, concluding that even later in life they "cling to my memory" (123). The home embodied, for Lumpkin looking back on it from the vantage point of the 1940s, a private cultural memory of family, of the Southern ethic of honor and etiquette. But the private memory reinforced the public memory. If culture is learned behavior, one sees how Southern children learned to be 'Southern'. She recreates how she as a young child must have learned her regional culture, in this case white supremacy in the 1890s when racial segregation and disfranchisement of African American voters were codified.

> We can be certain from the time I could sit in my high chair at table or play about the parlor floor while others conversed, my ears were saturated with words and phrases at all times intimately familiar to Southern ears and in those years of harsh excitement carrying a special urgency: "white supremacy," "Negro domination," "intermarriage," "social equality," "impudence," "inferiority," "uppitiness," "good darkey," "bad darkey," "keep them in their place." (130)

Lumpkin touches on the language of Southern white racial dominance and on fears of its being constantly threatened.

Obsession with race – white supremacy – was the ideological foundation after the Civil War for the cultural memory learned in homes as well as on the town squares, with their Confederate monuments where the broader community gathered to celebrate the Lost Cause. Despite defeat in the Civil War, Lumpkin writes, "Our fathers knew their way was good" (236). Southern white leaders after the war agreed, she writes, "they should keep their way of life" (236). Her father's way embraced a totality of Southern culture, but the rhetoric and language of the Confederate memory was the conceptual glue that made the South an entity to be defended. She remembered her father saying of his children: "Their mother teaches them their prayers. I teach them to love the Lost Cause" (121). She recalls his telling Southern men to "let your children hear the old stories of the South; let them hear them by the fireside, in the schoolroom, everywhere, and they will preserve inviolate the sacred honor of the South" (121). The term "sacred honor" sacralized a predominant regional value system that made defense of Southern tradition itself a mission. Connection between memory, cultural identity, and maintenance of an on-going, patriarchal, paternalistic, racially-conscious social system is seen in a comment by Lumpkin, looking back on what she learned as a child. There was "the glamorous, distant past of our heritage", but her family and most white Southerners thought "it was by no means our business merely to preserve memories" (127). They had to "keep inviolate a way of life" (127), and she indicates the foundation of that way of life was white supremacy. It was inconceivable, she recalls from her childhood, "that any change could be allowed that altered the very present fact of the relation of superior white to inferior Negro" (127–128). Her family understood this assumption to be "the very cornerstone of the South" (128). Her family, and the American South as a whole, embraced the centrality of white supremacy during the agrarian political turmoil of the Populist movement in the 1890s, which was perceived as threatening to split white Southerners and empowering African Americans politically.

Lumpkin grew up in the genteel environment of an elite family, but her racial awakening came through a very un-genteel experience. When she was a young girl, six years old, she heard her father beating their black cook for perceived impudence, one of the worst failings of an African American servant under the region's racially oppressive system of laws and folk expectations. She heard sounds "to make my heart pound and my hair prickle at the roots. Calls and screams were interspersed with blow upon blow" (132). Peeking in the kitchen window, she saw the family's African American cook "writhing under the blows of a descending stick wielded by the white master of the house. I could see her face distorted with fear and agony and his with stern rage" (132). The "white master" was her father, but the beating was never mentioned in the family nor was there any outside intervention, as the cook was a second-class citizen in the Jim Crow South. After that horrifying experience for the young Katharine, she began revising her rosy images about slavery and about the Ku Klux Klan, learned from her father's stories. She writes, "I was fully aware of myself as a white, and of Negroes as Negroes" (133). She became "self-conscious about the many signs and symbols of my race position that had been battering against my consciousness since virtual infancy" (133), signs and symbols that separated Southern public spaces sharply into 'White' and 'Black' worlds. Railroad coaches, streetcars, theaters – all such public spaces were cordoned off into separate racial spheres. Of particular importance in teaching the child Katharine about the Southern racial way was the taboo of eating with African Americans, for which she uses the term "sin" to characterize its religious significance, representing as it did "an unthinkable act of 'social equality'" (135). Never again after the beating of the cook could Lumpkin look upon the inherited family and region's assumptions about the benevolence of Southern ways of racial dominance and use of violence to enforce it as normal and beneficent. She could no longer embrace her home as a safe refuge from the moral contradictions of her society.

Lumpkin then traces with specificity in her memoir her awakening to an interracial consciousness when she leaves home for school. She saw the origins of "inter-racial cooperation" (180) in the South in Booker T. Washington's efforts to bring white and black Atlantans together after the 1906 Atlanta race riot to discuss the causes of the violence:

"Of course the term was quite unknown as well as inconceivable to us then. We remained ignorant of it even as first co-operative steps were taken during the First World War" (180).

Lumpkin's awakening to an interracial way came during the Progressive era of the early twentieth century and in the decades afterwards, a slow process to break away from the region's reigning worldview and one so deeply rooted in her family. One of the crucial reasons she became able to do so was her experience in the poverty-stricken Sand Hills of upcountry South Carolina. Her family had left the comforts of their Georgia home in 1909, when she was nine years old, to move there, where her father took a new job with the railroad. She found herself for the first time witnessing at close hand the terrible poverty of white and black people on rural farms. She was used to African American poverty, but here her white schoolmates were poor as well. In a chapter called "Sojourn in the Sand Hills", she notes that her family's farm was not actually in the Sand Hills, but that the family lived adjacent to "this desolate area", whose inhabitants had "pasty faces, scrawny necks, angular ill-nourished frames, straw like hair" (151). These poor whites were landowners, but "in name only; the heavy mortgages they carried were ever a threat to their tenure" (151). They mostly had a few acres of not very productive land and flimsy housing. Some were sharecroppers with even less. In the classroom she was able to observe how different the poor rural children of this rural area were from her own experiences and those of other town children. Even language was different. She notes: "I was a city child and talked like one" (159). She rememberes how "hard they would stare at me when I talked, as though I were some kind of foreigner, as indeed they regarded me" (159). She uses a Southern phrase to indicate these poor whites' sense of social class resentment, writing that they thought she was "putting on airs" (159) to flaunt her social superiority.

The poverty she saw there broadened her mind and spirit about social and economic injustices. She had learned from the beating of the cook about whiteness, its source of privilege and the violent extremes to which her father would go to defend the social boundaries with black people. From her experiences in the Sand Hills, Lumpkin learned of social class inequality, an understanding that would lead her soon to reject the conventional wisdom that black people were poor because they were inferior; white people could suffer from poverty, whose causes therefore could not rest on racial inferiority. The Sand Hills experience occurred during her "changing teens" and made her aware of the "glaring incongruities" (239) of life in the South. "Here in actuality was the moment when chance circumstance showed me our native Tree of Life, and had me eat its revealing fruit" (239). She confesses in her memoir: "[I] never again could return to the comfortable ignorance which would have let me assume as an unfortunate inevitability the destitution, the drabness of life, the spiritual and material exploitation, which was the lot of so many" (239).

Lumpkin's education was another factor in her conversion to the interracial Southern way. She attended Brenau College in Gainesville, Georgia, from 1912 to 1915, carrying with her in her mind the conviction that she "belonged to a people of a special mold" (178). She had experienced the "traits of geniality and generosity which were handed down and preserved as something precious" (178). She recites a litany of cultural traits that she believed constituted the Southern way of life of the early twentieth century. "In my head", she writes, "I carried the picture of the Southerner which we cherished, and whose likeness we had been reared to aspire to – of a courteous, kindly people, swift to sympathy, hospitable, gay, affectionate, withal proud, and of noble spirit and high ideals" (178). She knew "how warm a South it could be to its own, how outgoing, friendly" (178). Again, she paints a sensual portrait of this South she had grown up with, noting that "to me, the very soft air we breathed gave off an essence", and she prized "the welcoming wide-open doors of our homes, the little neighborliness in which we liked to excel – among our own kind, to be sure" (178). She recognizes that the region's "peculiar institution", as racial arrangements were called, was a key part of this Southern way of life, but "had it not also been fashioned by the hands of our fathers, who in passing it on to us told us to maintain it?" (178).

Lumpkin recalls that as she began college "there was certainly nothing visible to me to hint that contrary streams of influence were moving into the South" (179), but the Progressive era did witness early attempts at biracial dialogue and the emergence of reformers, including the interracial cooperative movement, trying to address the South's socioeconomic problems. "Here then", she writes of this potentially radical social interaction between white people and black people, "was a feebly breathing, hardly existing South" (180). Yet she notes, even if such influences got to her small town Georgia college, how could they "penetrate the thick overlay of the old-ways-are-right in which we Southern students were encased?" (180). Lumpkin realizes that she had an advantage in responding to these new influences, namely her childhood, in which she had been an avid reader and her parents had encouraged discussion of public issues, with a "Saturday Night Debating Club" (124) a part of their weekly routine. She met a small number of students who had similar backgrounds, and a faculty member encouraged them to "use our minds, go to the sources, have no truck with undocumented hearsay, keep our eyes on the vast play of forces" (186).

Lumpkin's Episcopal religious faith was important in giving her a vision of the scriptural basis of social justice; she became a passionate convert to the social gospel in college and came to believe in the idea of the Kingdom of God on Earth. She describes this theological discovery "as soaking into my consciousness" (189), and an opportunity soon appeared to put her new faith to work in regards to the central issue of race relations. She was involved in the work of the Young Women's Christian Association (YWCA), which was one of the most important institutions in exploring interracial interactions in the early twentieth-century South. In 1915, Lumpkin graduated from Brenau and was working on campus as a tutor. She attended a YWCA conference in Charlotte that year, and one of the speakers was an African American woman named "Miss Arthur", the "Miss" title being virtually unprecedented in the Jim Crow South for African American women. Miss Arthur spoke about Christianity and race, and Lumpkin and the other student leaders she was with feared the implications of this situation. "This really opened the door to thoughts we would like to avoid" (190), she remembers. "What would people say?" (190) she worried. The young white women listening to a black woman speak about race violated the fundamental expectation of Southern race relations of 'Keep them in their place' (191). But Lumpkin looked to the Bible for a metaphor for her experience here, writing that she and her fellow students were "like a little company of Eves" (191) for whom temptation arose. "We had been taught that it was wrong to eat this apple. Yet as it was put before us, we felt guilty not to" (191). Lumpkin conveys the psychological and emotional trauma of violating the racial norms, recalling "how our pulses had hammered, and how we could feel our hearts pound in our chests" (192). Lumpkin comes to realize that she and others in attendance, "by sheer force of unsought circumstance" had found "ourselves called upon to pluck from the Tree of Life the apple that would open our eyes to see what was good and evil" (191), using the same analogy she uses to describe her understanding of social class injustice learned in the Sand Hills. Yet she confesses that "the old Southern heritage could not be thrust aside, even momentarily, except by something insistently strong" (191). The Southern way of life's teaching of keeping African Americans "in their place" was heretofore believed "to be immutable and unchangeable", but the counterweight of the Kingdom of God on Earth "could even take precedence over our assumed racial verities" (191). Those racial verities had been "this tabernacle of our sacred racial beliefs untouchable" (193). And yet she "touched it", had reached out her hand "for an instance and let my finger-tips brush it", and "not the slightest thing had happened" (193). She admits that this change in consciousness affected only "a scattered few of us who were just coming into adulthood and had begun to wrestle with our Southernness" (198). Even by World War I, there were few Southern places where interracial discussions could take place.

Lumpkin returned to Brenau after this formative experience, realizing that "the heavens had not fallen, nor the earth parted asunder to swallow us up in this unheard of transgression" (192–193). Still, she was relieved to have experienced that moment of transformation and could now "breathe freely again, eat heartily, and even laugh again" (193). Important as this moment was, Lumpkin reveals an experience that suggests the slowness of conversion to a new Southern way. The film *The Birth of a Nation* came to the Brenau campus, and Lumpkin was eager to see it, having read as a younger woman the novel *The Clansman* by Thomas Dixon Jr., on which the film draws. The students and townspeople went wild over the film, as white audiences all across the South were embracing it. "All around me people sighed and shivered, and now and then shouted or wept" (200), over the tale of the horrors of an African-American dominated South in Reconstruction. Lumpkin herself admits that she "felt old sentiments stir, and a haunting nostalgia, which told me that much that I thought had been left behind must still be ahead" (200). Lumpkin is once again honest in admitting the cautionary emotional journey she went on before achieving a fuller conversion to an interracial Southern way of life.

After graduating from Brenau, she went to Columbia University to earn a master's degree in sociology, and then she earned a doctorate in economics in 1928 at the University of Wisconsin. In graduate school she learned of the work of North Carolina sociologist Howard Odum's mentor, Franklin H. Giddings, and his theory of "consciousness of kind" (1896: 17) and Herbert Spencer's social Darwinism. "It appeared that scientific minds surmised that the 'mores' were so imbedded in men's social habits as to make it nearly impossible to alter them – at best taking generations of time, at worst centuries" (204). She had grown up believing in the slowness of social change from her knowledge of the South's ways and now she had "a heavy sense of the authority of science confirming my own inclinations" (204) that she had grown to question. Still, she later learned that William Graham Sumner, who wrote of the immutability of folkways, had opposed organized efforts at worker rights, and she realized that "the author of the 'mores' himself believed enough in their possibility of change to consider it needful to put obstacles in the way" (204). She came to understand that people like Giddings, Spencer, and Sumner gave "a scientific name to describe what my eyes had seen, especially in our racial ways, and the solemn morality we attached to these practices which after all were but the creations of the brains of men" (204). That last phrase best indicates the understanding she had grown into of the predominant Southern ideology as a social construct. She discovered that the North had its own sense of racial division, observing that northerners "aped our Southern ways" (202) and identified with white Southerners' efforts to deal with the 'Negro problem', as it was known in the early twentieth century.

In graduate school, an African American woman, also from Georgia, was Lumpkin's classmate, and she took a key part in Lumpkin's conversion to the interracial way; from her, Lumpkin learned about the oppression and poverty of black Southerners in a region she had grown up idealizing. When her professor at Columbia had the class over for tea, including the black classmate, it meant violating the Southern racial way, committing the "grievous Southern sin" (206) of eating with a black person. Ironically, Lumpkin's consciousness had evolved so far by that point that she had no psychological moment of crisis, as she had when listening to Miss Arthur. Rather, "one could feel relief to have had the chance to prove that this taboo no longer held dominion over one's mind" (206). She reflects that this taboo was not even a personal matter: "It had a large social purpose which we white Southerners had summed up as keeping the Negro in his 'place.' It was for this it had been made a part of our life, and on this account that it was inserted into the minds of each white generation" (207). She grew increasingly savvy about the signs and symbols of the Southern way of life. She and her African American classmate found themselves traveling together through the South representing the YWCA. They entered a train station in North Carolina, but, as she writes, "by different doors: hers, 'For Colored,' mine, 'For White.' Presumably I was used to this. I had done nothing else all my life. But it was not the same. Every feature of these now peculiar-seeming arrangements thrust themselves against me as something shockingly new" (215). There were two ticket windows, her traveling companion standing at one and Lumpkin at the other. She notes the train station platform was the only place not segregated; "railroad platforms must have baffled our Southern ingenuity" (215), she writes sarcastically. She reflects that "one sign was meant to stigmatize, the other to assert superiority" (215). None of this was for "frivolous or capricious reasons. Never had I seen so plainly as on this day how deadly serious the white South was in its signs and separations, or understood in clearer focus its single-mindedness of aim" (215).

Lumpkin came home to Georgia in the early 1920s, observing a turbulent post-World War I South of restless African Americans and of whites determined to resist change. Her consciousness had so changed that what she once saw as normal now seemed strange. Lumpkin learned more about poor whites and came to work for their betterment through the organized labor movement. "I no longer used the term 'lower classes.' These were working people" (217). And she came to understand the South was not just a traditional culture with distinctive social ways. It was an economic system, and she wanted to figure out how it worked to maintain the status quo. She came to use the term "backward"ness to describe her region: "how meager were the protections that we afforded compared with those of other sections" (218). She worked briefly in a shoe factory to observe working conditions of long hours and low pay and to learn something of the concerns of working women. Her conclusion about the Southern economy was that "we were hardly more than instruments, it seemed, moved helplessly by a larger machine that ran all the smaller ones at which we worked, and which was operated by some remote control, a vast over-all mechanism that was not geared to human consequences" (220–221). Her grasp of capitalism's reaches led her to understand the exploitation of workers, resulting from expanding industry's reliance on the "profitability of our labor supply. This was our great attraction, our main drawing-card: we had a cheap, docile, abundant, native white labor force" (221). She notes that, in an economic sense, the mass of whites had a "place" where they were supposed to stay, but that meant that "surely wage-earning whites and Negroes were, functionally speaking, not so unlike after all" (222). This knowledge meant that "the proof of group incapacity, because of poverty or what the lowly working men did, lost it persuasiveness" (222).

Lumpkin notes in 1947, when her memoir appeared, that, despite her change in consciousness, for the South in general "the old ways still mold the lives of Southern children" (233). They still were taught "as sacrosanct the old abhorrences" (233), her use of that term suggesting her belief in the immorality of the Southern way of life. 'Colored' and 'White' signs still marked the landscape as visual enforcers of the Southern racial way of life, and white supremacy continued as a political mantra. Nonetheless, she saw by the 1940s that the old segregated life continued, "but not serenely, not without a struggle to maintain its existence" (233). The Depression, the New Deal, agricultural mechanization, and the growth of the organized labor movement all had brought unforeseen changes to Southern society. She recognizes the limitations at that point of deeper change as well, namely the white South's inability to "confront the full realities of what it does to a people on whom segregation is imposed – and also what it does to us whose hands impose it" (235). Here, she takes responsibility as a white Southerner for the system, even though she had come to oppose it. She glories that "strong forces have been battering against the South", and "it is not a slight thing that we strike some blows against these shackles" (234).

Lumpkin spent her career teaching economics and social science, although she was frustrated at the barriers to women's advancement in the American academic world. She also wrote on labor issues and general reform, and she worked as an activist on the ground to promote organized labor. She worked at the Council of Industrial Studies at Smith College and then at the Institute of Labor Studies that followed progress in unionization during World War II. Katharine Du Pre Lumpkin's ability to see the Southern way of life as a human construct of racial and social class hierarchies may also have benefited from the independence of her sexual identity. She lived with her same-sex partner, Dorothy Douglas (a radical economist in the interwar years), for three decades. Lumpkin became one of the most reflective of white Southerners on the interracial South, one she saw rooted in working people. As her biographer Jacquelyn Dowd Hall writes, "Katharine's project, her lifelong endeavor, was to convince southerners and northerners alike to tell a new story, a story in which the South ceased to figure either as the not-modern – a landscape of nostalgia, a touchstone of yearning and loss – or as the nation's collective unconscious, the repository of American nightmares that America could not face" (HALL 1998: 112). Moreover, she used her experience and her autobiographical reflections upon her experiences to place a woman at the center of Southern history. Coming from an elite family, she embodied the ability of a privileged individual to refashion the Southern way of life ideology of white supremacy into a progressive ideology of interracialism.

List of Works Cited

CASH, WILBUR JOSEPH (1956) [1941]: *The Mind of the South*. Garden City, NY: Doubleday.

GIDDINGS, FRANKLIN HENRY (1896): *The Principles of Sociology*. New York: MacMillan.

HALL, JACQUELYN DOWD (1998): Open Secrets: Memory, Imagination, and the Refashioning of Southern Identity. *American Quarterly* 50.1, March: 109–124.

LUMPKIN, KATHARINE DU PRE (1947): *The Making of a Southerner*. New York: A. Knopf.

SPENCER, HERBERT (1852): A Theory of Population Deduced from the General Law of Human Fertility. *Westminster Review* 57: 468–501.

SUMNER, WILLIAM GRAHAM (1906): *Folkways: A Study of Sociological Importance of Usages, Manners, Customs, Mores, and Morals*. n. p.: Ginn.

Life, Literature, Ecocriticism

Nature and Life Writing

A Comparative Study of Henry David Thoreau and Tao Qian

Zhang Longxi

In American literature, Henry David Thoreau (1817–1862) is probably the most well-known writer on nature, whose life in the woods laid the foundation for writing a philosophical reflection on nature and a narrative of his own life that became major works of American transcendentalism. His most important work, *Walden: or, Life in the Woods*, first published in 1854, is an American classic and an exemplary work of life writing, for much of that work is unabashedly autobiographical, about his own life and at the same time about the New England natural environment in which he lived for a period of time as an experiment in life. It is life writing par excellence. As a distinguished Americanist, Alfred Hornung has worked on life writing as a major area of his scholarly contributions, and therefore his insightful comments on Thoreau and life writing are of particular value and importance. "Thoreau and *Walden* serve as a perfect starting point for the correlation of nature and culture in life writing, for the alignment of ecology and life writing" (HORNUNG 2016: 336), he argues eloquently. In looking at ecology and life writing from a perspective beyond the usual horizon of American Studies, Hornung helps us understand Thoreau not just as a great American writer, but as a writer of global significance. "Thoreau's writing", he says, "not only encapsulates the romantic model and incorporates the whole universe in his individual existence, but his readings in Asian philosophies and the observation of Native American lives turn *Walden* into an ecoglobalist project of life writing" (HORNUNG 2016: 336). In a magisterial survey of ecology and life writing in Asian, American, and Canadian literary traditions, Hornung brings Thoreau into meaningful dialogue with many writers and poets long before and after him in different cultures, thus making Thoreau a great writer of world literature.

Such large-scale comparison of different works from very different traditions is Hornung's great contribution to American Studies, for his approach changes the discipline from one of national or regional coverage into transnational American Studies with global significance and implications. "The coordination of stages of life with evolutionary cycles of nature in all instances", says Hornung in examining ecology and life writing in different literatures, "transcends the narrow boundaries of fixed political or cultural frames and offers a transcultural perspective" (HORNUNG 2016: 345–346). In transcending narrow boundaries and thinking outside of boxes of fixed political or cultural identities, Hornung has made it possible to move out of a certain American exceptionalism, and thereby opens a whole new area with great potential for transnational American Studies, which lends legitimacy to our effort to read American literature in a much larger context, and to discuss Thoreau in connection with life writing on a global scale, as part of a new and exciting corpus of world literature.

It is in the spirit of transnational border-crossing and from a transcultural perspective that I shall put Thoreau's *Walden* and the writings of the fourth-century Chinese poet Tao Qian into cross-cultural dialogue. The linguistic, cultural, and historical differences between the two are huge and important, but what makes such a cross-cultural dialogue possible is the close correlation of nature and life in the works of both writers. Thoreau's *Walden*, as mentioned above, is unabashedly autobiographical. "In most books, the *I*, or first person, is omitted", says Thoreau; "in this it will be retained" (THOREAU 1982 [1854]: 259). He made it clear that his choice of living in the woods had a definite purpose of discovering the essentials of life, the truth about life. As he writes:

> I went to the woods because I wished to live deliberately, to front only the essential facts of life, and see if I could not learn what it had to teach, and not, when I came to die, discover that I had not lived. I did not wish to live what was not life, living is so dear; nor did I wish to practise resignation, unless it was quite necessary. I wanted to live deep and suck out all the marrow of life, to live so sturdily and Spartan like as to put to rout all that was not life, to cut a broad swath and shave close, to drive life into a corner, and reduce it to its lowest terms, and, if it proved to be mean, why then to get the whole and genuine meanness of it, and publish its meanness to the world; or if it were sublime, to know it by experience and be able to give a true account of it in my next excursion. (THOREAU 1982 [1854]: 343–344)

"Few declarations in American literature are as famous as this", says Harold Bloom when commenting on this passage. "For Thoreau then, work and life are a theory of fusion. Such fusion depends upon a radical isolation: from the post office, the newspaper, or in our day, the screen of all varieties" (BLOOM 2003: 1). In other words, living a simple life with only the basics is what Thoreau did in the small house he had built himself near Walden Pond in Concord, Massachusetts, but that was not just a way of living, but the practice of a philosophical theory, a theory about nature and life. The "radical isolation" Bloom thought to be the foundation of Thoreau's philosophical reflection is, however, probably not essential for his philosophy in a literal sense, but the manifestation of some personal eccentricity on the part of Thoreau as a man of an unusual disposition. After all, Thoreau did not consider himself completely isolated from the world. "I am naturally no hermit", he says. "I had three chairs in my house; one for solitude, two for friendship, three for society" (THOREAU 1982 [1854]: 390). His purpose of living alone in the woods, as he states in the passage quoted above, is to know life and to "publish" or "give a true account" of what he has learned. He wanted to know for himself what life really was, and then to tell the world about it.

For more than two years, Thoreau did live alone in the woods, and he felt completely at home with nature. "Every morning was a cheerful invitation to make my life of equal simplicity, and I may say innocence, with Nature herself" (THOREAU 1982 [1854]: 341), he writes. "I have been as sincere a worshipper of Aurora as the Greeks. I got up early and bathed in the Pond; that was a religious exercise, and one of the best things which I did" (THOREAU 1982 [1854]: 341). There is of course some basis for Bloom's comment on "radical isolation", for in the chapter on "Solitude", Thoreau insists that he had "never felt lonesome" (THOREAU 1982 [1854]: 383), except once for a short while, but soon recovered from that momentary sense of loneliness. "In the midst of a gentle rain", he remarks, "I was suddenly sensible of such sweet and beneficent society in Nature, in the very pattering of the drops, and in every sound and sight around my house, an infinite and unaccountable friendliness all at once like an atmosphere sustaining me, as made the fancied advantages of human neighborhood insignificant, and I have never thought of them since" (THOREAU 1982 [1854]: 383). This is indeed rather unusual, and Thoreau did live in deliberate isolation from what he considered insignificant "human neighborhood". Perhaps few, except for a fictional Robinson Crusoe, can live like that for a relatively long period of time. Thoreau, however, is no misanthrope, for his passion for the beauty and comfort of nature is deeply human, with a sense of human dignity removed from life's unessential trappings, far from the madding crowd. He felt a spiritual affinity with the ancient Greeks, which connected his appreciation of nature with an admiration of human culture. Nature and culture do not form an uncompromising dichotomy.

That sense of living alone with dignity is of course not uniquely Thoreau's, nor is it uniquely American or Western. In fact, more than a millennium before Thoreau, the great Chinese poet Tao Qian or Tao Qian, also known as Tao Yuanming (365–427) held much the same attitude. Much of Tao Qian's writing is also autobiographical; he not only wrote poems about himself and his lived experience, but he also wrote a fictional biography, *Life of Mr. Five Willows*, originally intended as a self-portrait or autobiography, and he even wrote a piece in mourning of his own death (see TAO QIAN *a*: 123; 162–163). That is indeed an unusually intense focus on one's self and self-knowledge, reminiscent of Michel de Montaigne.[1] The focus is, however, motivated by a profound interest in the correlation of nature with human life, not a self-centered, egoistic narcissism. One of Tao Qian's best-known poems expresses the idea of living alone, away from the hustle and bustle of the world:

> I built my humble house in the world of men,
> But there is no noise of carriages and horses.
> You may ask, sir, how is it possible?
> With the mind aloof, the place will be remote.
> Picking chrysanthemums under the eastern hedge,
> Unawares I catch sight of the southern hills.
> The mountain air is fair in the lovely sunset,
> And flocks of birds are returning to their nests.
> There is a true meaning in all of these,
> But when I try to explain, I forget my words.
> (TAO QIAN *C*: 63)[2]

In the very first line, Tao Qian sets up an opposition between a "humble house" he had built and "the world of men", and he makes it clear that right in the middle of "the world of men", his private world has "no noise of carriages and horses", that is, it is isolated from the busy world of the rich and powerful. Unlike Thoreau living alone in the woods, Tao Qian's solitude is not the result of physical distance from insignificant "human neighborhood", but rather a mental and psychological remoteness. "With the mind aloof", says the poet, "the place will be remote". Tao Qian's mental aloofness or detachment achieves the same "radical isolation" Thoreau did by living alone in the woods, and the opposition between the mental or spiritual aloofness and the "world of men" or "human neighborhood" reappears in several of Tao Qian's other poems. In a poem on "Returning to Dwell in My Fields and Gardens", for example, he again writes: "In the wild country, I have little to do with men, / In these poor lanes, wheels and harness are rare" (TAO QIAN *e*:

[1] See Sarah Bakewell's excellent study, *How to Live, or A Life of Montaigne*.
[2] All translations into English by the author.

36). In Chinese antiquity, only emperors and high-ranking officials had the privilege of riding on horse-drawn carriages, so "carriages and horses" and "wheels and harness" all refer metonymically to the ruling elites, evoking their rank and social status. By living in "poor lanes" that admit no "wheels and harness", Tao Qian, like Thoreau, achieved his own "radical isolation" from the world with a sense of dignity, pride, and spiritual superiority, but an isolation of a mental and psychological status rather than a physical ambiance.

It is true that Thoreau built a hut by Walden Pond and fenced off the world of men. "My nearest neighbor is a mile distant, and no house is visible from any place but the hilltops within half a mile of my own. I have my horizon bounded by woods all to myself" (THOREAU 1982 [1854]: 381), Thoreau writes in the chapter on "Solitude". But for him, as for Tao Qian, the mental aloofness is far more important for a sense of solitude than the physical condition, as he continues that "for the most part it is as solitary where I live as on the prairies. It is as much Asia or Africa as New England. I have, as it were, my own sun and moon and stars, and a little world all to myself" (THOREAU 1982 [1854]: 381). Thoreau here was thinking globally, beyond the New England of his time, and the world he created might as well be in Asia or Africa because it was a little world created all by himself in imagination, which had little to do with actual physical space. As Hamlet claims, "I could be bounded in a nut-shell, and count myself a king of infinite space" (SHAKESPEARE 2003 [1599–1602?]: II.ii.250, 72). Thoreau expressed that idea rather clearly in the "Conclusion" of *Walden*, where he bids his readers to "be a Columbus to whole new continents and worlds within you, opening new channels, not of trade, but of thought. Every man is the lord of a realm beside which the earthly empire of the Czar is but a petty state, a hummock left by the ice" (THOREAU 1982 [1854]: 560). In other words, Thoreau's physical isolation was but a concretization of his existing mental condition, and in that sense, then, the American writer could very well understand Tao Qian, the Chinese poet, across huge temporal gaps and cultural differences, and might carry on an imaginary conversation with him, for both found consolation in nature and quietude from the busy world of men in pursuit of wealth, power, and life's little vanities.

In the poem quoted above, Tao Qian goes on to describe a beautiful sunset with birds returning to their nests in the mountains and suddenly comes to the realization that there was a "true meaning" in what he had experienced in nature, although he could not find words to express it. For the poet, the beauty of nature and the truth therein thus remain inexpressible, beyond the power of language. In the last two lines, Tao Qian alludes to a famous passage of the philosophical work *Zhuangzi*, in which the Daoist philosopher states that words exist for the sake of meaning, just as a fish trap exists for the fish, so "once you've got the fish, you forget the trap", and "once you've got the meaning, you forget the word" (GUO QINGFAN (1844–1895?) 1954: xxvi, 407). By forgetting words, therefore, the poet may have got the "true meaning" of nature in a moment of epiphany at a beautiful sunset, but that meaning must remain unexpressed, something intuitively understood at heart but unsaid and unsayable in words. In that sense, then, forgetting words is not an indication of the poet's failure to speak, but rather a sign of a deeper understanding as well as a different approach to truth and its articulation in pregnant silence, in indirect, suggestive language.

The emphasis on a suggestive or oblique style of expression may be said to represent a prominent feature of poetics of not only the Chinese literary tradition, but of the Indian tradition as well. In Sanskrit poetics, according to R. S. Pathak, the concept of *vakrokti* is "nothing less than the basal principle of poetic language", and it mainly refers to "the curved or oblique diction, peculiar to poetic language" (PATHAK 1998: 99). Another Indian scholar, Chettiarthodi Rajendran, argues that "[i]t is the suggestive art which is the real touchstone of a poetic genius, and a person becomes a great poet only when he has mastered the art of suggestion" (RAJENDRAN 2001: 100). In Indian poetics, he remarks, the "essence of poetic art consists of leaving the deeper aspects of the experience unexpressed to be reconstructed by the reader using his imaginative faculty", and he compares that with William Empson's theoretical argument presented in the latter's well-known book on the oblique language of poetry, *Seven Types of Ambiguity* (RAJENDRAN 2001: 107). Indeed, poetic language is different from the everyday language of communication mainly because of its obliquity, ambiguity, suggestiveness, and openness to multiple interpretations. This is a general feature of poetic language in the East as well as the West, discussed not just by Empson, but by many other critics in the Western tradition. Indeed, silence may become the very inspiration for poetic articulation, as Rainer Maria Rilke writes beautifully in a poem: "*Schweigen. Wer inniger schwieg, / rührt an die Wurzeln der Rede*"(RILKE 1975 [1924]: 258), "Being-silent. Who keeps innerly / silent, touches the speech" (trans. by MOOD 1975: 85).

Interestingly, the realization of both the inadequacy and the suggestive power of language is also what Thoreau expresses towards the end of *Walden*, where he speaks of his "desire to speak somewhere *without* bounds" (THOREAU 1982 [1854]: 563). He realizes that "[t]he volatile truth of our words should continually betray the inadequacy of the residual statement. Their truth is instantly *translated*; its literal monument alone remains" (THOREAU 1982 [1854]: 563). Language is nothing but a "residual statement", but it is at the same time a "literal monument" referring to something else, something beyond or outside the literal sense. Thoreau's metaphorical expression gives us a memorable description of what language is and does. And yet, he also realized that it is absolutely necessary to speak, for words, though inadequate, can still point to what is beyond words, with the symbolic power of monuments. "The words which express our faith and piety are not definite; yet they are significant and fragrant like frankincense to superior natures", as Thoreau puts it beautifully (THOREAU 1982 [1854]: 563). By forgetting words, Tao Qian tried to preserve intact the unsayable true meaning, while Thoreau conceived of true meaning as certain "superior natures" towards which words, inadequate and yet significant and fragrant, point to gently, like a wisp of frankincense.

Tao Qian also wrote about solitude and his search for understanding and communication – for what the Chinese call a *zhi yin*, literally "one who knows the sound", namely, a sympathetic reader who truly understands and appreciates what the poet has to say. Again, the solitude the poet speaks of is more a psychological or spiritual loneliness than physical isolation. In the following poem, the images of a "solitary cloud" and a single "bird" effectively convey that sense of loneliness and solitude:

> Ten thousand creatures all have their reliance,
> Only the solitary cloud floats without support.
> Fainter and fainter, it dissolves in the sky,

When is the time we see its last glimmer?
The morning glow breaks the lingering mists,
Flocks of birds start their flight together.
Slowly, slowly, a bird soars out of the woods,
And comes back again before it is dark.
Knowing its strength, it keeps to the old route,
How can it escape from cold and hunger?
When no one is here to know the sound,
What use is there to strike a sad note?
(TAO QIAN *f*: 81)

The "solitary cloud" floating without support and the bird that "keeps to the old route" despite "cold and hunger" are all symbolic images of a lonely poet, and the poem ends with a gesture of resignation to the fact that there is no one around with sympathetic understanding. For Tao Qian, that was quite true of his time, for his poetry was not considered important by his contemporaries. He wrote in a seemingly simple and plain language, which suited his idea of simplicity in nature and life, but was fundamentally at odds with the trend of his time when poets of the Six Dynasties valued a much more elaborate and flamboyant style. The great critical work during that period, *The Literary Mind or the Carving of Dragons* by Liu Xie (465?–522), did not even mention Tao Qian's name, and another important critical work, *The Ranking of Poetry* by Zhong Rong (459–518), put him in the middle rather than the upper rank. Though he was known to poets of later generations, Tao Qian was not fully appreciated by many, and he had to wait for almost six hundred years before he found his *zhi yin* and his poetry would get sympathetic understanding and appreciation when the great poet Su Shi (1037–1101) became his true admirer and canonized Tao Qian for the Chinese literary tradition.

Even in this respect, in the reception of their works, there is something interestingly comparable between Tao Qian and Thoreau, for Thoreau's work was, and perhaps still is, sometimes dismissed by critics as uninteresting. "I certainly make no claim to being the first to recognize the boring quality of *Walden*" (SHWARTZ 1987: 79), says Ronald Shwartz. "Nathaniel Hawthorne called Thoreau a bore; so did the critic Theodore Baird. Even Thoreau called himself a bore, though he was not referring to Thoreau the writer of *Walden*. Stanley Cavell admitted that "[i]t cannot, I think, be denied that *Walden* sometimes seems an enormously long and boring book" (qtd. in SHWARTZ 1987: 79). It seems that a great writer or poet needs to wait patiently for the right reader and the right moment for getting the proper recognition due his work, and sometimes spiritual loneliness or solitude is part of a writer's career. The right reader, the one who knows the sound, needs to understand writing and life as one. "Thoreau makes life subtly lyrical. One might say that *Walden* domesticates through resonant language the irritatingly obscure word 'transcendental', makes it breathe", as Shwartz argues. "*Walden* does not merely 'describe' or 'illustrate' the Walden experience; in a real sense the language and the experience are inseparable; the feeling and the reflection upon it merge" (SHWARTZ 1987: 81). These remarks are as true of Tao Qian as of Thoreau because Tao Qian's poetry is also largely autobiographical, telling of his life in nature and reflecting on his life and nature. It is in the context of his life experience that we may understand the images of a "solitary cloud" and the lonely "bird" not just as poetic metaphors, but as metaphors that speak the truth of someone's life. In other words, it is from the perspective of life writing that we may come to a better understanding of the kind of autobiographical writings in Tao Qian and in Thoreau.

Solitude is not, however, just the unpleasant isolation from one's unappreciative contemporaries, but can also be a deliberate choice to stand aloof from those who lack understanding. In that sense, then, it becomes a conscious choice to be alone and different from those whose life is caught in the mindless pursuit of power and wealth, a choice we find as essential in Tao Qian's poetry as in Thoreau's *Walden*. In a poem that would be particularly pertinent in a dialogue with Thoreau living in the woods, Tao Qian speaks of his own inclination towards nature and of his return to nature from a brief assumption of a minor office as a momentary mistake. The poet writes:

> In youth, nothing in me fit the common taste,
> It's my nature to love mountains and hills.
> By mischance I fell into the net of dust,
> And was kept away for thirteen years.
> A fastened bird would long for old woods,
> A stranded fish would remember the deep pond.
> I've tilled some land at the edge of southern heath,
> Keeping simplicity, I return to my home ground.
> Around my house I have a couple of acres,
> And eight or nine rooms with thatched roof.
> Elms and willows shade the back eaves,
> And before the hall a peach and plum grove.
> Half-hidden is the village of secluded people,
> From their houses a wispy smoke arises.
> A dog barks in the depth of a small lane,
> On top of a mulberry tree a rooster cries.
> No dust soils the pure air within my doors,
> In my bare rooms I find plenty of leisure.
> Too long I have been caged like a prisoner,
> Oh, at last, I now come back to nature.
> (TAO QIAN *e*: 35)

The background of this poem is Tao Qian's leaving a minor office he had held for about a dozen years and had finally quit when an inspector came and he was told to dress up to meet his apparently not very intelligent superior. As we read in his biography, he quit his office in indignation, famously saying, "how can I bend myself to bow to a country bumpkin just for five bushels of grain!" (XIAO TONG (501–531), qtd. in TAO QIAN *e*: 2) The "five bushels of grain" refers to the meager remuneration he received for his low-ranking office, and his refusal to bow to a higher-rank official with no intelligence or integrity certainly showed the poet's mental aloofness from the officialdom with all its pomp and stupidity, and also his sense of dignity and pride. Tao Qian was only too glad to come back to his home in the country, for it had always been his "nature to love mountains and hills". His brief entanglement in officialdom was now seen as a mistake, like falling into the "net of dust", restrained like a "fastened bird" or a "stranded fish", and "caged like a prisoner". The scene of a "village of secluded people" with a dog barking and a rooster crying makes a nod to the great Daoist philosopher Laozi, who envisioned an ideal social condition with as little human interference as possible, where "neighboring countries can see one another, and the crowing of roosters and the barking of dogs can be heard, but people would never associate with one another all their lives, even till death" (WANG BI (226–249) 1954: 47). This is one of many allusions in Tao Qian's work that indicate a significant Daoist influence, particularly its naturalism, on his thinking and poetry. "No dust soils the pure air" in his "bare rooms", says the poet, and the poem is a celebration of a kind of utopian simplicity, of his return to the simple life in nature, to his home and garden in the country.

Home is a man's bastion against the coldness of the outside world, and that is what Tao Qian returns to for comfort and consolation; his home is deeply connected with nature. If, in addition to his two-year stay at Walden Pond, Thoreau lived as a handyman and friend in Emerson's home and several other places, published essays and poems, surveyed land and gave lectures, Tao Qian returned to his home and lived the simple life as a farmer in the fields. He wrote a rhyme-prose on his homecoming to express his joy of return, realizing that he is now free from the mistake of being trapped in a minor office that had kept him away from the wonders of nature[3]:

> Oh, let me go home!
> Why not go as my garden and field lay barren?
> Since my heart has been enslaved by the body,
> Why still feel sad and sullen?
> I realize that the past is beyond rescue,
> But the future is still possible to pursue;
> I have not gone too far on the wrong road,
> Yesterday was false, but today is true.
> (TAO QIAN *g*: 135–136)

To come back to nature is to return to his self, to the healing effect, the catharsis of one's wounds in nature's purifying ambience. What is important is that nature has the power to help one understand better the true meaning of temporality, and in a way the true meaning of life and death. "Trees are all lush and green; / And streams flow and grow wide. / All ten thousand things have their time, / And I know there'll be the end of my life", Tao Qian writes. The realization that all things have their time and so does human life, however, does not lead to fear or panic, but to the quiet acceptance of one's life as part of nature's "transformation". Thus Tao Qian ends the piece on a note of calm and tranquility:

> How long in this universe
> Can we have our body reside?
> Why not let our heart be the guide?
> Why hurry to follow every empty tide?
> Wealth is not my wish;
> Nor the immortal's abode for me to abide.
> I walk alone in the lovely morning,
> Or work in the fields, my stick put aside.
> Climb up the eastern hill to howl aloud,
> Or compose a poem by the river's side.

[3] Rhyme-prose sounds like an oxymoron, and the Chinese original is 賦 *fu*, a special literary genre that is considered to be prose, but with rhyme and often parallelism.

> I follow the transformation to the very end,
> Without hesitation, but with my fate content.
> (TAO QIAN *g*: 136)

The "transformation" is again an allusion to a Daoist idea, as expressed in a beautiful passage from the *Zhuangzi*, where the philosopher gives an account of a most peculiar dream:

> Once Zhuang Zhou dreamed of himself being a butterfly, he was really a butterfly fluttering around, happy and comfortable, knowing not that he was Zhou. After a while, he woke up, and he was surprisingly Zhuang Zhou himself. It is not clear whether it was Zhou who had dreamed of being a butterfly, or it was a butterfly that had dreamed of being Zhou. Yet there must be differentiation between Zhou and the butterfly, and this is called the transformation of things. (GUO QINGFAN (1844–1895?) 1954: 53–54)

The idea is that all things are equal, and everything, including human life, is engaged in the process of endless changes in time, that is, endless "transformation", while definite, rigid, and fixed identities are perhaps one's own illusions. With typical poetic brilliance and a bold, counter-intuitive paradox, *Zhuangzi* gave the idea a memorable expression. The uncertainty about whether dream is reality, or reality is but a dream, or whether the man is really a butterfly, or the butterfly is the philosopher, effectively shatters our fixation on narrow identities. In an unexpected way this resonates remarkably well with the words of Hornung, quoted at the beginning, when he writes: "The coordination of stages of life with evolutionary cycles of nature […] transcends the narrow boundaries of fixed political or cultural frames" (HORNUNG 2016: 345). Here again, from the perspective of transnational American Studies, we find it possible to relate Tao Qian to Thoreau in the two writers' enlightened understanding of the meaning of life in nature's purifying embrace. In an important passage of *Walden*, Thoreau writes:

> Sometimes, in a summer morning, having taken my accustomed bath, I sat in my sunny doorway from sunrise till noon, rapt in a revery, amidst the pines and hickories and sumachs, in undisturbed solitude and stillness, while the birds sang around or flittered noiseless through the house, until by the sun falling in at my west window, or the noise of some traveler's wagon on the distant highway, I was reminded of the lapse of time. I grew in those seasons like corn in the night, and they were far better than any work of the hands would have been. They were not time subtracted from my life, but so much over and above my usual allowance. I realized what the Orientals mean by contemplation and the forsaking of works. (THOREAU 1982 [1854]: 363–364)

Like Tao Qian feeling content with his fate, Thoreau also found a peace and quietude in nature that makes him feel as if he is growing "in those seasons like corn in the night". He was of course aware of "the lapse of time", but "not time subtracted from [his] life, but so much over and above [his] usual allowance". In both Tao Qian and Thoreau, then, nature and life are correlated in such a harmonious way that they both find living in nature to be a kind of participation in the cycles of nature, the change of seasons, the transformation of all things in the universe. Such a symbiotic harmony of nature and life informs their writings as exemplary life writing with particular elegance and depth of meaning.

The healing or cathartic effect of nature is of course an important aspect of ecology and ecocriticism. Tao Qian and Thoreau, though more than a thousand years apart, were both able to live in nature with harmony and peace, and their writings about harmony in nature become particularly significant and especially relevant to our own time because of the serious problems we now face in our environment – global warming and climate change, pollution of water and air, and the many other environmental catastrophes we experience in the world. "It is not surprising that these deep ecological ideas surface at a time when modern technologies and urban life styles have produced destructive features to the human environment which even threaten the preservation of the planet earth" (HORNUNG 2016: 340), as Hornung points out. "This combination of life writing and ecology is now in the service of recuperation and healing for both human and physical nature" (HORNUNG 2016: 340). Tao Qian has always been revered in the Chinese tradition as a great poet of nature, and Thoreau, in the words of Lawrence Buell, has become "the patron saint of American environmental writing" (BUELL 1995: 115). Reading Tao Qian and Thoreau in cross-cultural dialogue, then, may provide some valuable insights into the symbiotic relationship between man and nature, and may bring the two writers to us and have them speak to our time and our problems with particular urgency and persuasion.

List of Works Cited

BAKEWELL, SARAH (2010): *How to Live: Or, a Life of Montaigne in One Question and Twenty Attempts at an Answer.* New York: Other Press.

BLOOM, HAROLD (Ed.) (2003): *Henry David Thoreau*. Philadelphia: Chelsea House (Bloom's Bio-Critiques).

BUELL, LAWRENCE (1995): *The Environmental Imagination: Thoreau, Nature Writing, and the Formation of American Culture*. Cambridge, Mass.: Belknap Press of Harvard University Press.

GUO QINGFAN (1844–1895?) (Ed.): Zhuangzi jishi [Variorum Edition of the Zhuangzi]. In *Zhuzi jicheng* [*Collection of Masters Writings*]. Beijing: Zhonghua, 1954, vol. III.

HORNUNG, ALFRED (2016): Ecology and Life Writing in Transnational and Transcultural Perspective. In HUBERT ZAPF (Ed.): *Handbook of Ecocriticism and Cultural Ecology*. Berlin/Boston: De Gruyter, 334–348.

MOOD, JOHN L. (1975): *Rilke: On Love and Other Difficulties. Translations and Considerations of Rainer Maria Rilke*. New York/London: Norton.

PATHAK, R. S. (1998): *Comparative Poetics*. New Delhi: Creative Books.

RAJENDRAN, CHETTIARTHODI (2001): *Studies in Comparative Poetics*. New Delhi: New Bharatiya.

RILKE, RAINER MARIA [1924]: (Für Frau Fanette Clavel) Schweigen. Wer inniger schwieg. In Rilke Archive in conjunction with RUTH SIEBER-RILKE and ERNST ZINN (Eds.): *Sämtliche Werke*, 12 vols. Frankfurt a.M.: Insel., 1975, vol. II, 258.

SHWARTZ, RONALD B. (1987): Private Discourse in Thoreau's Walden. In HAROLD BLOOM (Ed.): *Henry David Thoreau's Walden*. New York: Chelsea House Publishers (Modern Critical Interpretations), 79–88.

SHAKESPEARE, WILLIAM [1599–1602]: *Hamlet*, ed. by BURTON RAFFEL and HAROLD BLOOM. New Haven: Yale University Press, 2003.

TAO QIAN (365–427) *a*: Life of Mr. Five Willows. In WANG YAO (Ed.): *Tao Yuanming ji* [*Tao Yuanming's Works*]. (Beijing: Renmin wenxue, 1957).

TAO QIAN *b*: In Mourning of Himself. In WANG YAO (Ed.): *Tao Yuanming's Works*.

TAO QIAN *c*: Twenty Poems on Drinking Wine. No. 5. In WANG YAO (Ed.): *Tao Yuanming's Works.*

TAO QIAN *d*: Five Poems on Retuning to Dwell in My Fields and Gardens. No. 1. In WANG YAO (Ed.): *Tao Yuanming's Works*.

TAO QIAN *e*: Five Poems on Retuning to Dwell in My Fields and Gardens. No. 2. In WANG YAO (Ed.): *Tao Yuanming's Works*.

TAO QIAN *f*: Seven Poems on Poor Scholars. No. 1. In WANG YAO (Ed.): *Tao Yuanming's Works*.

TAO QIAN *g*: Oh, let me go home! In WANG YAO (Ed.): *Tao Yuanming ji* [*Tao Yuanming's Works*].

THOREAU, HENRY DAVID [1854]: *Walden.* In CARL BODE (Ed.): *The Portable Thoreau*. New York: Penguin, 1982 [1947].

WANG BI (226–249): *Laozi zhu* [*The Annotated Laozi*]. In *Zhuzi jicheng* [*Collection of Masters Writings*], 8 vols. Beijing: Zhonghua, 1954, vol. III, chapter 80.

XIAO TONG (501–531): Tao Yuanming's Biography. In WANG YAO (Ed.): *Tao Yuanming's Works*.

Humanimagic Relations

Cabeza de Vaca's Account (1542) and Posthumanism

Nadja Gernalzick

During the Fourth International Auto/Biography Association (IABA) European Section Conference on "Dialogical Dimensions in Narrating Lives and Life Writing" at the Centro de Estudos de História do Atlântico in Funchal, Madeira, in 2015, a conversation with Alfred Hornung about *La Relación* by Álvar Núñez Cabeza de Vaca (1542) and Andrés Serrano's *Cabeza de Vaca* (1984)[1] suggested to me a correlation between posthumanism and Cabeza de Vaca's account. Might Serrano's conceptual art be read as part of posthumanist discourse? Might *La Relación*, its provenance from the sixteenth century notwithstanding, be read as posthumanist?

FIG 1. *Cabeza de Vaca*, Photograph by Andrés Serrano (1984, Cibachrome, 27.5 x 40 in./69.85 x 101.6 cm)

In the course of answering these questions affirmatively, I argue that the title of Cabeza de Vaca's account – *La Relación* [*The Relation*][2] – signifies not only the genre of

[1] I thank my students for critical discussions in seminars on Cabeza de Vaca's *La Relación* and its adaptations at the universities of Bern and Mainz in 2004–2005, 2016 and 2017.

[2] The complete title is *La relación que dio Álvar Núñez Cabeça de Vaca de lo acaescido en las Indias en la armada donde iva por governador Pánphilo de Narbáez, desde el año de veinte y siete hasta el año de treinta y seis que bolvió a Sevilla con tres de su compañía* [The account that Álvar Núñez Cabeça de Vaca gave of what occurred in the Indies on the expedition of which Pánfilo de Narváez served as governor, from the year [15]27 to the year [15]36 when he returned

the text but also stands for the principle of meaning generation in semiosis, and, in particular, semiosis in first contact as it is the topic of the account: relationality as the textual creation of relativity of signifiers between languages and life styles, across systemic boundaries and despite instances of incommensurability. Concurring with and semiotically extending José Rabasa's reading (2000) of *La Relación* as allegory, I treat the title *La Relación* as denoting the production of connections between signifying systems and agents across spatial and temporal codes. Connecting the semiotic contexts by relativity of signs across temporalities of historiography and of narrative generates meaning transgenerically, transmedially and translingually. A reading of *La Relación* through relationality affords the crossing of temporal categories of chronology or historiography as well as the recognition of an *avant-la-lettre* posthumanist discourse in the sixteenth century resulting from the semiotization of first contact. Further, it methodologically offers critical vocabularies that open up multiple inversive directionalities of reading. What remains incommensurate within the posthumanist conjuncture producible between *La Relación*, its narrator and characters, Serrano's *Cabeza de Vaca* and the engaged reader of the twenty-first century, I call humanimagic.

The posthumanist dissolution of the superiority of the human subject in history is considered to involve a movement from "hubris to humility" (MIAH 2008: 10) and a questioning of agency as defined by will power or consciousness. "Humanism is the philosophical view that understands persons to be the unique and unified source of meaning and agency. By contrast, post-humanism is that form of thinking that displaces the idea of the whole person as being the most significant level of analysis and understanding", so that there is a "de-centring of human agents from the heart of inquiry" (BARKER 2004: 151), with also the consequence of the dissolution of established, identified units of critical practice into relational procedures and the search for new critical vocabularies. In a passage frequently read to describe the fantastic, the narrator of *La Relación* describes precisely such an experience of decentring between European proto-scientific and Indigenous shamanistic practices and affirms the social viability of the latter:

> On that island about which I have spoken, they [the Indigenous people] tried to make us physicians without examining us or asking us for our titles, because they cure illnesses by blowing on the sick person, and with that breath of air and their hands they expel the disease from him. And they demanded that we do the same and make ourselves useful. We laughed about this, saying that it was mockery and that we did not know how to cure. And because of this, they took away our food until we did as they told us. And seeing our resistance, an Indian told me that I didn't know what I was saying when I said that what he knew how to do would do no good, because the stones and other things that the fields produce [*que se crían por los campos*] have powers, and that he, by placing a hot stone on the abdomen, restored health and removed pain, and that it was certain that we, because we were men [*hombres*], had greater virtue and capacity. In short, we found ourselves in such need that we had to do it, without fearing that anyone would bring us to grief [*pena*] for it. (CABEZA DE VACA 1542, trans. Adorno and Pautz: 113; 112)

to Seville with three members of his company.] (CABEZA DE VACA 1542, trans. Adorno and Pautz: 14, 15)

"Stones and other things that grow in the fields" (CABEZA DE VACA, trans. Frances M. López-Morillas, qtd. in RABASA 2000: 57) is a different translation of the words *que se crían por los campos*, a translation which more closely renders the Spanish phrasing that 'the stones bring themselves into being through or by way of the fields' than the phrase 'the fields produce' that makes the stones inactive. The Spanish source provides the stones with agency in the most relational of the phrasings. The text demonstrates the confounding of the narrator's expectations regarding qualities of and qualifications for agency; it is a confusion that decenters and destabilizes the narrator's and his Old-World companions' understanding of themselves as subjects, an understanding which seemed guaranteed by professional titles as they are produced in the Spanish system of medical training, for example. In the Indigenous semiosis – "an interpretative moment in the *Naufragios* [… :] Cabeza de Vaca has an Indian (using indirect speech, as Maureen Ahern [1993] has put it in her brilliant reading) explain why magic works" (RABASA 2000: 56) – the human beings – Indigenous and Christians alike – share the capacity for agency with the stones, and the resulting relational practices are affirmed as viable and productive of meaning.

La Relación is an autobiographical account of the years Cabeza de Vaca and three other survivors of the shipwrecked imperial and military expedition lived among Indigenous peoples before they met again the *conquistadores* in New Spain and returned to serve Emperor Charles I of Spain (reigned 1516–1558) and, in personal union, Charles V of the Holy Roman Empire (reigned 1519–1558). The text is a classic narrative of early colonial exploration, travel and captivity and a rare ethnographic document. Between 1528 and 1536, in areas that are today in the states of Florida, Louisiana, Mississippi, Texas, New Mexico and Arizona in the southern United States of America as well as in the states Tamaulipas, Nuevo León, Coahuila, Chihuahua, Sonora, Sinaloa, Durango and San Luis Potosí of the northern United Mexican States, Cabeza de Vaca and three other men, the only survivors of several hundred persons on six ships, traveled along the coast of what is today called the Gulf of Mexico and the Pacific, largely uncharted then by transatlantic explorers.[3] The distance eventually covered on foot by Cabeza de Vaca and three other surviving expeditionaries in company with semi-nomadic Indigenous peoples of diverse tribes totals approximately 1800 kilometers. In their eight years of wandering, the four men come to share the languages, customs and community of the Indigenous tribes. Returned to the imperial settlements, the men follow the obligation to write a report on the lost expedition for the Emperor. This first, so-called *Joint Report* (1536–1537) is no longer extant.[4] As an autobiographical account of first transatlantic contact with Indigenous peoples, Cabeza de Vaca also writes and publishes *La Relación* in Spain after his return from the colony La Florida. The narrator describes the loss of the Spanish ships due to storms as well as the remaining expeditionaries' incapacity of steering the ships; the building and the loss of rafts; the loss of supplies; stealing food from and fighting with

[3] Maps of the reconstructed course of the expedition and of the survivors by sea and land in ADORNO/PAUTZ 1999, vol. I: xxvi–xxix; vol. II: xxvi–xxxv; and vol. III: xviii.

[4] Details from the *Joint Report* along with references to *La Relación* are rendered by Gonzalo Fernández de Oviedo y Valdés in his *Historia general y natural de las Indias* written between 1525 and 1548 (ADORNO/PAUTZ 1999, vol. III: 12–45).

Indigenous peoples; separation from other survivors of the expedition; hunger and starvation; captivity among Indigenous tribes; physical duress and forced labor; learning to communicate in sign language and in Indigenous spoken languages; becoming a trader among the Indigenous peoples; reunification with other survivors of the transatlantic expedition; becoming healers among the Indigenous peoples; syncretic healing practices; integration into a migratory pan-tribal Indigenous community and taking on Indigenous lifestyle; reunification with the Spanish army; briefly taking action as a protector of Indigenous peoples in New Spain; concluding with the eventual return to Spain.

Much debated among readers since the publication of *La Relación* have been the reports on healing practices observed and performed by Cabeza de Vaca and the other three survivors among the Indigenous peoples. In an ethnographic reading of *La Relación* after Michael Taussig and Claude Lévi-Strauss, Rabasa summarizes that a contemporary reading of the "empathetic descriptions of difference" ought to be "attentive to the historiographical difficulties Cabeza de Vaca encountered in telling the story of his experience of customs contrary to Western values" (RABASA 2000: 49). In order to transcribe and decipher Indigenous practices and worldviews, the narrator of *La Relación* as well as the contemporary reader across history, Rabasa suggests, must perform an inversion of perspective, required in encounters with the unknown, the unfamiliar and the new. This imaginative inversion is comparable to the cosmological inversion associated with the so-called Copernican turn of the sixteenth century and its uses in postcolonial theory (GERNALZICK 2010: 221–223). Gayatri Chakravorty Spivak outlines the inversive process as part of "planet thought", by which "we imagine ourselves as […] planetary creatures", living on the planet Earth while it "belong[s] to another system" and so we "inhabit it, on loan" (SPIVAK 2003: 72). "[T]his peculiar mindset" is necessary because "alterity remains underived from us; it is not our dialectical negation, it contains us as much as it flings us away" (SPIVAK 2003: 72). In first contact between groups, the inversive process "is not even 'learning *about* cultures.' This is imagining yourself, really letting yourself be imagined (experience that impossibility) without guarantees, by and in another culture" (SPIVAK 2003: 52). As Rabasa and others have demonstrated, the narrator of *La Relación* partially succeeds in such a procedure, for example by "corrod[ing] stock New World images" (RABASA 2000: 52) in ways that "manifest a mastery of the code" (RABASA 2000: 49), or by associating first-person plural narrative perspective changeably with different groups: the imperial army from Europe called *cristianos*; [5] the

[5] *La Relación* participates in pre-nation-state, feudal discourses of the fifteenth and sixteenth centuries. Indigenous peoples are called *indios* by the narrator, after Columbus's and his contemporaries' belief that the whereabouts of the Americas were in India, whereas persons from the Holy Roman Empire in the account are called Christians, *cristianos*. The narrator "follow[s] the practice common since the Castilian conquest of southern Spain, when narratives about Castilians at war with Muslims referred to the former as Christians and the latter as 'infidels'" (ADORNO/PAUTZ 1999, vol. III: 43–44), which practice, on the one hand, excludes also the Jewish population in the Holy Roman Empire and Spain (GOMEZ-GALISTEO 2013: pos. 165–177) and, on the other hand, signifies that "not everyone who came to Spanish America under the banner of Castile, was a Spaniard" (ADORNO/PAUTZ 1999, vol. III: 43–44). "Rather than a national sense of being Spaniards, the important social status marker was being a Christian" (GOMEZ-GALISTEO 2013: pos. 165–177). The pre-nationalist discourses that inform *La Relación* underline that the interest the account has for Transnational American Studies lies in non-national patterns of group formation.

four survivors from Europe and North Africa; or the four survivors together with the Indigenous,[6] *indios*. With the ending of the narrative, upon reuniting with the Spanish military at an early colonial outpost on the Pacific coast of Northern Mexico, the narrator notes his attempts to save the Indigenous people with whom the survivors lived from enslavement by the *conquistadores* (CABEZA DE VACA 1542, trans. Adorno and Pautz: 249–263). Describing his altercations with some members of the imperial military about the enslavement of the Indigenous, the narrator, by manner of an identitarian reconstitution that undoes having joined the Indigenous groups, realigns himself as an "authority" on behalf of the Indigenous peoples and as a person who commands them (CABEZA DE VACA 1542, trans. Adorno and Pautz: 255, 261). He continues to position himself, nevertheless, between the "Indians" and the "Christians"; even though paying respect to "God our Lord", he does not once again until the very end of the text count himself and the 'we' of the four survivors among "the Christians" (CABEZA DE VACA 1542, trans. Adorno and Pautz: 247–279). The narrator emerges as a writing subject of the empire versed in legitimation as well as subversion of the hispanophone context.

Rabasa underlines that critical readings of *La Relación*, by contrast, often condescend to the descriptions of the Indigenous healing practices by treating them as fictions within the generally non-fiction account, thereby repeating the colonialist discourse about the primitive as opposed to the civilized and rational, Christian European. The first critical evaluation of Cabeza de Vaca's *La Relación* by Gonzalo Fernández de Oviedo y Valdés in his *Historia general y natural de las Indias* sets the precedence for such criticism of Cabeza de Vaca's work, considering it to show "a lack of clarity" (RABASA 2000: 49). Oviedo's reading of *La Relación* is, according to Rabasa, the earliest example of how "commentators [...] have negated Cabeza de Vaca's testimony of experiences that are alien to the common sense of Western rationality" (RABASA 2000: 51) by calling them 'magic.' Regarding such a tradition of critical reception of the descriptions of shamanism

[6] "We" in a single textual instance does not mean 'we survivors' but 'we' as including the surviving expeditionaries together with the Indigenous peoples while excluding the members of the imperial army: "a language that they [the Indigenous] had among them by which we understood one another [*una lengua que entrellos avía con quien nos entendíamos*]" (CABEZA DE VACA 1542, trans. Adorno and Pautz: 251, 250). Despite some ambiguity regarding the referent for "quien", which in some translations is taken to be "entrellos" so that the "we" remains restricted to the survivors (FAVATA/ FERNÁNDEZ 1993 and FRYE 2013), Adorno and Pautz's translation is more plausible since 'quien' in the sixteenth century could likely still be used synonymously with 'que' (see also MOLINER 2007, entry for "quien": "(del lat. 'quem', accusativo del pron. 'quid') I (inacentuado) pron. rel. Equivale al pronombre 'que'"), and the remaining syntax also supports the reference to "lengua". The statement is on Primahaitu, an Indigenous *lingua franca* (GIL-OSLE 2018) used for communication across a great variety of tribal languages (CABEZA DE VACA 1542, trans. Adorno and Pautz: 187 and *passim*), learned by the four survivors and first described in *La Relación*. Moreover, in the general "complexity of the language situation in North America nearly five hundred years ago" (BONVILLIAN et al. 2009: 154), Cabeza de Vaca and the group of survivors become "quite adept at the sign-communication system used by the Native Americans around" (BONVILLIAN et al. 2009, 150) them, which is a skill that, inversely, also has to be attributed to the Indigenous peoples who commmunicate with the expeditionaries.

in *La Relación*, Rabasa asks if, like Oviedo, "contemporary critics domesticate the uncanny by classifying passages as novelesque, as made up, fictional stories [...] intercalated in an account of real events" (RABASA 2000: 50; 45). By assigning the status of fiction rather than chronicle to the descriptions of healing practices, the "uncanny coexistence of two worlds in the *Naufragios*" (RABASA 2000: 51) and the survivors' "immersion in an Amerindian worldview" (RABASA 2000: 52) are devalued as contrived. By European standards of rationalism, readers have dismissed and silenced Amerindian knowledge that the narrator Cabeza de Vaca brings into hispanophone semiosis; "careful comparison of those passages purported to be fictions with shamanic practices" (RABASA 2000: 54) by Silvia Spitta (1995) demonstrates that "those passages read by critics as novelesque actually contain anthropological information on shamanism" (RABASA 2000: 45). Consequently, Rabasa demands that "[w]e should [...] resist the impulse to define Cabeza de Vaca's function as a shaman in the *Naufragios* with the topoi of the Western hero whose perspicacity enables him to play the role of quack doctor" (RABASA 2000: 83) or to become "a manipulator of fear or gullibility, [...] an astute as well as benevolent, savvy, colonial frontier-type, when not a picaro" (RABASA 2000: 54). We should not read shamanism as "miracles effected by God" so as to turn Cabeza de Vaca "into a saint of the conquest" (RABASA 2000: 54). Instead, according to the narrator's description, the surviving expeditionaries are given power by the Indigenous from within their world system to perform and succeed as shamans. The narrator, as Lévi-Strauss writes of shamanistic processes, "did not become a great shaman because he cured his patients; he cured his patients because he had become a great shaman" (LÉVI-STRAUSS 1949*a* [1963]: 180, qtd. in RABASA 2000: 58; compare ADORNO 1991: 173). The healing practices denote not the single agency of Cabeza de Vaca but agency dissipated, and, inversely, foremost including Indigenous knowledge and agency. Critical of the critics, Rabasa concludes that Oviedo's and others' "ascription to the text of a lack of clarity manifests an ethnocentric view" (RABASA 2000: 49).

Semiotic incommensurabilities have produced critical shipwreck of the colonialist interpretations of the text. The semiosis by and narrative form of *La Relación* requires the reader to refrain from attribution of passages to the known and familiar. Incommensurability of European and Indigenous discourses, of Indigenous and Christian knowledge and cultural practices, is precisely the gist of *La Relación*, as most evident in the descriptions of the healings, in strategies of indirect speech (AHERN 1993) and allegory. For the same reason, "*irony* in the *Naufragios* is not accidental" (RABASA 2000: 50), and, consequently, the reception of *La Relación* produces an aesthetic surplus of semiosis at the contextual location of systemic incommensurability. In the tradition of reception and adaptation, this excess has frequently been attributed with spiritual significance [Fig. 2]: In the eighteenth century, the Christian reading of *La Relación* as spiritual shipwreck under the new title of *Naufragios*[7] became popular.

[7] The word *naufragios* appears in *La Relación*; however, the title *Naufragios* [*Shipwrecks*] was first used with an edition of 1749 (ADORNO/PAUTZ 1999, vol. III: 383). By the metaphorization of *naufragios*, the account is interpreted as a de-Europeanization and primitivization, attributed with formal failure due to 'lack of clarity', or read as a trial of the narrator in spiritual terms.

FIG 2. Iconography of Cabeza de Vaca as Christ in the filmic adaptation *Cabeza de Vaca* (1991) directed by Nicolás Echevarría.

Yet the spiritual travails that the narrator of *La Relación* is supposed to have undergone according to such interpretations seem minor compared to the difficulties of communicating the experiences in America to Europeans. To the transcription of realities that in the narrator's discourse of provenance would have been fictions, Rabasa ascribes the quality of "a series of narrative loops" (RABASA 2000: 52), in the manner of interactive feedback loops discussed in cybernetics and considered part of the autopoietical processing of systems (MATURANA/VARELA [1972] 1980). There is a "shuttling back and forth between the canny and the uncanny" that Rabasa, along with Hayden White, reads as "integral to what makes the *Naufragios* an allegorical text" (RABASA 2000: 52). It is a text that creates meaning by evoking a surplus of signification beyond the given context, or, that is, like any historical text, "allegorical" in "saying one thing and meaning another" (White qtd. in RABASA 2000: 50), and a text that is allegorical of knowledge yet unencodable for the narrator (RABASA 2000: 83) and yet indecipherable to the reader. Adorno and Pautz elaborate that the four survivors of the expedition

> faced the enormous challenge of communicating to their countrymen in an intelligible way where they had been for the previous eight years, what had happened to them, and what was contained in the places they had lived in and traversed. Their task was made more difficult by the fact that they were uncertain about the location of the point along the coast of the Gulf of Mexico whence they had started, the extensive distance they had traveled, and the length of time they had been gone. In a sense, virtually everything was relative, and the circumstances of their experience placed them at great distance in space and time from any established point of reference. (ADORNO/PAUTZ 2003: 18)

Details in *La Relación* show that, based on the geographical, navigational and cosmographical knowledge available, the leading personnel of the expedition, including Cabeza de Vaca, miscalculated the distances between landmarks along the coast and the distance to their destination port on the Gulf of Mexico to a degree that the "magnitude of the error" (ADORNO/PAUTZ 2003: 8) according to a contemporary standard of measure amounts to approximately 1600 kilometers. The relativity observed by Adorno and Pautz is descriptive of the process of dead reckoning in nautics and seafaring still in use in the sixteenth century when the position of a ship on the ocean was calculated from the compass course, the North Star and the speed of the ship by measuring each successive position in relation to the previous one, without any further astronomic, projectional or coordinate data with which to locate the positions according to a general measure. The information processing of the expeditionaries, therefore, is structuralist on all accounts; it becomes poststructuralist by the mobilization of their initial system of signification in the contact with the Indigenous system and code.

Through relativity and relationality, the semiotic incommensurability of European and Indigenous life worlds is overcome and the violence of distinction and segregation is subverted. The "colonial communication divide" brings about semiosis in the form of "new rituals, rites of conquest and colony formation, mystiques of race and power, little dramas of civilization tailoring savagery" that "bound Indian understandings of white understandings of Indians to white understandings of Indian understandings of whites' (TAUSSIG 1987 qtd. in RABASA 2000: 121). Relationality processes and dissolves division. The wording "bound [...] to" in the passage signifies the creation of a contingent relation between signifiers and thereby describes a connection, to a degree, to have taken place between the respective semiotic systems as well as the production of a shift in the semiotic systems – languages, cultures, disciplines, histories – that becomes readable at different times. For Rabasa, "[r]adical incommensurability [...] does not preclude the existence of two (incommensurable) worlds in one consciousness without incurring a contradiction. Rather, contradiction results from the attempt to translate one world into the other" (RABASA 2000: 51), as critics attempt to do. Instead of translation between distinct codes, *La Relación* produces relation and linkages between in/commensurable codes. By his descriptions, the narrator performs semiosis in a process related to the cooperative semiosis in shamanistic curing: "[S]hamanistic cures are effective when the ill person incorporates the structure of the narrative recited by the shaman. Thus, the 'shaman provides the sick woman with a *language*,' that is, with a structure bearing a connection between psychic and physical phenomena" (LÉVI-STRAUSS [1949*b*] 1963: 198, emphasis in original, qtd. in RABASA 2000: 57). I congrue with Rabasa when he insists, with Taussig (1992), that in the process, the sick person does not even need to understand the language of the shaman and the spirits. The expeditionaries share much of Indigenous life – clothing, food and provision practices, social roles, rituals and language – but also maintain certain Old-World practices, such as the inclusion of Christian elements in the healing rituals. While the "shaman must learn the practices of the community [... ,] he can also experiment, as in Cabeza de Vaca's introduction of Christian prayers" (RABASA 2000: 58), or employ the sign of the cross in the healings otherwise following Indigenous procedure. This syncretism means "transforming any binary order into a field of plurivalent points in a continuous flux" (BRUCE-NOVOA 1993: 17).[8] During the healing rituals in which the expeditionaries use Christian prayers, "the Indians did not understand Cabeza de Vaca's prayers" (RABASA 2000: 57), which were presumably pronounced in Latin or Spanish. Rabasa insists that the Indigenous did not require linguistic understanding of the prayers because they assumed the shaman addressed the spirits and spoke in

[8] Bruce-Novoa considers *La Relación* to create Cabeza de Vaca as a "malleable point of syncretism" (1993, 17); other readings describe him as "syncretic shaman" (LÓPEZ 2013: 152) or "syncretic Messiah" (JUAN-NAVARRO 2013: 76). Since the latter two noun phrases distinguish the shaman and the Messiah in mutually exclusive ways, however, they obstruct syncretism defined as semiotic flux by Bruce-Novoa. In Nicolás Echevarría's filmic adaptation *Cabeza de Vaca* (1991), depiction of religious syncretism is also avoided, so as to keep images of Indigenous shamanism and Christianity clearly and visually distinct.

their language. The pragmatics of semiosis in the creation of signs and sounds in physical contact are sufficient for a successful healing. In other words, the determination of clear-cut language boundaries and the strict logical separation between understanding and incomprehension is not feasible regarding the linguistic and significatory transactions described in *La Relación* as healing practices. As in the reception process created by literary translinguality (GERNALZICK 2013), communication between the agents in *La Relación* takes place more by pragmatic codes, affective channels and faculties of semiotization than by linguistic material alone. The communication must be considered to have included a tolerance for vagueness and ambiguity with resulting temporal extensions until confirmation, or not, of interpretive assumptions as well as a reliance on intuitive interpersonal and situational knowledge. Like the Indigenous people do for him, the narrator provides the hispanophone reader with access to shamanistic ritual and knowledge. The narrator's prose provokes the imaginative inversion of the narrative and signifying agency in *La Relación*; the readers may or may not collaborate in this type of relational semiosis.

Nevertheless, despite instances of inversion and agential dissipation, *La Relación* ineluctably participates in and remains determined by the discourse and semantics of colonialist terror in New Spain (RABASA 2000, Chapter 1). Even though this statement seems self-evident, it requires repetition because of iconizations and glorifications of the narrator in readings of *La Relación* in hispanophone and anglophone criticism as well as in adaptations of the past thirty years. Moreover, the translation of *La Relación* by Rolena Adorno and Patrick Charles Pautz, for example, sentimentalizes the style of telling and, thereby, sentimentalizes sixteenth-century discourse of class and power relations by privileging emotional semantics and vocabularies in the English rendering of Spanish terms. By the Catholic beliefs under the Inquisition, such actions as the healings would make the narrator accountable and punishable for "heresy, witchcraft, and superstition" (RABASA 2000: 49). The explanation that not "anyone would bring [them] to grief [*pena*] for it" (CABEZA DE VACA 1542, trans. Adorno and Pautz: 113; 112, my insertions) implies that the Indigenous people do not punish the expeditionaries but also that there were no Christians witnessing the procedures who might have found fault with Cabeza de Vaca's group. By the word *pena*, the line bespeaks more than the "grief" or, in other translations, the "scorn" it might bring on the survivors of the expedition who turned into shamans since the Spanish *pena* (CABEZA DE VACA 1542: 112) also means 'punishment'. This translation is frequently used. By translating the word as 'grief,' Adorno and Pautz choose a more emotional and sentimental vocabulary than is appropriate in the context of the legal, inquisitional semantics of the source text. Other instances of the translation by Adorno and Pautz evince a similar sentimentalization whereas the Spanish idiom would seem to connote a more legalistic description. The narrator uses phrases that indicate that he finds himself at risk regarding the transcription of Indigenous ritual into Spanish. In addition, the narrator's use of the collective first-person plural 'we' and his speaking on behalf of a variety of groups, particularly of the entire group of four survivors, and rarely of himself alone, is frequently ignored in the reception of *La Relación*. Generally, readings turn the narrator-as-author into a singular, autonomous self and heroic figure.[9] Rabasa summarizes that critical

[9] Rabasa derives the catalogue of positions that create a 'good' Cabeza de Vaca from the critical

> preferences for a Cabeza de Vaca who undergoes a conversion from what can only be a stereotype of a greedy conquistador to a panoply of 'good' traits – critic of empire [...], advocate of peaceful conquest [...], first Chicano [...], first Spanish transculturator of Indian culture [...] – suggest a need for a homey *Madre Patria*, for a counterdiscourse to the *leyenda negra*, for a founding moment of Latin America and modernity where imperialism was not always 'bad.' Thus, these readings manage to critique imperialism while retaining a redeemable view of Spanish colonialism in exceptional individuals. Have we been seduced by Cabeza de Vaca into an uncritical participation in and reproduction of the culture of conquest? (RABASA 2000: 35)

Andrés Serrano's Cabeza de Vaca *(1984)*

Cabeza de Vaca (1984) by Andrés Serrano [Fig. 1] responds to the scholarly and popular iconization of the narrator of *La Relación*. In Serrano's *Cabeza de Vaca*, Rabasa encounters his very concern that "interpretations" of *La Relación* tend to "share a common need to impose order on magic, hence to kill, as it were, the spirit of the *Naufragios*" (RABASA 2000: 54). Implying decapitation, the dead cow's head signifies the violence of conquest that destroys the conquered, severs established relations and reorganizes them by aggressive imposition of power. In addition, the image plays on the function and meaning of a personal name across languages.[10] The work means a move from *La Relación* as a hispanophone text – with two words, "arraca" for "look over there" and "xo" for "dogs" (CABEZA DE VACA 1542: 187) in an Indigenous language – to the adaptation that as a photograph has no words of written or spoken language except the hispanophone title. "[T]he photograph says 'This is Cabeza de Vaca, and only if you speak Spanish will you know that this is not a cow's head, but also that it is'" (RABASA 2000: 55–56, with LIPPARD 1990). The photograph is conceptual art and meta-discursive: As an intermedial adaptation of *La Relación* as well as of the discourse attached to *La Relación* and to the name of Cabeza de Vaca, the photograph addresses the transmedial and transtemporal relationality produced by the interactions with the sixteenth-century text.

tradition from 1972 to 1997 (RABASA 2000: 35); moreover, there are readings that create the opposite, 'bad' Cabeza de Vaca (qtd. in RABASA 2000: 45; GOMEZ-GALISTEO 2013: pos. 2816). The adaptations of *La Relación* by Haniel Long and Echevarría, for example, also focus on and identify the narrator with the individual and author Cabeza de Vaca. By contrast, Laila Lalami's rewriting (2014) of *La Relación* moves the focus from its narrator and from the iconization of Cabeza de Vaca to the figure of Estevanico.

[10] Cabeza de Vaca is supposed to have traced his name to the early period of the Christian *reconquista* of the Iberian Peninsula from the Muslims, with the "origin of the name" 'Cabeza de Vaca' legendarily found in "the name given to the ancestor who in 1212 aided Christians during the *reconquista* by using a cow's skull to point out a passage through the mountains that would be undetected by the Muslim army" (RABASA 2000: 55). ADORNO/PAUTZ (1999, vol. I: 298–303) dismiss this legendary origin of the name Cabeza de Vaca. The legendary origin with a reference to Islam and the *reconquista* appears to have been developed in the eighteenth century when the Christian reading of *La Relación* as spiritual shipwreck under the title of *Naufragios* became popular.

The work consists of a photograph of a mixed-media object created from the head of a dead cow on a faux marble pedestal. The photograph has three sections – the cow's head, the pedestal and the background – and, in size, the cow's head approximates realistic dimensions. The visual-art genres of sculpture, photography and bioart are involved. Since the dead cow's head has a bloody snout and neck, the experience of the photograph provokes, on the one hand, questions concerning the decomposition of the biological matter, and, on the other hand, the "eye is particularly disturbing [...]. It gives the sensation that the head is still warm, not quite dead" (Rabasa 2000: 55). Moreover, the head appears served up "for our safe consumption", as Rabasa states, like a dish of roasted meat on a table, "sitting on a pedestal, or is it a platter?" (Rabasa 2000: 55). The photograph plays with the expectations of the observer regarding the established visual arts media of the portrait and the sculptured bust, in particular regarding the tradition of sculptures and busts of heroes and celebrities through the ages, an effect due to the marbled, precious appearance of the pedestal, with marble a signifier of the heroic tradition in art since antiquity. Intermedially, the image by Serrano also relates to a postage stamp in honor of Cabeza de Vaca that was issued in Spain in 1960 [Fig. 3]:

FIG 3. Postage stamp in honor of Cabeza de Vaca, issued in Spain in 1960.

The ear of the cow in Serrano's photograph looks like the feather or plush accessoire on the hat of the figure on the stamp. There is even a similarity of shape and expression in the eye of the dead cow and the eyes of the figure on the stamp. In both depictions, the gaze is directly at the observer. The celebratory purposes of the stamp in anniversaries of the conquest are mocked by Serrano's *Cabeza de Vaca*, just as iconization is mocked in associations of the image by Serrano with the biblical story of the golden calf, evoked by the golden-colored tint of the fur of the animal and the reddish-golden pedestal and background of the photograph. By association with idolatry, the photograph satirizes the celebrity the figure of Cabeza de Vaca has received by the reception of *La Relación* in literary and cultural studies.

Contrary to a masculine heroic tradition, however, the head of the animal is attributed to a cow, *vaca*, not to a bull, *toro*, that would be expected to have horns. The cow is white, not black, innocent rather than devilish, according to Christian iconography. There are no horns on the cow's head, which makes it appear less combative and less symbolically loaded than an animal head with horns, whether male or female. The heads of cows in Cabeza de Vaca's coat of arms, by contrast, are depicted with horns, above the four fields and between the towers and the bird's necks [Fig. 4]. By using a model without horns for his photograph, Serrano creates an image calling for exemption from contemporary associations with bullfights and toreros and the violence of that tradition. Still, on closer research and observation, the hornlessness may be the result of selective breeding or of the violence of surgical removal. The horns of the model may have been removed before the head was installed for the photograph, as the bloody back of the head above the ears suggests. On a further zoological note, the cow of Serrano's work is not a bison, not of an American species at all, so that the transatlantic encounter, rather, is figured.

FIG 4. Coat of Arms of Cabeza de Vaca.

The cow's mimics, due to the slightly grinning appearance of the raised corner of its mouth, seem knowledgeable yet resigned to all kinds of interpretation. Concerning perspective, the art object is ambiguous: the 'first-person', disturbingly non-fiction gaze of the cow's eye at the observer is mediated through the 'objective' camera perspective and thereby becomes fictionalized, 'made up'. Moreover, the head of an unnamed cow takes on the quality of a species rather than an individual, so that the first-person gaze may also be read as a first-person plural, a 'we' rather than an 'I/eye'. This 'we', in turn plays on the several meanings the name and figure Cabeza de Vaca have collected in the critical tradition and repeats the shift from first-person singular to first-person plural narrative perspective in *La Relación*.

Serrano's photographic conceptual art is postmodernist – "ironic allegory" (RABASA 2000: 55) – in the sense of the satirical inversions and hybridities it generates for the observer: multiple perspectives, fictionality and non-fictionality, portraiture and conceptual art, animal and man, genetic engineering and wildlife, name and person, life and death. Through transgeneric mimicry rather than mimesis, the work provides a meta-discourse on a name and on words themselves. The soft and wise grin of the cow's mouth mocks aggression. Identifications enforced by words as tools of distinction or as name-calling are warded off; they glance off the image. Serrano's *Cabeza de Vaca* animalizes as well as humanizes Cabeza de Vaca. By depicting the narrator and author of *La Relación* as a dead animal, the distinctions 1) of the European subject from Indigenous peoples considered animal-like or primitive according to chronologically later, dehumanizing discourse,[11] 2) of human being and animal in general as well as 3) between individual, mortal corporeality and transtemporal discursive practice are destabilized and ironized. Relationality of sense making as a process between textual work, visual artwork and observer across historical periodization is foregrounded.

Posthumanism, or, Walking in Skins

I consider the junctures, intersections and relations produced by Serrano's *Cabeza de Vaca* to signal the posthumanism of the photograph as much as the posthumanism already of *La Relación*. By the photograph and the text, the posthumanist decentering of the human as subject in the sense of a dispersal of agency is performed, in a way similar to the dispersal of agency in the scene of learning the practice of healing in *La Relación*.

The decentering of the human in posthumanism is supported by materialism: "'[T]he human' is achieved by escaping or repressing not just its animal origins in nature, the biological, and the evolutionary, but more generally by transcending the bonds of materiality and embodiment altogether. [... P]osthumanism [...] opposes the fantasies of disembodiment and autonomy, inherited from humanism itself" (WOLFE 2010: xv). In *La Relación*, there are several descriptions of the blurring of the boundary between humans and animals that revolve around the skin. The skin as the surface of bodies signifies their delimitation from the environment. Undecidability between human and animal body matter and a proximity between human and animal corporeality in death is found in repeated mention of the animal hides worn by the narrator, the group of expeditionaries and the Indigenous people as well as in a passage with a description of human corpses dressed in deerskins. The animals die at human hands, by human agency, yet their cadavers and body parts in the posthumanist discourse of *La Relación* and of Serrano's photograph figure a critique of the triumphalist concept of humanity and mark the finitude of all flesh. Like in Serrano's photograph of the dead cow's head, the mortality of animals signifies the end of the concept of the human as the exceptional and superior rational being such as we have long considered ourselves.

The first instance of significatory instability is developed by the trope of animal skins – bison hides or deerskin – used as clothing by the Indigenous people, the narrator and

[11] This racist discourse is not yet entrenched in texts of the early sixteenth century, just as slavery is in transition from being based on conquest in war as in antiquity (PHILLIPS 1996) to being widely race-based as in modernity. The European debate on the humanity of the Indigenous people that was ongoing in the Holy Roman Empire and the Catholic church at the time of the writing of *La Relación* is not found in the text itself. There is a single exception in the address to the emperor in which the Indigenous people are called barbaric (CABEZA DE VACA 1542: 18); however, this is not in the voice of the narrator of the text but in the voice of the imperial subject that is subverted by the text. *La Relación* does not question the humanity of the Indigenous people, suggesting the position of Bartolomé de las Casas and of the papal decision in *Sublimis Deus* (1537) on the humanity of Indigenous tribes as rational beings with souls who should not be enslaved. The humanity of the Indigenous people, nevertheless, does not prevent the violence of conquest as part of imperial warfare for territorial gain.

the other three expeditionaries. The narrator describes the killing of the animals for food and hides in a detached, perfunctory, proto-humanist way. The animals are considered to supply to and serve the human in a description that is in the voice of a *conquistador* evaluating the resources available in the New World. As Adorno and Pautz point out, the American bison is described by the narrator of *La Relación* for the first time in the Euro-American textual tradition (CABEZA DE VACA 1542, trans. Adorno and Pautz: 147):

> Cows sometimes range as far as here [the Texas coast], and three times I have seen and eaten of them. And it seems to me that they are about the size of those of Spain. They have small horns like Moorish cows, and their fur is very long. Some are brown and others black, and in my opinion they have better meat and more of it than those from here [Castile]. From the young ones the Indians make robes to cover themselves, and from the mature animals they make shoes and shields. These cows come from the north forward through the land to the coast of *Florida* and they extend over the land for more than four hundred leagues. And along this entire route throughout the valleys through which they come, the people who inhabit them come down and sustain themselves on them, and they supply the land with a great quantity of hides [*grande quantidad de cueros*]. (CABEZA DE VACA 1542, trans. Adorno and Pautz: 147, 146, my insertions)

The utilitarian approach to the animals is complicated by the approximation of human and animal matter in the wearing of skins. By the killing of the animal its skin is turned into a hide which human beings wear as a second skin. Walking in skins brings the Christians and the Indigenous people close, literally, to animals; the borders of the human body are extended, changed and made slippery by taking on another skin, the skin of another being, the skin of a dead body. The animal skin becomes a double for the human skin and an interface with the environment; it is as close to the human body as to the surroundings. Moreover, the description of cows in the passage connotes the narrator's name, so as to bring on, as in Serrano's photograph, a further blurring of the distinction of animals and human beings. The narrator walks in skins, takes on another skin that is not categorically different from his own skin. This layering and doubling underlines the cognitive challenge spelled out in *La Relación*, the challenge to the Spanish explorers as well as to the Indigenous peoples, who frequently hold power over the four Spanish men, to bear and make pragmatically feasible the borderline fuzziness and in/commensurability of semiotic systems and worldviews as part of their relations and as part of the transtemporal relations of readers to *La Relación*.

In the vocabulary of its hispanophone source version, the passage is related to the address to the emperor by which the narrator begins his work: "I walked lost and naked [*anduve perdido y en cueros*]" (CABEZA DE VACA 1542, trans. Adorno and Pautz: 19, 18, my insertion). In the anglophone translation, *en cueros* is rendered as 'naked' whereas in the source text, the Spanish phrase connotes the animal skins of bison or deer that provide the bodies of the Indigenous and the Christians with protection against cold or injury. Adorno and Pautz's translation as 'naked' anticipates one of the most frequently quoted statements from the last sentence of the address to the emperor: "[T]his alone is what a man who came away naked could carry out with him [*éste solo es el que un hombre que salió desnudo pudo sacar consigo*]" (CABEZA DE VACA 1542, trans. Adorno and Pautz: 21, 20, my insertion). In this instance in the source text and in the translation, the word *desnudo* is rendered as 'naked', which is of greater semantic equivalence than *en cueros* and 'naked'. It is not clear why the translators do not render that the narrator describes himself as dressed in animal skins – rather than as naked – in the first instance of the address to the emperor as he does throughout the account. If it were clear that the people usually wore animal skins – were dressed *en cueros* – rather than went naked, the uncommon appearance of *desnudo* in the last line of the address to the emperor would become more easily recognizable as the metaphorical exaggeration rather than realistic description that it is in the source text.

The metaphorical use of nakedness is part of the narrator's rhetorical strategy. The shifting of the meaning of the text regarding the physical appearance of the narrator between naked in his own skin and covered by the skin of an animal creates an ambivalence regarding the use of nakedness as a biblical metaphor in colonial writings on the Americas and in the semantics of first contact between Christians and Indigenous peoples (GLANTZ [1992/1993] 2005) in which nakedness is taken to denote the Indigenous world as a primordial or even paradisiacal state. The religious discourse is reduced in *La Relación* since it changes into a cultural one when the narrator is literally dressed in skins and is naked metaphorically only by European standards of rationalism and 'world' explanation. Rabasa's claim that "[s]hipwreck in Cabeza de Vaca's narrative marks the transition to a primordial time signified by physical nakedness and the revelation that European civilization is a very thin veneer, easily forgotten" (RABASA 2000: 50) has to be modified in that the narrator is described as at least partially dressed in animal hides. The nakedness of the last line of the address to the emperor then takes on the qualities of a philosophical *tabula rasa* of the mind, a state of ignorance more so than moral innocence, particularly in the context of the address to the emperor that foregrounds the bringing of information and knowledge to Europe. Rabasa explains that the "return to a first time entails not only a complete loss of material civilization, but also a complete dependence on Amerindian knowledge – including a plurality of possible worlds in which magic makes sense, works" (RABASA 2000: 50).

Another frequently discussed passage of *La Relación* signifies a transitional process of relationality between animal and human matter: "[W]e found many crates belonging to Castilian merchants, and in each one of them was the body of a dead man, and the bodies were covered with painted deer hides. This seemed to the commissary to be a type of idolatry, and he burned the crates with the bodies in them" (CABEZA DE VACA 1542, trans. Adorno and Pautz: 37, 39). The scene marks and is marked by the instability of the border between Christians and Indigenous peoples, inanimate and animate, between assemblage and inchoate decay, between animal and human, between Indigenous ritual and a burning reminiscent of autodafés by the Spanish Inquisition. Bruce-Novoa argues that

> this hybrid assemblage of European boxes, native deerskins, and male cadavers; these bodies that drift between pagan and Christian, between Native American and Native European, even between inanimate and animate; these body signs created by Native Americans and recreated again by a once Spaniard turned Indiano: Americano [...] in their ambiguous location within and among codes of signification, float back and forth across multiple borders of identity demarcations. (BRUCE-NOVOA 2011: 27)

For Bruce-Novoa, 'Americanness' becomes a synonym for the poststructuralist semiotics he discovers in the semiotization of human and animal bodies in *La Relación*.[12] The attribution of the corpses to a group is as instable as the sixteenth-century navigational and geographical data circumscribing the area where the boxes were found and is as unreliable and as prone to misunderstanding as seems the communication "[b]y means of signs" (CABEZA DE VACA 1542, trans. Adorno and Pautz: 39) – 'sign language,' that is, doubly layered 'sign signs' – as the source of information during first contact further described in the passage. The reader, like the first observers, is called upon to make sense of the scene of corpses in deerskins in boxes.

The textual examples – on the healing power of stones and men and on walking and decaying in skins that signify the crossing of codes and a connection of all matter – demonstrate how *La Relación* functions as a narrative of the decentering of the human by Old-World and Christian concepts. The narrator describes himself as transforming from a self-governing, autonomous European man of reason – counting himself among "gente de razón [men of reason]" (CABEZA DE VACA 1542, trans. Adorno and Pautz: 150) – into an agent in a relational network that includes the members of the imperial army, the Indigenous people, the readers, the animals, and the stones. Through descriptions of the semiosis by the Indigenous peoples that relativizes European textual traditions and images of the human, *La Relación* decenters the human as subject. Humanimagic emerges as a practice of relationality that seeks to acknowledge the multiplicity and relativity of agential positions in any communication and description, contrary even to syntax and and its often mono-directional or linear logic. Such a practice includes the proposition of exchange across conventionally stabilized borders, such as in the exchange with a dead animal, that is, exchange across the line between life and death and the species boundary as by the gaze of the cow from Serrano's image. 'Magic' becomes a synonym for sign production that is less fantastic than it is creative of a relation between in/commensurable discourses and semiotic systems. The modification of visuality and rationality by other faculties of perception is involved in this aesthetic and poetic process.

Through the relational decentering of the narrative perspective and subject, *La Relación* and Serrano's *Cabeza de Vaca* share criteria of posthumanist discourse. Posthumanism, then, is not bound to a chronological allocation after, or to the bringing about of an end to, Renaissance humanism and its linear continuations until a contemporary era. The

[12] As is well known and much discussed, in the appended chapter thirty-eight, provided as if by an afterthought to complete the official accounting for the lost expedition, the narrator attributes the dead bodies to Christians. In a passage that resembles a nautical logbook by its style of reporting, the narrator mentions the dead bodies in connection with the retracing of a good place for anchoring that had been overlooked earlier by members of the expedition (CABEZA DE VACA 1542, trans. Adorno and Pautz: 277). The passage suggests that the bodies are claimed to have been of Christians because the area where they were found was in the vicinity of the anchoring place that was frequented by Spaniards with their ships. By contrast, as Adorno and Pautz point out, Oviedo notes that by rules of the church the bodies ought not to have been burned if they had been of Christians (CABEZA DE VACA 1542, trans. Adorno and Pautz: 39 note 1), which detail supports the interpretation that the clerical commissary who ordered the burning considered the bodies to be of Indigenous persons.

progression, therefore, from humanism to posthumanism along a linear temporality, a progression Cary Wolfe, for example, argues, becomes questionable. Wolfe holds that

> posthumanism names a historical moment in which the decentering of the human by its imbrication in technical, medical, informatic, and economic networks is increasingly impossible to ignore, [...] a new mode of thought that comes after the cultural repressions and fantasies, the philosophical protocols and evasions, of humanism as a historically specific phenomenon. (WOLFE 2010: xv–xvi)

The befores and afters of a discourse determined by linear temporality also become questionable with respect to the narrative of the progress of civilization. In the preface to an edition of *Interlinear to Cabeza de Vaca*, the adaptation of *La Relación* by Haniel Long (1936), Henry Miller argues that the "important thing to bear in mind is precisely what the Interlinear [...] brings out, namely that the civilized European of four centuries ago had lost something that the Indians still possessed" (Miller 1946 qtd. in Rabasa 2000, 56). "Miller's contention that Indians still possessed a link to spirituality no longer available to the West" (RABASA 2000: 56) is founded on the discourse of civilization that describes a temporal linearity and a teleology from primitive to civilized. According to this discourse, the Indigenous, on the one hand, are always earlier, before – or, therefore, spatially behind, as it were – the more advanced and civilized Europeans and can never reach across that distance. The Europeans or Euro-Americans, on the other hand, as in primitivist modernism (LEMKE 1998), are supposed to find rejuvenation with them that are styled as primordial and innocent. In such a primitivist way, Miller inverts the values of the civilizatory tale and the linear temporality criticized by Johannes Fabian in *Time and the Other* ([1983] 2014). The Indigenous are nostalgically placed in a supposedly more spiritual time that is considered not to be same time as that of the narrator Cabeza de Vaca nor of the contemporary readers and critics. Such a discourse, however, does not inform *La Relación* of 1542 nor its narrator's rendering of Indigenous life. The coevalness, instead, of the Indigenous peoples and the expeditionaries in *La Relación*, like the engaging relationality in the rendering of in/commensurability in their depiction, supports a posthumanist reading of the account.

A transtemporal posthumanist relationality is at work in and through *La Relación*. Temporalities of historiography and evolutionary theory are relativized in *La Relación* as well as in the discourse and works it generates, effecting a coevalness of positions in a plurinodal network relationality and in transtemporality. This is not *posthistoire* since we are still writing and reading. Andy Miah defines posthumanist thought as oriented by concepts of temporariness and processuality as features of perpetual becoming (MIAH 2008: 23). "[P]osthumanism encounters an ongoing undecidability over the value of transgressing boundaries [...]" (MIAH 2008: 18). In respect of *La Relación*, I find a posthumanist mode of thought in the critique of Old-World, Christian anthropocentrism and in the transtemporal engagement of the reader through the practices described by the narrator Cabeza de Vaca, so that "magic works" (RABASA 2000: 56). The narrator challenges us in a similar way as Spivak calls on us to "persistently educate ourselves into this peculiar mindset" (SPIVAK 2003: 72) of perspectival inversion.

> '[A]ny notion of the posthuman that is to be more than merely an extension of the human, that is to move beyond the dialectic of control and lack of control, superhuman and inhuman, must be premised upon a mutation that is ongoing and immanent,' and this means that to become posthuman means to participate in – and find a mode of thought adequate to – 'processes which can never be entirely reduced to patterns or standards, codes or information.' (RUTSKY qtd. in WOLFE 2010, xviii)

The posthuman thinking described by R. L. Rutsky and Wolfe through characteristics such as surplus, excess and incommensurability and the contemporary task of further conceptualizing relativity across disciplines correlates with the problematics of accounting for in/commensurability in comparative literature and culture studies, as summarized by Susan Stanford Friedman (2012).

Friedman revisits the methodological uses of relationality as conceptualized by Éduard Glissant or Fernando Ortíz and follows in Spivak's footsteps by arguing for a "poetics of relation on a planetary landscape" (FRIEDMAN 2012: 513), even if her argument for a "polycentric framework" still emphasizes items according to binary distinctions of "identities of self and other" (FRIEDMAN 2012: 512). The direction of Glissant's argument, however, is towards the relational "*possibility for each one at every moment to be both solidary and solitary there*" (GLISSANT [1990] 1997: 131), a description that is congenial to the way the narrator creates himself in *La Relación*. In the aesthetic theory of the *Poetics of Relation*, Glissant describes two approaches to science: "A science of conquerors who scorn or fear limits" as "a science of conquest" and "the other direction, which is not one", and that

> distances itself entirely from the thought of conquest; it is an experimental meditation (a follow-through) of the process of relation, at work in reality, among the elements (whether primary or not) that weave its combinations. A science of inquiry. This 'orientation' then leads to following through whatever is dynamic, the relational, the chaotic – anything fluid and various and moreover uncertain (that is, ungraspable) yet fundamental in every instance and quite likely full of instances of invariance. (GLISSANT [1990] 1997: 137)

The "effortful epistemic shift" (SPIVAK 2003: 114, note 1) from distinguishing to relating that is called for by Glissant and Spivak is a process of gradual modification of assembly of contiguous elements, including temporalities and speeds. *La Relación*, a text that describes and is received as part of this epistemic shift, has been a posthumanist enterprise since 1542.

List of Works Cited

ADORNO, ROLENA and PATRICK CHARLES PAUTZ (2003): Introduction. In: *Álvar Núñez Cabeza de Vaca: His Account, His Life, and the Expedition of Pánfilo de Narváez*. Trans. and ed. by ROLENA ADORNO and PATRICK CHARLES PAUTZ. Lincoln/London: University of Nebraska Press, 1–37.

ADORNO, ROLENA and PATRICK CHARLES PAUTZ (1999): *Álvar Núñez Cabeza de Vaca: His Account, His Life, and the Expedition of Pánfilo de Narváez*. 3 vols. Lincoln/London: University of Nebraska Press.

AHERN, MAUREEN (1993): The Cross and the Gourd: The Appropriation of the Ritual Signs in the *Relaciones* of Alvar Núñez Cabeza de Vaca and Fray Marcos de Niza. In JERRY WILLIAMS and ROBERT LEWIS (Eds.): *Early Images of the Americas: Transfer and Invention*. Tucson: Universiy of Arizona Press, 215–244.

BARKER, CHRIS (2004): Post-Humanism. *The SAGE Dictionary of Cultural Studies*. London: SAGE, 151–152.

BISHOP, MORRIS (1933):*The Odyssey of Cabeza de Vaca*. New York: Century Company.

BONVILLIAN, JOHN D., VICKY L. INGRAM and BRENDAN M. MCCLEARY (2009): Observations on the Use of Manual Signs and Gestures in the Communicative Interactions between Native Americans and Spanish Explorers of North America: The Accounts of Bernal Díaz del Castillo and Álvar Núñez Cabeza de Vaca. *Sign Language Studies* 9.2: 132–165.

BRUCE-NOVOA, JUAN (2011): Unpacking America's Boxed Gifts: From Cabeza de Vaca to Donald Duck. In ASTRID FELLNER (Ed.): *Body Signs: The Latino/a Body in Cultural Production*. Zürich: LIT, 23–51.

BRUCE-NOVOA, JUAN (1993): *Reconstructing a Chicano/a Literary Heritage: Hispanic Colonial Literature of the Southwest*. Tucson: University of Arizona Press.

CABEZA DE VACA, ÁLVAR NÚÑEZ [1542]: The 1542 *Relación* (Account) of Álvar Núñez Cabeza de Vaca. Trans. and ed. by ROLENA ADORNO and PATRICK CHARLES PAUTZ. *Álvar Núñez Cabeza de Vaca: His Account, His Life, and the Expedition of Pánfilo de Narváez*. 3 vols. Lincoln/London: University of Nebraska Press, 1999. Vol. I. 1–279. after ÁLVAR NÚÑEZ CABEZA DE VACA [1542]: *La relación que dio Álvar Núñez Cabeça de Vaca de lo acaescido en las Indias en la armada donde iva por governador Pánphilo de Narbáez, desde el año de veinte y seite hasta el año de treinta y seis que bolvió a Sevilla con tres de su compañía*. Zamora: Printed by Augustín de Paz and Juan Picardo for Juan Pedro Musetti.

Cabeza de Vaca. Dir. Nicolás Echevarría. color/sound, 112 min. Mexico, 1991. Paris: E.D. Distribution.

FABIAN, JOHANNES ([1983] 2014): *Time and the Other: How Anthropology Makes Its Object*. New York: Columbia University Press.

FAVATA, MARTIN A. and JOSÉ B. FERNÁNDEZ (Trans.): *The Account: Álvar Núñez Cabeza de Vaca's* Relación. Houston: Arté Publico Press, 1993.

FRIEDMAN, SUSAN STANFORD (2012): World Modernisms, World Literature, and Comparativity. In MARK A. WOLLAEGER (Ed.): *The Oxford Handbook of Global Modernisms*. New York: Oxford University Press, 499–525.

FRYE, DAVID (Trans.): *Chronicle of the Narváez Expedition*, by Álvar Núnez Cabeza de Vaca. Ed. by Ilan Stavans. New York/London: W.W. Norton, 2013.

GERNALZICK, NADJA (2013): Translinguality and Transculturality. In ALFONSO DE TORO (Ed.): *TRANSLATIO: Transmédialité et transculturalité en littérature, peinture, photographie, et au cinéma (Amériques – Caraïbes – Europe – Maghreb)*. Paris: L'Harmattan, 81–95.

GERNALZICK, NADJA (2010): Teleskop und Erzählperspektive in der amerikanischen Renaissance: Emerson, Thoreau, Fuller, Melville. In ULRIKE BERGERMANN, ISABELL OTTO, and GABRIELE

SCHABACHER (Eds.): *Das Planetarische: Kultur – Technik – Medien im postglobalen Zeitalter*. München: Wilhelm Fink Verlag, 221–233.

GIL-OSLE, JUAN PABLO (2018): Cabeza de Vaca's Primahaitu Pidgin. *Journal of the Southwest* 60.1: 253–269.

GLANTZ, MARGO ([1992/1993] 2005): El cuerpo inscrito y el texto escrito o la desnudez como naufragio: Álvar Núñez Cabeza de Vaca. In: *La desnudez como naufragio: Borrones y borradores*. Madrid: Iberoamericana and Frankfurt: Vervuert, 67–101.

GLISSANT, ÉDOUARD ([1990] 1997): *Poetics of Relation*. Trans. by Betsy Wing. Ann Arbor: The University of Michigan Press.

GOMEZ-GALISTEO, CARMEN M (2013): *Early Visions and Representations of America: Álvar Núñez Cabeza de Vaca's* Naufragios *and William Bradford's* Of Plymouth Plantation. New York: Bloomsbury, Kindle edition.

JUAN-NAVARRO, SANTIAGO (2001): Constructing Cultural Myths: Cabeza de Vaca in Contemporary Hispanic Criticism, Theater and Film. In SANTIAGO JUAN-NAVARRO and THEODORE ROBERT YOUNG (Eds.): *A Twice-Told Tale: Reinventing the Encounter in Iberian/Iberian American Literature and Film*. Newark: University of Delaware Press and London: Associated University Presses, 67–79.

LALAMI, LAILA ([2014] 2015): *The Moor's Account*. New York: Vintage.

LEMKE, SIEGLINDE (1998): *Primitivist Modernism: Black Culture and the Origins of Transatlantic Modernism*. Oxford/New York: Oxford University Press.

LÉVI-STRAUSS, CLAUDE ([1949*a*] 1963): The Sorcerer and His Magic. *Structural Anthropology*. (1958). Trans. by Claire Jacobson and Brooke Grundfest Schoepf. New York: Basic Books, 167–185.

LÉVI-STRAUSS, CLAUDE ([1949*b*] 1963): The Effectiveness of Symbols. *Structural Anthropology*. (1958). Trans. by Claire Jacobson and Brooke Grundfest Schoepf. New York: Basic Books, 186–205.

LIPPARD, LUCY R. (1990): Andres Serrano: The Spirit and the Letter. *Art in America* 78 (April): 239–245.

LONG, HANIEL ([1936] 1985): *Interlinear to Cabeza de Vaca: His Relation of the Journey from Florida to the Pacific 1528–1536*. Tucson: The Peccary Press.

LÓPEZ, KIMBERLE S. (2001): Naked in the Wilderness: The Transculturation of Cabeza de Vaca in Abel Posse's *El largo atardecer del caminante*. In SANTIAGO JUAN-NAVARRO and THEODORE ROBERT YOUNG (Eds.): *A Twice-Told Tale: Reinventing the Encounter in Iberian/ Iberian American Literature and Film*. Newark: University of Delaware Press and London: Associated University Presses, 149–168.

MATURANA, UMBERTO and FRANCISCO J. VARELA ([1972] 1980): *Autopoiesis and Cognition: The Realization of the Living*. Dordrecht/Boston/London: Reidel.

MIAH, ANDY (2008): A Critical History of Posthumanism. In BERT GORDIJN and RUTH CHATWICK (Eds.): *Medical Enhancement and Posthumanity*. Heidelberg: Springer, 71–94.

MOLINER, MARÍA (2007): *Diccinario de uso del español*. 2 vols. 3rd ed. Madrid: Gredos.

PHILLIPS JR., WILLIAM D. (1996): Slavery in Space and Time: Continuities. In: *Slaves with or without Sugar*. Funchal: Atlantic History Study Center, 127–142.

RABASA, JOSÉ (2000): *Writing Violence on the Northern Frontier: The Historiography of Sixteenth-Century New Mexico and Florida and the Legacy of Conquest*. Durham/London: Duke University Press.

SPITTA, SILVIA (1995): Shamanism and Christianity: The Transcultural Semiotics of Cabeza de Vaca's *Naufragios*. In: *Between Two Waters: Narratives of Transculturation in Latin America.* Houston: Rice University Press, 29–54.

SPIVAK, GAYATRI CHAKRAVORTY (2003): *Death of a Discipline*. New York: Columbia University Press.

TAUSSIG, MICHAEL (1987): *Shamanism, Colonialism, and the Wild Man: A Study in Terror and Healing.* Chicago: University of Chicago Press.
TAUSSIG, MICHAEL (1992): Homesickness & Dada. In: *The Nervous System.* New York: Routledge, 149–182.
WOLFE, CARY (2010): *What Is Posthumanism?* Minneapolis and London: University of Minnesota Press.

List of Figures

FIG 1

Cabeza de Vaca, photograph by Andrés Serrano (1984, Cibachrome, 27.5 x 40 in./69.85 x 101.6 cm). *theartstack.com/artworks/cabeza-de-vaca.*

FIG 2

Iconography of Cabeza de Vaca as Christ in *Cabeza de Vaca* (1991), directed by Nicolás Echevarría. Echevarría 1991. Screenshot.

FIG 3

Postage Stamp in Honor of Cabeza de Vaca, Issued in Spain in 1960. *https://colnect.com/de/stamps/stamp/173687-Cabeza_de_Vaca-Discovery_of_America-Spanien.*

FIG 4

Coat of Arms of Cabeza de Vaca. Detail from a manuscript in the Archivo General de Indias, Seville, Spain. Reproduced from Bishop 1933, 278, after Edward J. Gallagher, *digital.lib.lehigh.edu/trial/reel_new/films/list/0_5_12_3.* Also reproduced in ADORNO/PAUTZ 1999, vol. I, 335.

Sustainability and Literature

Hubert Zapf

Literature as Cultural Ecology[1]

A cultural ecology of literature is based on a functional–evolutionary view of cultural and literary history, in which literary texts *as imaginative and artistic forms of textuality* have acquired specific qualities, modes, and features of writing that are both interrelated with and different from other forms of writing. Literature is described as a transformative force of language and discourse that combines civilizational critique with cultural self-renewal in ways that turn literary texts into forms of sustainable textuality. Literature uses the resources of language, imagination, and discourse for the creation of long-term, self-reflexive models of ecosemiotic complexity. If sustainability in a *biological* sense means the ways in which living systems remain alive and productive over time, then the cultural ecosystem of literature fulfills a similar function of sustainable productivity within *cultural* discourses. And if sustainability in a cultural sense means the ways in which the life of culture can be kept in "equilibrium with basic ecological support systems" (STIVERS 1976: 187), then this criterion applies in a special degree to literary culture, which is characterized in its functional dynamics by maintaining a deep-rooted affinity between its modes of (re-)generation and the ecological processes of life that it both reflects and creatively transforms.

On the one hand, this approach is grounded in a general theory of cultural ecology as a field of transdisciplinary studies that has gained considerable visibility in recent ecological thought, bringing together the formerly separate epistemic domains of ecology and culture, biological life sciences and the sciences of mind, systems theory and textual theory, and natural and cultural evolution in manifold and promising new ways. Primary references are Gregory Bateson's *Ecology of Mind* (1973), which explores connecting patterns of mind and life beyond disciplinary boundaries, and Peter Finke's notion of *cultural ecosystems*, which he develops from Bateson's ecology of mind and from Jakob von Uexküll's distinction between "Umwelten" and "Innenwelten", between external environments and internal worlds, which Uexküll ascribes to nonhuman as well as to human life. In a dialogue between evolutionary biology, social systems theory, and linguistics (UEXKÜLL [1909] 2014), Finke points out that the characteristic environments of human beings are not just external but internal environments, the inner worlds and landscapes of the mind, the psyche, and the cultural imagination which make up the habitats of humans as much as their external natural and material environments. Language as a cultural ecosystem is especially important here as a shaping factor in the process of cultural evolution. Language represents a "missing link" between cultural and natural evolution (FINKE 2006: 202) because it relates back to concrete biophysical forms of

[1] In my paper, I present some ideas on the relationship between sustainability and literature that are based on a cultural ecology of literature that I have proposed in my recent work In my argument, I am drawing in part on my book *Literature as Cultural Ecology: Sustainable Texts* (London: Bloomsbury, 2016).

information and communication in the precultural world of nature, but also transforms them into more abstract, symbolic systems of human interpretation and self-interpretation. Language thus decisively contributes to the emergence of internal worlds of consciousness and culture that are characteristic of cultural evolution. Language and other cultural sign systems, in turn, are the material and the medium of art and literature, whose task is the constant critical examination, imaginative exploration, and creative self-renewal of these cultural sign systems.

In this more specific sense, literature can itself be described as the symbolic medium of a particularly potent form of cultural ecology. Literary texts have staged and explored the complex interactions between culture and nature in ever new scenarios, and have derived their specific power of innovation and cultural self-renewal from the creative exploration of this boundary. This attention to the life-sustaining significance of the mind/body and culture/nature interaction became especially prominent in the era of romanticism, but continues to be characteristic of literary stagings of human experience up to the present. The aesthetic mode of textuality involves an overcoming of the mind/body dualism by bringing together conceptual and perceptual dimensions, ideas and sensory experiences, reflective consciousness and the performative staging of complex dynamical life processes.

From the beginnings of modern aesthetic theory in Alexander G. Baumgarten's *Aesthetica* (1750–58), Immanuel Kant's *Critique of Judgment* (1790), G.W.F. Hegel's *Lectures on Aesthetics* (1835–38) and Theodor W. Adorno's *Aesthetic Theory* (1970) up to Gernot Böhme's contemporary ecophilosophical *Aesthetics of Nature* (1989), theory has struggled with the double status of the aesthetic as both an experience and a form of knowledge, a paradoxical, nonsystemic form of *sinnliche Erkenntnis*, or sensuous knowledge, in which the tension and ambiguous co-agency between mind and body, thought and life was part of the way in which the productivity of aesthetic and imaginative processes was conceived. Literature as a medium of cultural ecology thus specifically focuses on this interactivity of mind and life staged in literary texts as a liminal phenomenon on the boundary between culture and nature, self and other, anthropocentric and biocentric dimensions of existence. Literary texts provide a transformative site of cultural self-reflection and cultural self-exploration, in which the historically marginalized and excluded is semiotically empowered and activated as a source of artistic creativity, and is thus reconnected to the larger cultural system in both deconstructive and reconstructive ways. As the medium of a potentially radical civilizational critique, literature at the same time provides a sustainable generative matrix for the continuous self-renewal of the cultural ecosystem.

The Cultural Dimension of Sustainability

In view of the general relevance of sustainability as a concept, it has taken a surprisingly long time to be acknowledged and find serious attention as a phenomenon of *culture*. In the general public, the three pillars of sustainability comprise ecology, economy, and society – but not usually culture. At universities, typical disciplines involved in sustainability studies include economics, materials sciences, physics, biology, chemistry, environmental history, geography, sociology, and political science – but rarely disciplines from cultural and literary studies. It is true that a growing number of the sustainability programs in university curricula do include the occasional inputs from the social sciences and the humanities. Also, there have been attempts to implement ideas of sustainability within programs of education and teacher training, in order to raise the awareness of educators and students for responsible learning cultures of the future in terms of an "ecological literacy" (STONE/BARLOW 2005).

There has also been a growing discussion of sustainability in contemporary art and art theory, pioneered by developments in landscape and urban art such as Alan Sonfist's *Time Landscape* reintroducing a precolonial indigenous forest in New York City, or Joseph Beuys's project *7000 Oaks – City Forestation Instead of City Administration* at the 1982 *documenta 7* in Kassel, which involved the planting of oaks and of accompanying basalt stones over several years and which, extending from the exhibition site into the city, still shapes the cityscape today. This links up with experimental forms of architecture not only in terms of providing green spaces in cities, but of creating new concepts of urban living in which technomorphic and biomorphic forms of architectural composition are interfused, pioneered already in Friedensreich Hundertwasser's inner-city biotopes, and successively spreading into different architectural styles, green building programs, and concepts of "sustainable design" (JARZOMBEK 2003).

On the other hand, sustainability as a concept has been viewed rather critically in parts of the humanities because of its usurpation by primarily economic–technological models of environmental epistemology and agency. As Stacy Alaimo, a member of the Institute of Sustainability and Global Impact at the University of Texas at Arlington, observes, the dominance of a "sanitized term of sustainability" that does not "in any way question capitalist ideas of unfettered expansion" creates a problem particularly for the humanities and for literary studies, because its adherence to the "gospel of efficiency" involves a preference for disciplines such as "engineering, the sciences, and maybe architecture", at the expense of "philosophical questions, social and political analyses, historical reflections, or literary musings", which seem a waste of time in the face of pressing environmental realities and responsibilities and thus "irrelevant for the serious business of sustainability" (ALAIMO 2012: 560). In its adaptation to cultural and humanist studies, then, the discourse of sustainability needs critical questioning and epistemic extension from such a narrow "techno-scientific focus" towards an inclusion of "issues of human choice involved in putting sustainability into effect and [...] over the socio-cultural practices, behaviours, and structures such choice involves" (GOEMINNE 2011: 20). It requires recognition that "one's very self is substantially interconnected with the world" (ALAIMO 2012: 561) and that this entails a "regrounding of the subject in a materially embedded sense of responsibility [...] for the environments she or he inhabits" (BRAIDOTTI 2006: 137). Sustainability in this cultural sense would then involve the transformation of a "technocratic, anthropocentric perspective" towards "more complex epistemological, ontological, ethical, and political perspectives", which counter the tendency "to externalize and objectify the world" and instead broaden this revised concept of sustainability by incorporating the "lively relationalities of becoming of which we are part" (BARAD 2007: 393).

Sustainability and Literature

The relation of sustainability to literature has so far rarely been explicitly addressed. Apart from the occasional journal contribution, a 2012 issue of *American Literary History* has been devoted to the subject, in which the concept of sustainability is examined in a spectrum of contributions addressing topics such as the relation between the humanities and the sciences (WOOD 2012); environmental justice aspects of sustainability implied in the "indigenous cosmopolitics" in literary works by indigenous authors (ADAMSON 2012); the interwined aspects of race and labor within a critical socioeconomic contextualization of sustainability; re-imaginings of oil-dependent economic practices in texts that confront "the challenge of powering down to create smaller-scale, post-oil economies" (qtd. in SLOVIC 2012: 185); disruptive weather and water conditions as an environmental-historical subtext of William Faulkner's novel *The Sound and the Fury* (PARRISH 2012); and more general epistemological questions on the potential contribution of the humanities to sustainability discourse in terms of a critical and self-reflexive metadiscourse on the categories defining that discourse (PHILIPPON 2012); all of them revealing, as Scott Slovic rightly points out, that sustainability is not a fixed concept, content or program but "a moving target, a distant goal, not a permanently achievable plateau of being" (SLOVIC 2012: 187).

In a *PMLA* issue in 2012, the topic was addressed from different critical angles, ranging from a radical critique of the concept as an instrument of corporate greenwashing to the postulate formulated by Stephanie LeMenager and Stephanie Foote that "we scholars of literary and cultural studies need to claim our stake in sustainability" (LEMENAGER/FOOTE 2012: 577), and to Lynn Keller's contention that "the arts and the human imagination deployed by the arts have significant roles to play" if, as she puts it, "popular ideas of sustainability are to be reclaimed from the blurry, feel-good realm of corporate advertising and given meaningful, hard edges" (KELLER 2012: 581).

All of these perspectives are promising and useful, and they suggest that the dialogue between the discourses of literature and sustainability may have a considerable potential for the future of ecocritical thought. For the most part, though, these are still first steps that are largely focused on thematic issues and environmental content rather than on art and literary aesthetics itself as a site and medium of cultural sustainability.

Two short contributions, however, can indicate complementary ways in which this relation can be conceived. Both of them consider sustainability as a concept connected with long-term ethical perspectives of human living that is transmitted in texts. One comment is John P. O'Grady's article in *ISLE* on "How Sustainable is the Idea of Sustainability?", in which the author questions the predominance of a managerial, economic-developmental and scientific approach to sustainability. O'Grady exposes fundamental ambiguities of the term. For one thing, the reality of both life and nature is not characterized by unchanging constancy but by constant change, since "all things flow" and "everything is in flux" (O'GRADY 2003: 3), and therefore predictions about future developments, which are required by any rational sustainability management, are quite uncertain and unreliable. For another thing, the notion of sustainability involves not just external but internal, ethical values, which have to do with the question of the 'good life' in the ancient classical sense of *eudaimonia*, the sense of living well in a fulfilled, responsibly balanced relation between the self, other humans, and the nonhuman environment. This ethical sense of a "good or sustainable life" (O'GRADY 2003: 7), however, is not objective but a question of the imagination, of literary texts, which can help to reconnect the abstract modern mind to the "lost face of the world" (HILLMAN qtd. in O'GRADY 2003: 7). O'Grady exemplifies this in a poem by Wendell Berry, "A Meeting in a Part", in which the very mutability and changeability of the world, whose existentially most distressing fact is death, becomes a source of sharing and "understanding whatever it is that truly sustains us" (O'GRADY 2003: 8). The poem, which deals with the return of a dead friend in a dream, becomes the medium of a spiritual form of sustainability, which both reflects and redeems what is continually lost in the material world of nature, time, and history.

While O'Grady emphasizes the fundamental difference between poetic and scientific concepts of sustainability, Hannes Bergthaller insists on the relevance of the latter for the ecocritical analysis of literature in his response essay to O'Grady in *ISLE* on "Humanism and the Problem of Sustainability in Margaret Atwood's *Oryx and Crake and The Year of the Flood*" (BERGTHALLER 2010). Criticizing O'Grady's approach as symptomatic of a romantic ecology that posits a pristine, precultural state of nature as an ideal of human cultural self-realization, Bergthaller points out how Atwood, in the dystopian, postapocalyptic scenarios in the first two novels of her MaddAddam trilogy, shows how human nature is no reliable basis for a sustainable future but is fundamentally flawed and driven by egocentric rather than ethical or environmentally responsible motives. Human nature therefore needs the correctives of rational cultural self-management and self-domestication that are represented by science and technology, but also by "anthropotechnologies" (SLOTERDIJK qtd. in BERGTHALLER 2010: 729) like the arts. The creation of a new, ecologically perfectly well-adapted posthuman species, which the social-genetic engineer and 'mad scientist' Crake achieves, is the extreme, perverted manifestation of a civilizational impulse of human self-immunization and self-optimization, which the novel opposes to the traditional, flawed humanism of Snowman alias Jimmy. According to Bergthaller, neither of these poles can claim validity, and the failure of both can only demonstrate that human nature needs the "imaginary order" of culture that "transcends and, as it were, extenuates the biological givens" (BERGTHALLER 2010: 739) for its successful adaptation to the goal of sustainability. Sustainability in this sense does not result from the adaptation of humans to nature but from cultural attempts to adapt human nature to imperatives of survival that are posed precisely by the disastrous results of the uncontrolled and ruthless, but nevertheless 'natural' species expansion of humans.

Whereas O'Grady locates the contribution of texts to sustainability in their liberating of human nature and its spiritual potential from the restrictions of economic and scientific control, Bergthaller, in contrast, assigns the sustainability of texts to their role as part of a larger civilizational program of "bio-political control" and cultural self-domestication of the human species (BERGTHALLER 2010: 729). O'Grady's concept of sustainability is internal and mystic while Bergthaller's is scientific and rational. O'Grady's concept looks to texts for the recovery of a lost past whereas Bergthaller considers them a medium of probing viable perspectives for a yet-to-be gained future. Both approaches tend to link literary texts with a certain agenda rather than with the functional potential of their own evolved forms and aesthetic procedures.

Perhaps the figure of Snowman/Jimmy in *Oryx and Crake* points towards characteristic ambiguities involved in the question of literature and sustainability. He is a half-imaginary figure "existing and not existing, flickering at the edges of blizzards [...] known only through rumours and through its backward-pointing footprints" (ATWOOD 2003: 7–8). As Danette DiMarco writes: "These mythic and multi-directional footprints (they point backward as they move forward) represent Snowman's liminal position and potential power – to repeat a past cycle of aggression against nature in the name of personal profit, or to re-imagine a way for future living grounded in a genuine concern for others" (DIMARCO 2005: 170). This double orientation toward past and future is underlined in the flashback technique of the narrative. It also involves a double ambiguity, which seems to me an important feature in the relation between literature and sustainability. While the look backwards can become a retrogressive fantasy preventing change and development, it is also necessary for developing sustainable, sufficiently complex perspectives for the future. And while the look forward without a sufficiently complex awareness of the past can lead to unsustainable solutions, it is likewise essential in the attempt to search for "new beginning[s]" (DIMARCO 2005: 170) after past catastrophes, which is inscribed into this and other novels. Literature acts between these poles in interconnected zones of radical ambiguities, and the open ending of *Oryx and Crake*, where Snowman/Jimmy meets the human strangers intruding from the past into a posthuman world, is an exemplary case since it illustrates both the recursive connection of past and future in the exploration of new beginnings and the dialogic openness of the text, which is the condition of its co-creative reception by the reader.

Thinking sustainability is thus by no means opposed to innovation and creativity as such. While it contradicts and endeavors to overcome the currently prevalent short-term, instrumental, and profit-driven form of economic and scientific innovation, it necessarily presupposes an alternative, more complex notion of cultural creativity oriented on the long-term survival of cultural and natural ecosystems as interdependent realities enabling the continuation of life on the planet. Thinking in terms of this dynamic, cultural-ecological concept of sustainability has to constantly negotiate between the poles of continuity and change in the imaginative anticipation of possible future scenarios in a newly conceived, democratically legitimated form of cultural evolution, which combines the awareness of its natural-historical conditions of emergence with the consideration of the ethical-ecological consequences of its future agendas. Thinking sustainability in this sense involves "no dogma, no fixed set of formulas and rules that tell you you have to do this and that in order to be sustainable". Rather, it provides "a playing field where one can experiment" (DÜRR qtd. in GROBER 2002: 175 [trans., H.Z.]). And it seems to me that art and literature represent a form of cultural creativity that provides important playing fields for such experiments in the interest of long-term cultural evolution.

In spite of the semantic openness and variable use of the concept of sustainability in culture and literature, a provisional definition of the notion of 'sustainable texts' seems possible on the basis of the various aspects discussed so far. It involves the basic assumption that imaginative literature as a special, artistic form of cultural textuality is characterized by the following traits of a sustainable cultural practice: (1) a *long-term perspective* of culture/nature coevolution vs. short-term concerns; (2) a double orientation toward *continuity and change*, past and future, cultural memory, and cultural creativity; (3) a sensitivity to the *multi-layered forms of relationality* between self and other, mind and life, humans and the nonhuman world, encompassing perceptual, sensory, emotional, cognitive, communicational, and creative dimensions; (4) an attention both to life-sustaining *diversities* and to patterns of *connectivity* across the boundaries of categories, discourses, and life-forms; and (5) an implicit but crucial relevance of this ecocultural potential of imaginative texts for the continuing *capacity of self-renewal* of the cultural ecosystem in its long-term coevolution with natural ecosystems. It is important to note that the aspects of sustainability just described imply no self-evident or objectively given set of properties but a potentiality of texts that only comes alive through its ever new actualizations within always changing historical, social, and individual conditions.

Concluding Remarks

The notion of literature as a form of sustainable textuality is connected with the basic assumption of cultural ecology that literature acts as an ecological force within the larger system of cultural discourses. Even though this force takes on multiple shapes and is actualized in various forms and degrees in individual texts, it indicates a shared generative potential which enables literature to critically reflect and aesthetically explore a given state of civilizational development from a set of relational complexities that are indispensable in maintaining the vitality of cultural ecosystems.

As ecological metanarratives of their culture, literary texts follow an underlying dynamic of transgression and polysemic excess which enables processes of revitalization and symbolic regeneration – even if such regeneration is almost never fully achieved on the level of mimesis and plot but only in an aesthetic reflexivity of discourse that is to be realized in the cognitive-emotional participation of the reader. As Alfred Hornung has shown in various publications, the "life" to which this culturally transformative dynamic of literary texts relates includes, but also goes beyond, individual life (see especially HORNUNG/BAISHENG 2013). "Life" as a precarious process of constant semiosis, interpretation, and adaptation between self and other, autopoiesis and ecopoiesis, is also a crucial dimension of the ways in which imaginative texts, *as* texts, are acting as an ecological force within culture. In their performative and communicative dimensions, they are primary examples of what has been distinguished as "in vivo knowledge" in contrast to the "in vitro knowledge" of the objectifying natural sciences (NICOLESCU 2008: 3). From the microstructure of tropes to the macrostructure of narratives, the imaginative processes of texts are made up by tensions and connecting patterns which transgress the separations of hegemonic discourses and release creative energies that can be activated for the self-criticism and self-renewal of the cultural ecosystem.

Long before contemporary debates about local vs. global issues in society and ecology, literary texts have at least implicitly included this transcultural and (eco-) global dimension in their aesthetic processes. Wai Chee Dimock has called this transnational and potentially global dimension the "deep time" encoded in literature, a time beneath the actual narrative that reflects and refracts in multiple ways the mutual influences and dialogic connections of national literatures to transnational literatures, connections which do not simply supply an additional frame but constitute the very substance of literary texts (DIMOCK 2009). With regard to American literature, Dimock points out the degree to which the transnational, mutual influences of European, African, Indian, Chinese, and other literatures provide formative intertexts for classical and modern American texts. I fully agree here with Dimock and others in their conviction that literature, and not only American literature, has always already been coded in such a transnational way, that literature is always, in principle, world literature (ARAC 2007). Alfred Hornung has taken up and further expanded this thought by explicitly including the ecological dimension in this transnational and transcultural conception of literature and literary life writing (HORNUNG 2016).

In this view, the deep time implied in the rich intertextual fabric of literature that results from its innovative recycling of previous models of genre, style, and aesthetics, is not just the signature of a *cultural memory* of transnational interactivity and interdependence that is part of the very ways in which literary texts become what they are. It is also the signature of the deep time of culture/nature coevolution, which is inscribed into the generative code of texts as a *biosemiotic memory* (WHEELER 2006) that must repeatedly be reconnected to cultural memory in order to find new ways of continuing and renewing cultural and literary creativity. This creativity consists not primarily of the eco-didactic transmission of thematic issues, ideological beliefs, or ecologically revised moral systems. It rather emerges from the complex staging of semantic tensions, ideological conflicts, and discursive indeterminacies, which are inevitably bound up with the issues and problems of the changing evolutionary relationship between culture and nature, human and nonhuman world that is a central generative matrix of literary texts. In this in-between status, literature is, both by its deep evolutionary signature and by its evolved modern cultural function, a multiply coded and highly indeterminate form of discourse, which invites and is dependent on the creative activity of its readers to actualize its rich semantic potential in ever new ways under always changing historical and cultural conditions. The sustainability of literary texts consists in their potency to represent ever renewable sources of creative energy across time and space for ever new generations of readers, not only for its culture of origin but also for other cultures. In this transcultural dimension as well, literary texts provide a sustainable matrix for an ongoing process of ecocultural communication, criticism, and self-renewal that can potentially be shared by a worldwide literary community.

List of Works Cited

ALAIMO, STACY (2012): Sustainable This, Sustainable That: New Materialisms, Posthumanism, and Unknown Futures. *PMLA* 127.3: 558–564.

ADAMSON, JONI (2012): Indigenous Literatures, Multinaturalism, and Avatar: The Emergence of Indigenous Cosmopolitics. *American Literary History* 24. 1: 143–162.

ARAC, JONATHAN (2007): Global and Babel: Language and Planet in American Literature. In WAI-CHEE DIMOCK and LAWRENCE BUELL (Eds.): *Shades of the Planet: American Literature as World Literature*. Princeton, NJ: Princeton University Press, 19–38.

ATTRIDGE, DEREK (2004): *The Singularity of Literature*. London/New York: Routledge.

ATWOOD, MARGARET (2003): *Oryx and Crake*. New York: Doubleday.

BARAD, KAREN (2007): *Meeting the Universe Halfway: Quantum Physics and the Entanglement of Matter and Meaning*. Durham/London: Duke University Press.

BATESON, GREGORY (1973): *Steps to an Ecology of Mind*. London: Paladin.

BECK, ULRICH (1999): *World Risk Society*. Cambridge/Malden: Blackwell.

BERGTHALLER, HANNES (2010): Housebreaking the Human Animal: Humanism and the Problem of Sustainability in Margaret Atwood's *Oryx and Crake* and *The Year of the Flood*. *English Studies* 91.7: 728–743.

BÖHME, GERNOT (2016): Ecological Aesthetics of Nature. In HUBERT ZAPF (Ed.): *Handbook of Ecocriticism and Cultural Ecology*. Berlin/Boston: De Gruyter, 123–134.

BRAIDOTTI, ROSI (2006): *Transpositions: On Nomadic Ethics*. Malden: Polity.

BROCCHI, DAVIDE (2008): The Cultural Dimension of Sustainability. In SACHA KAGAN and VOLKER KIRCHBERG (Eds.): *Sustainability: A New Frontier for the Arts and Cultures*. Frankfurt a. M.: VAS, 26–58.

CAPRA, FRITJOF (2002): *The Hidden Connections: A Science for Sustainable Living*. New York: Random House.

CLARK, TIMOTHY (2011): *The Cambridge Introduction to Literature and the Environment*. Cambridge: Cambridge University Press.

DIMARCO, DANETTE (2005): Paradice Lost, Paradise Regained: *homo faber* and the Makings of a New Beginning in *Oryx and Crake*. *Papers on Language and Literature* 41.2: 170–195.

DIMOCK, WAI CHEE (^{2}2009): *Through Other Continents: American Literature across Deep Time*. Princeton, NJ: Princeton University Press.

DIMOCK, WAI CHEE, and LAWRENCE BUELL (Eds.) (2007): *Shades of the Planet: American Literature as World Literature*. Princeton, NJ: Princeton University Press.

FINKE, PETER (2006): Die Evolutionäre Kulturökologie: Hintergründe, Prinzipien und Perspektiven einer neuen Theorie der Kultur. *Anglia* 124.1: 175–217.

FLUCK, WINFRIED, ERIK REDLING, SABINE SIELKE, and HUBERT ZAPF (Eds.) (2014): *American Studies Today: New Research Agendas*. Heidelberg: Universitätsverlag Winter (American Studies – A Monograph Series 230).

GOEMINNE, GERT (2011): Once upon a Time I Was a Nuclear Physicist: What the Politics of Sustainability Can Learn from the Nuclear Laboratory. *Perspectives on Science* 19.1: 1–31.

GOODBODY, AXEL, and KATE RIGBY (Eds.) (2011): *Ecocritical Theory: New European Approaches*. Charlottesville: University of Virginia Press.

GROBER, ULRICH (2002): Modewort mit tiefen Wurzeln. Kleine Begriffsgeschichte von ‚sustainability' und ‚Nachhaltigkeit'. In GÜNTER ALTNER et al. (Eds.): *Jahrbuch Ökologie 2003*. München, 167–175.

GROBER, ULRICH (2012): *Sustainability: A Cultural History*. Transl. by Ray Cunningham. Totnes, Devon: Green Books.

HORNUNG, ALFRED (2014): Response to Hubert Zapf. In WINFRIED FLUCK, ERIK REDLING, SABINE SIELKE, and HUBERT ZAPF (Eds.): *American Studies Today: New Research Agendas*. Heidelberg: Universitätsverlag Winter, 254–259.

HORNUNG, ALFRED (2016): Ecology and Life Writing in Transnational and Transcultural Perspective. In HUBERT ZAPF (Ed.): *Handbook of Ecocriticism and Cultural Ecology*. Berlin: DeGruyter, 334–348.

HORNUNG, ALFRED, and ZHAO BAISHENG (Eds.) (2013): *Ecology and Life Writing*. Heidelberg: Universitätsverlag Winter (American Studies – A Monograph Series 203).

JARZOMBEK, MARK (2003): Sustainability – Architecture: Between Fuzzy Systems and Wicked Problems. *Blueprints* 21 (1): 6–9, *http://web.mit.edu/mmj4/www/downloads/blueprints21_1.pdf* [21 March 2014].

KELLER, LYNN (2012): Beyond Imagining, Imagining Beyond. *PMLA* 127.3: 579–585.

LeMenager, Stephanie, and Stephanie Foote (2012): The Sustainable Humanities. *PMLA* 127.3: 572–578.

Müller, Timo (2011): From Literary Anthropology to Cultural Ecology: German Ecocritical Theory since Wolfgang Iser. In Axel Goodbody and Kate Rigby (Eds.): *Ecocritical Theory: New European Approaches*. Charlottesville: University of Virginia Press, 71–83.

Müller, Timo, and Michael Sauter (Eds.) (2012): *Literature, Ecology, Ethics: Recent Trends in Ecocriticism*. Heidelberg: Universitätsverlag Winter.

Nicolescu, Basarab (Ed.) (2008): *Transdisciplinarity: Theory and Practice*. Cresskill, NJ: Hampton Press.

O'Grady, John P. (2003): How Sustainable is the Idea of Sustainability? *ISLE: Interdisciplinary Studies in Literature and Environment* 10.1 (Winter): 1–10.

Parrish, Susan Scott (2012): Faulkner and the Outer Weather of 1927. *American Literary History* 24, 1: 34–58.

Philippon, Daniel J. (2012): Sustainability and the Humanities: An Extensive Pleasure. *American Literary History* 24 (1): 163–179.

Rueckert, William ([1978] 1996): Literature and Ecology: An Experiment in Ecocriticism. In Cheryll Glotfelty and Harold Fromm (Eds.): *The Ecocriticism Reader: Landmarks in Literary Ecology*. Athens: University of Georgia Press, 105–123.

Slovic, Scott (2012): Commentary. *American Literary History* 24.1: 180–188.

Smith, Stephanie, and Victor Margolin (Eds.) (2005): *Beyond Green: Toward a Sustainable Art*. Exhibition catalogue. Chicago/New York: Smart Museum of Art and Independant Curators International.

Stivers, Robert L. (1976): *The Sustainable Society: Ethics and Economic Growth*. Philadelphia: Westminster Press.

Stone, Michael K., and Zenobia Barlow (Eds.) (2005): *Ecological Literacy: Educating Our Children for a Sustainable World*. San Francisco: Sierra Club Books.

Uexküll, Jakob Johann von ([1909] 2014): *Umwelt und Innenwelt der Tiere*. Ed. by Florian Mildenberger and Bernd Herrmann. Berlin/Heidelberg: Springer.

UN Documents: Report of the World Commission on Environment and Development: Our Common Future (Brundtland Report). World Commission on Environment and Development A/42/427. 1987. *http://www.un-documents.net/wced-ocf.htm*.

Westling, Louise (2014): *The Cambridge Companion to Literature and the Environment*. Cambridge: Cambridge University Press.

Wheeler, Wendy (2006): *The Whole Creature: Complexity, Biosemiotics and the Evolution of Culture*. London: Lawrence & Wishart.

Wood, Gillen D'Arcy (2012): What Is Sustainability Studies? *American Literary History* 24, 1: 1–15.

Zapf, Hubert (2013): Cultural Ecology and Literary Life Writing. In Alfred Hornung and Zhao Baisheng (Eds.): *Ecology and Life Writing*. Heidelberg: Universitätsverlag Winter, 3–25.

Zapf, Hubert (2016): *Literature as Cultural Ecology: Sustainable Texts*. London/New York: Bloomsbury.

Zapf, Hubert (Ed.) (2016): *Handbook of Ecocriticism and Cultural Ecology*. Berlin/Boston: De Gruyter.

Life Writing and Medicine

Lives without Memory

Alzheimer's Narratives

Rüdiger Kunow

When Mind Comes to Self: Human Life and the Narrative Form

Bodies, it is said, have stories, and we are willing, almost intuitively, to grant that. Life writing scholarship – much of it inspired by the work of Alfred Hornung – has theorized in more detail than I can show here how these stories function as mediations between body, self, and the world of social beings. But then there are cases in which bodies and stories seem to work against one another. Extreme physical anguish, shock, aphasia are such cases; my focus in this paper will be on Alzheimer's disease.

The illness defined by the American Psychiatric Association as "Senile Dementia of the Alzheimer's type" (Diagnostic and Statistical Manual of Mental Disorders, DSM-5, 2013)[1] is more than a grim presence haunting senior residences and geriatric care wards; it "permeates the cultural consciousness" of many countries all over the world, including the United States (BASTING 2003: 87).[2] In contrast to other mass diseases of our time, such as coronary defects or diabetes, whose progression often remains silent and unnoticed by the patient, Alzheimer's disease is highly 'visible' – not only because its effects can be meticulously measured by standardized tests[3] and also by techno-scientific imaging methods. Alzheimer's high profile is due also to the fact that it is, like cancer, an eminently narratable disease: like the AIDS/HIV virus, Alzheimer's sneaks in on the unsuspecting self and then takes over, step-by-step, body and mind; it even turns the mind against the body and its functions. And even though not all dementias are Alzheimer's and even though the disease afflicts not all old people, 'AD', as it is popularly called, has become a cultural idiom for the later stages of the human life course. This is deeply ironic, a case of speaking about rather than with AD patients, as the actual experience of the suffering almost always remains hidden from the public.

From the disciplinary perspective of cultural critique which cannot treat the illness but hopes to alleviate some of its cultural burdens, one of the first things that needs to be noticed is that AD is a disease where the jurisdiction of the medical profession has long eroded and everybody has his or her say on the disease. In the context of an overall "biomedicalization" (CLARKE et al. 2010: 1) of United States culture, Alzheimer's has travelled from the clinical domain into the general public, and in the process it has also become the object of intense practices of life writing in all kinds of media. Films such as

[1] About 5.1 million; in the next ten years numbers are expected to grow by 14 %. *https://www.alz.org/facts/downloads/facts_figures_2015.pdf.*

[2] Shrenk's landmark book *The Forgetting* brings together many of the cultural resonances of this disease, often with a fearful undertone.

[3] In particular, the 'mini mental', a ten-item routine examination of a patient's cognitive abilities with a heavy emphasis on memory, thus functions as a litmus test for future access to sociable forms of life.

Iris (2001) or *The Notebook* (2004)[4] come to mind here, but then there is also a growing archive of grassroots life writing in diaries, blogs and other forms. Among many other sites you will find a "Dealing with Alzheimer's Blog",[5] and there is even a site for "Best Alzheimer's Blogs of 2016".[6]

Even a cursory look at the inexhaustible mass of life writing material will reveal that something like a cultural master narrative of AD is often at work here, a master narrative which de- and prescribes how the entry of Alzheimer's into a person's life is to be scripted, what the intermediary steps are, how that person fights the disease, etc. The core element of this master narrative might be called a *Bildungsroman in reverse*: As the illness progresses and cognitive impairments become more severe, many things the mind had learned during a lifetime are unlearned. Alzheimer's narratives can thus be classified as identity narratives *manqués*; they portray identity – as we conventionally understand it – in the process of collapsing, so that in the end Alzheimer's patients are disconnected from their past (POST qtd. in BASTING 2003: 96), living lives without memory. In her autobiographical blog *Truthful Loving Kindness*, the eponymous author[7] reflects on the progression of her symptoms and the downward spiral towards total disconnection:

> First times for new symptoms are always difficult – the realization that you just slipped a notch.
> Yes, it is late; I was starting preparations for bed. Husband and I had enjoyed two hours of time together watching the show, "John Adams". Fifteen minutes ago I walked in the bathroom, turned on the light … and had no idea where I was. For a moment nothing looked familiar, and I was extremely confused. Where am I? I forgot where I was and why I was there … just standing in the room in shock because I did not recognize where I was.
> It only took a moment and reality clicked back again. I returned to the living room and hugged my husband … and then I cried.
> It is scary to realize I am losing … everything.
> (TRUTHFUL LOVING KINDNESS, "First Time of Where Am I")

In addition, people in advanced stages of Alzheimer's experience considerable difficulty in matching words with the ideas in their mind (METEYARD/PATTERSON 2009), and they do so in ways that afford parallels to the Saussurean notion of the troubled relationship between signifier and signified, as this recorded exchange with an Alzheimer's patient may show:

> ELINOR: How are you, Mother?
> LIL: Oh, in a fast muff, getting out of the wet ditches.
> ELINOR: Wet ditches, well, that's interesting.
> LIL: Oh, I'm in a dedeford, they're, they're having a beurz. I mean, they're having a cressit. And would be considered hijardi. Would be picking dependent stuff. I mean they're

[4] Other examples are: *Extreme Love* (2012), a TV documentary by Louis Theroux on Alzheimer's; and Alice Munro, "The Bear Came Over the Mountain" (1999), a short story about a man who loses his wife to Alzheimer's and then to another man.

[5] *http://creatingmemories.blogspot.de*.

[6] *http://www.healthline.com/health/alzheimers-disease/best-blogs-of-the-year#1*.

[7] She changed her legal name to Truthful Loving Kindness to remind herself and others of the importance of these attributes. *https://truthfulkindness.com/about/*.

> showing up prepays and other things.
> ELINOR: That's good.
> (FUCHS 2005, n. p.)

As the last quoted examples show, Alzheimer's can perhaps best be understood as a figure of interruption: it interrupts the 'normal' progression of the human life; it intrudes into the fabric of relations between self and others, self and words, 'virtual' and physical reality. And this makes "the possibility of narrative life to the human form" (JAMESON 2015: 13) seem remote. Here, Paul John Eakin's "autobiographical imperative", namely that of "narrating the self into existence" (qtd. in DONALDSON-MCHUGH 2010: 355) seems to reach its limit: in the face of such a text we might as well ask what self? What narrative?

Both are weighty, emotionally and ethically charged questions to which I cannot do justice in the short span of the paper at hand. I will here focus on the narrative aspects, because the principal interest of this paper is on the cultural presence (or absence) of the disease. The other reason is the strong elective affinity between the narrative form and Alzheimer's disease. Clinical as well as cultural gerontologists frequently argue that, especially for patients with cognitive impairments, telling the story of their life is a therapeutic act which helps shore up and stabilize their sense of self and identity (DE MEDEIROS 2009: 97–99). However, from the narrative point of view, such storytelling as the disease progresses must remain an incomplete project, haunted by the increasing loss of memory.[8] Oftentimes, patients find themselves caught in a struggle between keeping up with the symptoms and wanting to continue their participation in social interactions as well as sharing their experiences.[9] In such a situation, the next best thing is a textual form which might provisionally be identified as 'Alzheimer's memorials'. These are authored by family, friends, or sometimes by clinical personnel, and to these I will now turn.

Living in the Words of Others

It is frequently assumed that since Alzheimer's patients can no longer speak for and of themselves – at least not in the ways ordained by our culture – others must take over the job and thus secure a presence even if that presence exists only in memory. So one of the most popular, if not *the* most popular form of Alzheimer's life writing is the testimonial; and there are indeed many blogs featuring the disease and the associated decline of a loved one.[10] Testimonials have become a recognized cultural genre. After emerging

[8] In a highly popular Alzheimer's autobiography, Jeanne Lee even manages to make fun of this. She tells the incident of meeting with a friend of hers who says to her: "I wanted to take you to a really neat place, but I couldn't think of anywhere new. So, I decided to take you to this restaurant we've already been to, because I figured you wouldn't remember it anyway" (35).

[9] Truthful Loving Kindness regularly informs her readers about her condition and her fading ability to continue her blog and social media profiles. Posts like "Won't be around much" show her strong wish to continue but also the reality of fighting the illness. *https://truthfulkindness.com/2016/04/03/wont-be-around-much/*.

[10] Some examples of Alzheimer's testimonial blogs are *https://dealingwithdementia.wordpress.com*; *http://journeywithdementia.blogspot.de* and *http://helpparentsagewell.blogspot.de*.

mostly as a response to victimization, the form has now migrated into other contexts, and particularly so into illness narratives.

In September of 2001, US-American author Jonathan Franzen published a piece in *The New Yorker* called "My Father's Brain: What Alzheimer's takes away".[11] Its opening words "Here's a memory" (FRANZEN 2001: 81) place it squarely with the testimonial form. Throughout, Franzen makes clear that this memoir of his father Earl who had died from Alzheimer's in 1996 is conceived as a *compensatory project*, in Franzen's words "protecting the specificity of Earl Franzen from the generality of a named condition" (FRANZEN 2001: 85). While Alzheimer's is progressively taking away the social identity of Franzen's father, turning him into just another case, the telling of his life story can restore some sense of individual selfhood. After all, Franzen says, assertively, "[t]his was his disease. It was also, you could argue, his story. But you have to let me tell it" (FRANZEN 2001: 82).

As the text chronicles how Earl Franzen gradually succumbs to the "subtractive progress of Alzheimer's" (FRANZEN 2001: 90), the memories of him that are recorded become invested with a *double entendre* – which is quite typical of the memorial type of Alzheimer's life writing. There are events that happen in the life of the Alzheimer's patient, but these events also happen in the parallel universe of the living through the disease. And so, every gap in memory, every slip or search for a word becomes ominously significant, a sign for yet another step of the descent into dementia. Alzheimer's narratives are thus often suffused by a *hermeneutics of suspicion*, or, in less lofty theoretical language, they are curiously like the two levels of a detective story: events occurring on one level serve on a second level as so many clues as to the mysterious workings of the disease.

Throughout, Franzen avoids the ventriloquizing posture adopted in many other Alzheimer's memoirs written by next-of-kin or care personnel. He does not speak for, but about his father. At the same time, Franzen is curiously ambivalent about whose story this really is.[12] Even as it poses as a memoir, there are certain ambitions connected with this biographical project. As in so many AD biographies, telling the patient's fate is not enough; there is a larger moral message behind it. Hayden White, about whom I have more to say in a moment, has told us that we cannot narrativize without moralizing (WHITE 1981: 23), and certainly Franzen cannot do so, either. You might call it Franzen's version of the Cartesian dualism when he argues that telling the story of his father, setting it down "in permanent words, seems to me akin to the conviction that we are larger than our biologies" (FRANZEN 2001: 90). I would call this a compensatory project, if not even a *redemptive fantasy*: Not only does Earl Franzen live on in the words of his son, but his life and suffering are endowed with a larger cultural critical purpose. They are directed against what Franzen calls "the charms of materialism" (FRANZEN 2001: 90) in contemporary culture. One of the sinister effects of "our increasing willingness to see psychology as chemical, identity as genetic" (FRANZEN 2001: 90) is in his view to reduce people to the materiality of their bodies, to "a lump of meat" (FRANZEN 2001: 82). One

[11] It was also subsequently published in Franzen's essay collection *How to Be Alone*.

[12] He openly admits his ambivalence when he writes: "My memories of my father's initial decline are vividly about things other than him. Indeed, I'm somewhat appalled by how large I loom in my own memories, how peripheral my parents are" (82).

may or may not concur with the author's diagnosis; the point here is that in this as in many other Alzheimer's memoirs, the patients live on, but in the words of others – which also means they live on in the *worlds* of others, namely the interpretive universe which energizes and sustains the narrative and which has prompted it in the first place. This, however, has also been criticized by patients themselves. When Truthful Loving Kindness discusses the importance of mutual communication, she reminds the readers by using the words of a friend of hers: "Give us a VOICE – listen to us: we Tell You what Dementia friendly means" ("Importance of Communication").[13]

Can the Illness Speak? Does the Illness Speak?

Most Alzheimer's autobiographies are therefore created by patients during the early stages of the disease, and these are often narratives *haunted by temporality*[14], by the loss of time, both the time told and the time of telling. Hence they are most of the time not *auto*biographical in the strict sense of the word. Oftentimes, people close to the sufferer feel the urge to 'normalize' the original narrative or to add their own 'finishing touches'. So most of the time, we as critics find ourselves in a situation we have known from dealing with slave narratives or early women's writing like Mary Rowlandson's text. There as here, then as now, it is hard to know what amount of intervention or editorializing is involved.[15]

In view of this I decided to rely on material which, while older, is already published. My first examples here are two Alzheimer's autobiographies by Thomas DeBaggio (1942–2011), a journalist and freelance writer diagnosed with the disease at age fifty-seven. His first autobiography, *Losing My Mind: An Intimate Look at Life with Alzheimer's* (2002), created quite a stir when it first came out. Situating itself astutely within the discourses of difference, this text – DeBaggio declares – wants "to break through the sense of shame and silence [concerning] Alzheimer's […] and to tell the world what it is like" (DEBAGGIO 2002: 141). In other words, there is no outside observer mediating the narrative; here the Alzheimer's self ostensibly speaks of and for itself. But there is a catch, as I hope to show later on in this argument.

As *bona fide* Alzheimer's life writing, DeBaggio's narrative must necessarily remain incomplete, without closure. The authorial voice acknowledges this dilemma: "I knew I was unable to write about all stages of Alzheimer's disease because the disease causes cognitive decline and I will lapse into a world without language and memory" (DEBAGGIO 2002: 7). And, indeed, the story ends when the illness takes over. Or it does not. A year later, DeBaggio published another autobiography, *When It Gets Dark: An Enlightened Reflection on Life with Alzheimer's* (2003).

DeBaggio's autobiographical projects rely on but also run short of the key element of all forms of life writing, memory. Memory, or, rather its loss, are, as we all know, a

[13] My thanks to Juliane Strätz for alerting me to this material.

[14] On "the time quandary" of Alzheimer's patients cf. BASTING 2003: 95.

[15] In this regard, Alzheimer's online blogs might also offer the opportunity to publish unfiltered memoranda more easily. As they are mostly not edited by third parties and as they can be published immediately after writing, they also bypass the time lag of other media.

pivotal part of the epidemiology of Alzheimer's. As DeBaggio notes in his second book, without memory, "writing is like walking through a dark room … to find a path through the silent jungle where words are not easily picked and meaning is untrustworthy" (DEBAGGIO 2003: 17). Such a tropological move, faintly echoing, however, the colonialist 'heart of darkness' motif, would in itself invite critical commentary, for which there is no space here; instead, let me point out that DeBaggio's life writing here as elsewhere is not without rhetorical or more general aesthetic ambitions. You will find in his texts a well-organized shuffling of chronologies, a rich register of metaphors, leitmotifs, and a carefully orchestrated intertextuality through which Alzheimer's disease becomes something that Judith Butler would call a "signifying absence" (BUTLER [1990] 1999: 137). Thus, it can be said of DeBaggio's texts that they deny on the level of *discours* what the narrative presents as *histoire*, namely the story of Alzheimer's disease as a story to end all storytelling.

My second example is Cary Smith Henderson's *Partial View: An Alzheimer's Journal* (1998). Henderson, a former professor of history, had been diagnosed with Alzheimer's at the age of fifty-five. Six years later, at the beginning of this journal which spans roughly a year, he finds himself in what he calls a "living halfway" (HENDERSON 1998: 35) condition, already suffering from severe cognitive impairments, already living in a care facility, already incapable of writing, but still able to communicate his observations with the help of a tape recorder. You might call the result a blog *avant la lettre*, a collection of "journal entries arranged in loose groupings" (BASTING 2003: 94), which was later transcribed and edited by his daughter.

It is one of the defining characteristics of Henderson's *Partial View* that everything that gets (re)presented remains partial,[16] speech in progress, a rambling narrative in which connections between the entries, which would allow us to read them chronologically, are missing most of the time. Presentation and representation thus seem to coincide. Here is an example:

> The scariest thing is, I guess, the fact that I have no sense of time. I have not the slightest idea – my brain doesn't – what's ten hours away or what's two hours away.
> And if I think that somebody's been, that my wife had been gone a while, I get very antsy. And it may be just a short time that she's been away – it feels like forever.
> I feel like it's time long before anybody else feels like it's time.
> (HENDERSON 1998: 47; paragraph order original)

One of the last entries suggests that the effort to capture verbally, textually, life with Alzheimer's is almost exhausted: "I think I've said all that I can say" (HENDERSON 1998: 93). Cary Henderson, after living sixteen years with the disease, died from Alzheimer's-related symptoms in 2001, three years after publication of the book.

Partial View has been characterized as one of the few authentic first-person narratives *really* written from the inside of Alzheimer's (BASTING 2003: 152 et pass.). Here, the contours of a lived life, however tenuous at times, are still recognizable, but as you read on, they progressively disintegrate. The text also reflects, albeit rarely and only early on, its own precarious status: "I may not know all the time what I'm talking about, but I, damn it, still I can talk" (HENDERSON 1998: 3).

[16] The book cover with its facial image half covered seeks to also draw out this aspect.

If we follow the accepted practice in life writing scholarship and write auto/biography with a slash between the auto and biography, *Partial View* can be said to be located precisely *at* this slash. We still have a recognizable but gradually fading authorial self; we have (at least initially) an autobiography, although disassembled into tidbits of isolated moments.[17] In a second step we can then put the fragments together to get a *biography* with the help of two forewords by Smith's wife and daughter and of photos taken by Nancy Andrews, award-winning photographer from *The Washington Post*. These act as secondary support systems which help provide the *gestalt* of a recognizable life.

In comparing the two autobiographies last discussed here, one could say that in DeBaggio's texts Alzheimer's is *thematically* present while in the Henderson text it is narratively present, or perhaps better, present as an enactment, as "embodied autoreferentiality" (JAMESON 2015: 261). Maybe this is a slight exaggeration, but one can perhaps detect in the Henderson text the contours of what I want to call a *performative mode* of life writing, one where the illness is not talked or written *about* but performed.[18] In the words of Judith Butler, performance is a "discursive practice that enacts or produces that which it names" (BUTLER 1993: 13).[19] The name here would of course be 'Alzheimer's'; other names would be randomness, contingency, loss of meaning. What that might mean will be the topic of my concluding section.

Alzheimer's and the Ideology of Narrative

Life writing has an elective affinity with the real which few other genres of narrative can claim. Alzheimer's narratives are a showcase example of this close connection. Meanwhile, they are a motley genre; most of them, like Franzen's text, come from outside the illness and are witness texts, memoirs of love, care, and sorrow. Others, such as Henderson's narrative, are written from inside the illness, under its shadow, one might say. From a cultural critical point of view, all these texts have one thing in common: in their various ways they answer to the "challenge[s] of conveying broken human corporeality into the

[17] Truthful Loving Kindness, as a patient herself, reflects on fading of the self. She stresses that a fading of abilities does not necessarily imply a fading of the self: "Sometimes I hear the PWD is 'fading'. That word always makes me angry because it is important to differentiate between abilities and personhood. Yes the ABILITIES of PWD (Person With Dementia) are fading – including the abilities for various types of communication. Because the PWD communication ability is fading, their PERSONHOOD appears to be fading. This is a totally-unproven theory. In fact, sometimes in their last days persons who had seemed to be 'vegetable' will almost-supernaturally briefly recover, and verbally communicate. That could not happen if their personhood was gone!" *https://truthfulkindness.com/2016/01/26/import-communication-pwd/*.

[18] An example of projects counteracting the reliance of life writing on narrative are Anne Basting's TimeSlips and Penelope projects which seek to elicit in moments of improvisation, the activity, even creativity, from people with cognitive deficits; cf. *http://www.timeslips.org/about/history*; *http://www.thepenelopeproject.com/about/development-of-the-project*.

[19] The recourse to Butler is plausible also because, for her, "[o]ne is not simply a body, but, in some very key sense, one does one's body and, indeed, one does one's body differently from one's contemporaries and from one's embodied predecessors and successors as well"; performing (gender) is seen as "*a corporeal style*, an 'act,' as it were [...]" (BUTLER 1990: 272).

body of the text" (Athanasiou in BUTLER/ATHANASIOU 2013: 132), in the words of Athena Athanasiou. In this concluding section, I would like to dwell some more on these challenges.

It is Theodor W. Adorno to whom we owe the insight that objects of representation are not indifferent to the means by which they are represented. Especially when human life in its precarious condition was concerned, Adorno was wary that this precariousness should not be falsified by clichéd expressions, or the jargon of sympathy. For him, only the exposure of "the inadequacy of [...] language", of our means of representation, was the condition of possibility "to say what [somebody] suffered" (ADORNO 1991: 83).[20] In other words, and very broadly speaking, only a representation that represents its own shortcomings or its utter failure is an acceptable representation of human suffering. Very much all of Adorno's critique of Modernism with Samuel Beckett as central exemplar makes that same point.

Given today's anti-essentialist fashion, one may take umbrage with the judgmental position underwriting Adorno's argument, but the more important point for the present context is his truly dialectical idea that the impossibility of representing suffering through the available cultural archives opens up new ways of communicating "what is most real, in the form of a wild, unleashed lament" (ADORNO 1991: 83). Against this background we may want to take another, critical look at *narrative* as the principal conduit through which human life finds 'its' representation. And here we can engage one of the principal voices of the narrative turn in the humanities, that of Hayden White, who was in fact quite upfront about the shortcomings, the ideological blinders of the narrative form. In the world of narratives, he states, reality wears the mask of meaning. Narratives "arise [ ] out of a desire to have real events display the coherence, integrity, fullness, and closure of an image of life that is and can only be imaginary. [...] Does the world really present itself to perception in the form of well-made stories, with central subjects, proper beginnings, middles, and ends, and a coherence that permits us to see 'the end' in every beginning?" (WHITE 1981: 23). The world of Alzheimer's surely does not. Here, as in other cases, the experience of a severe illness will have the tendency to disrupt the narrative order. In view of this, Alzheimer's researchers and activists have come to see the prevalence of conventional narrative in Alzheimer's representation as a strategic choice at best to make the illness accessible to the general public while the fact remains that fully developed "narrative form contradicts the experience of the disease" (BASTING 2003: 94).

Registering, as I am attempting here, the resistance of the Alzheimer's experience to narrativization is not a specialist's sport; rather, it marks an important ideological-critical point of critique concerning life writing and especially its autobiographical variants. That which refuses to be included in the well-made form of a story, the "storm of shattered

[20] Truthful Loving Kindness also addresses the lack of shared meaning with regards to the term "suffering": "I don't think I have ever called someone other than myself a 'sufferer'. Until the recent uproar about the language guidelines proposed by several small groups, I considered the 'sufferer' issue a somewhat minor difference of opinion. But now I am beginning to conclude that 'suffer' is a useless term in communication BECAUSE the term often carries a large emotional aura but does not communicate at all the same meanings amongst groups of people. Lack of shared meaning for vocabulary facilitates mis-understandings instead of unity". *https://truthfulkindness.com/2016/02/02/sufferer-part-3-the-linguisticcommunication-issues/.*

references" (FUCHS 2005: 109) may just be that which matters in a life with Alzheimer's. And there is another point to be made here. If some selves do not fit into the established narrative order, then living a narratable life may not be the only form of having a self. There may be others. And if today we speak of post-humanist life forms, Alzheimer's may be an occasion to reflect also on post-narrative life forms. I admit right away that one would *not* normally go to dementia life writing *first* for such reflections; indeed, they weave through the writings of modernists and postmodernists, for example of Gertrude Stein or Samuel Beckett. Lennard J. Davis has coined the term "dismodernism" to point to this unlikely convergence in the idea of a new sense of self "based on the partial, incomplete subject" (DAVIS 2002: 30). Acknowledgment of such parallels which are even more plausible in the field of poetry may make us entertain the idea that at the point where the Cartesian self is losing its claim, the contours may be lurking of another self, another creativity.[21] To explore this speculation further, however, would be stuff for yet another paper.

List of Works Cited

ADORNO, THEODOR W. (1991): Heine the Wound. In ROLF TIEDEMANN (Ed.): *Notes to Literature, Volume One*. Trans. by Shierry Weber Nicholsen. New York: Columbia University Press, 80–85.

BASTING, ANNE (2003): Looking Back from Loss: Views of the Self in Alzheimer's Disease. *Journal of Aging Studies* 17.1: 87–99.

BUTLER, JUDITH, and ATHENA ATHANASIOU (2013): *Dispossession: The Performative in the Political.* Malden: Polity Press.

BUTLER, JUDITH (1990): Performative Acts and Gender Constitution: An Essay in Phenomenology and Feminist Theory. In SUE-ELLEN CASE (Ed.): *Performing Feminisms: Feminist Critical Theory and Theatre*. Baltimore: Johns Hopkins University Press, 270–282.

BUTLER, JUDITH [1990] (1999): *Gender Trouble: Feminism and the Subversion of Identity.* New York: Routledge.

BUTLER, JUDITH (1993): *Bodies That Matter: On the Discursive Limits of 'Sex.'* New York: Routledge.

CLARKE, ADELE E. et al. (2010): Introduction. In ADELE E. CLARKE, LAURA MAMO, JENNIFER RUTH FOSKET, JENNIFER R. FISHMAN, and JANET K. SHIM (Eds.): *Biomedicalization: Technoscience, Health, and Illness in the U.S.* Durham: Duke University Press, 1–47.

DAVIS, LENNARD J. (2002): *Bending Over Backwards: Disability, Dismodernism, and Other Difficult Positions*. New York: New York University Press.

DEBAGGIO, THOMAS (2003): *When It Gets Dark: An Enlightened Reflection on Life with Alzheimer's*. New York: The Free Press.

DEBAGGIO, THOMAS (2002): *Losing My Mind: An Intimate Look at Life with Alzheimer's*. New York: The Free Press.

DE MEDEIROS, KATE (2009): Suffering and Generativity: Repairing Threats to Self in Old Age. *Journal of Aging Studies* 23.2: 97–102.

[21] It has long been recognized that autism, conventionally understood, often involves special creative abilities, for example in dealing with numbers and figures. See for example Jamie Craig and Simon Baron-Cohen (1999): Creativity and Imagination in Autism and Asperger Syndrome. *Journal of Autism and Developmental Disorders* 29.4: 319–326. *SpringerLink.* Web.

DONALDSON-MCHUGH, SHANNON (2010): Performing Autobiographical Limits: Jeannette Winterson's *Oranges Are Not the Only Fruit*. In ALFRED HORNUNG (Ed.): *Auto/Biography and Mediation*. Heidelberg: Universitätsverlag Winter, 351–361.

FUCHS, ELINOR (2005): *Making an Exit: A Mother-Daughter Drama with Alzheimer's, Machine Tools, and Laughter*. New York: Metropolitan Books.

FRANZEN, JONATHAN (2001): My Father's Brain: What Alzheimer's Takes Away. *The New Yorker*, 10 September: 80–91.

HENDERSON, CARY S., JACKIE HENDERSON MAIN, RUTH D. HENDERSON, and NANCY ANDREWS (1998): *Partial View: An Alzheimer's Journal*. Dallas: Southern Methodist University Press.

HORNUNG, ALFRED (2010): Auto/Biography and Mediation: Introduction. In ALFRED HORNUNG (Ed.): *Auto/Biography and Mediation*. Heidelberg: Universitätsverlag Winter, XI–XVIII.

JAMESON, FREDRIC (2015): *The Ancients and the Postmoderns: On the Historicity of Forms*. New York: Verso.

LEE, JEANNE L. (2003): *Just Love Me: My Life Turned Upside down by Alzheimer's*. West Lafayette: Purdue University Press.

METEYARD, LOTTE, and KARALYN PATTERSON (2009): The Relation between Content and Structure in Language Production: An Analysis of Speech Errors in Semantic Dementia. *Brain and Language* 110.3: 121–134.

RICOEUR, PAUL (1984): *Time and Narrative*. Vol. I. Trans. by Kathleen McLaughlin and David Pellauer. Chicago: University of Chicago Press.

SHRENK, DAVID (2003): *The Forgetting: Alzheimer's Portrait of an Epidemic*. New York: Anchor.

TRUTHFUL LOVING KINDNESS: First Time of Where Am I. *https://truthfulkindness.com*, 8 May 2016 [15 August 2016].

TRUTHFUL LOVING KINDNESS: Importance of Communication with PWD. *https://truthfulkindness.com*, 26 January 2016. [15 August 2016].

WHITE, HAYDEN (1981): The Value of Narrativity in the Representation of Reality. In W. J. T. MITCHELL (Ed.): *On Narrative*. Chicago: University of Chicago Press, 1–23.

An Eye for an I

Autobiographical Representations, the Medical Gaze, and the Transnational in Nineteenth-Century America

Carmen Birkle

Nineteenth-century America saw a number of significant transformations that were to change and establish America as a new nation. After political independence came the attempt to declare cultural independence as well. However, leaving behind "the courtly muses of Europe" (EMERSON [1837] 1957: 79), as Ralph Waldo Emerson (1803–1882) famously suggested in his speech "The American Scholar", proved to be impossible and unnecessary. After all, exchange, contact, and collaboration did not mean dependence but a phenomenon that seems to have been widely acknowledged and more often practiced then than now, namely internationalization and, in its wake, transnationalization. Immigration and the Grand Tour, albeit quite different in essence, made visible the tremendous relevance of mobility, triggered by very different reasons but always marked by movement between nations and continents. One aspect that I would like to single out is the intimate relationship between the medical profession in Europe and the United States. Students of medicine and practicing doctors in the United States were aware of the American lag in medical innovation and flocked in great numbers to major centers of medical excellence such as Vienna, Zurich, Paris, London, Edinburgh, and Berlin. They criss-crossed the Atlantic in search of knowledge and became mediators between nations. The group that was particularly eager to participate in these journeys consisted of both women doctors and female students of medicine who had to overcome substantial obstacles to get any medical education on either side of the Atlantic. Some were certified doctors, such as Elizabeth Blackwell (1821–1910) and Mary Putnam Jacobi (1842–1910); some were nurses, such as Nancy Prince (1799–ca. 1856) and Mary Seacole (1805–1881); and some were practicing doctors without degrees, such as Harriot K. Hunt (1805–1875). In their autobiographical narratives, the women describe their ordeals; they look out for means of education, and they explore their own inner motivations, desires, and will to succeed and, in this process, reveal how the "I" of identity gradually claims an "eye of power" (see FOUCAULT [1977] 1980).

In the following, I will attempt to show how the physical or bodily "eye" is embedded in cultural practices, on the one hand, and, on the other hand, simultaneously contributes to a dis/empowerment of the self who is in the process of developing as subject and agent into the "I" of identity. To do so, I will focus on Elizabeth Blackwell's autobiography *Pioneer Work in Opening the Medical Profession to Women* of 1895 in order to show how vision in a multiplicity of actual material manifestations contributes to the formation of the autobiographical self represented in narrative. Blackwell's *Pioneer Work* is at once an embodied act of writing, a cultural act that writes women into the history of medicine, and a narrative act of self-formation through self- and other-identification. Moreover, this formation is embedded in and shaped by Blackwell's environment. As Emerson claims in "The American Scholar", the "world, – this shadow of the soul, or *other me*, – lies wide around. Its attractions are the keys which unlock my thoughts and make me acquainted with myself" (EMERSON [1837] 1957: 70). My Emerson analogy, however, fails in one major aspect, which is that Blackwell could never have been Emerson's "*Man Thinking*" (EMERSON [1837] 1957: 65), "One Man" who "is all" (EMERSON [1837] 1957: 64) and who feels "all confidence in himself [...]" (EMERSON [1837] 1957: 73). Blackwell turns into 'woman thinking' who has to muster up all her self-confidence to challenge the medical mainstream. What she shares with Emerson, however, is the focus on sight, on the power of the eye, and on the connection of the eye to nature, which is, in Blackwell's case, the nature of the physical-biological human body. Both look, as Emerson proclaims for himself in his essay "Nature", "at the world with new eyes" (EMERSON [1836] 1957: 55). Yet Blackwell is not Emerson's "transparent eyeball" (EMERSON [1836] 1957: 24), though she claims in her autobiography what Emerson states: "I am nothing" (EMERSON [1836] 1957: 24). While he is self-confident enough to further suggest "I see all" (EMERSON [1836] 1957: 24), Blackwell aspires to seeing all in the symptoms of the bodies of her patients by gaining perfection in her profession. If Emerson describes how "the currents of the Universal Being circulate through me; I am part or parcel of God" (EMERSON [1836] 1957: 24), Blackwell comes to her final decision to pursue medical studies when she cries out to God for help and experiences the Divine presence.[1] This spiritual manifestation gives her the self-confidence and self-knowledge to pursue her medical goals. She embraces Emerson's advice in his essay "Self-Reliance" (1840): "Trust thyself: every heart vibrates to that iron string. Accept the place the divine providence has found for you, the society of your contemporaries, the connection of events" (EMERSON [1836] 1957: 148). Ultimately, the biology of the "eye", the psychology of the "I", and the spirituality of Emerson's "other me" merge in narrative, which, in turn, becomes "eye", "I", and "other me".[2]

"I" Is for Identity

In the context of the frequently discussed medical humanities, Rita Charon has introduced the concept of "narrative medicine" for the purpose of better understanding patients and

[1] "A glorious presence, as of brilliant light, flooded my soul. There was nothing visible to the physical sense; but a spiritual influence so joyful, gentle, but powerful, surrounded me that the despair which had overwhelmed me vanished" (BLACKWELL [1895] 2005: 80–81).

[2] Elizabeth Blackwell was highly educated and, when living in Cincinnati, Ohio, beginning in 1838, was aware of the New England Transcendentalist movement, which gradually spread to the West. Some of the New England Transcendentalists, such as James Perkins, C. P. Cranch, William Greene, and Judge Walker (BLACKWELL [1895] 2005: 61), had moved to Cincinnati and gathered around Reverend William Henry Channing (1810–1884) – a nephew of Dr. Ellery Channing of Boston. Channing's enthusiastic introduction of Emerson's essays so strongly impressed Blackwell that she and her family "joined the Church of which Mr. Channing was minister", which was the Unitarian Church of Cincinnati (BLACKWELL [1895] 2005: 62). Emerson himself had been an ordained Unitarian minister but eventually resigned and continued as an independent thinker of the Transcendentalist group. Blackwell was shaped by her Unitarian acquaintances as well as her early reading of Emerson's essays so that the analogies I have drawn between her and some of Emerson's thoughts might not be too far-fetched.

their illnesses, leading "to more humane, more ethical, and perhaps more effective care" (CHARON 2006*a*; 2008: vii). She describes "narrative medicine" as "[a] form of clinical practice […], defined as medicine practiced with the narrative competence to recognize, absorb, interpret, and be moved by the stories of illness" (CHARON 2006*a*; 2008: vii). The patients' storytelling becomes an important focus for the doctors, which they have to study and understand in order to more fully grasp the individual patient's identity as a significant aspect in diagnosis and treatment. Let me extend this idea to the profession of the literary and cultural scholar who reads and analyzes texts with the aim of understanding both texts and contexts. To stretch the analogy even further, readers, critics, and scholars become *doctors* in their approach toward the patient-text, even more so if the narrative is an autobiographical one that, if scrutinized properly, reveals significant insight into the identity construction of author and narrator. As Paul John Eakin argues, "narrative is not merely something we tell, listen to, read, or invent; it is an essential part of our sense of who we are" (EAKIN 2008: ix). And in writing such a text, "we draw on – but are not wholly determined by – the physical and social constraints of our lives in human culture" (EAKIN 2008: x–xi). For Eakin, "the somatic and the cultural come together […] in the lived experience of ordinary individuals telling stories about themselves" (EAKIN 2008: xi). Eakin argues that we are "operating under the discipline of a rule-grounded identity regime" that also includes the language we use (EAKIN 2008: 17). An autobiography tells us as much about the autobiographer as about the culture from which it has emerged. Therefore, I consider my reading of a female doctor's autobiography part of the medical humanities and Blackwell's narrative to be "in the service of life sciences" (HORNUNG 2015: 41). My analysis is also meant to enable "the chance to respond to criticism of scientific theories within a narrative framework" (HORNUNG 2015: 42) and to constitute "not just a derivative but an independent, specifically complex and multilayered form of cultural knowledge in its own right" (ZAPF 2015: 3).[3] The medical humanities are ultimately based on what Birgit Däwes considers the fundamental mechanism of interdisciplinarity, which, for her, is "the complex, dynamic, multidirectional exchange of knowledge and methodologies in continuously changing educational environments. […] [I]nterdisciplinarity happens at the crossroads and overlaps between disciplines, in the encounters and dialogues taking place between different cultures of knowledge" (DÄWES 2013: 542).

Self and identity are key terms in Eakin's theory of autobiography. For Eakin, the self consists of the ecological, interpersonal, extended, private, and conceptual self (EAKIN 2008: xii-xiii), with identity being most closely associated with the latter as "the version of ourselves that we display not only to others but also to ourselves whenever we have occasion to reflect on or otherwise engage in self-characterization" (EAKIN 2008: xiv).[4]

[3] While these statements might support David Greaves's claim that "the medical arts are essentially an ornament to medicine" because they aim at "humanising practitioners" (GREAVES 2001: 22), I would rather argue that, in our case, literature is included in what he calls the "medical humanities", which aim "at humanising medicine" (GREAVES 2001: 22). The humanistic element is what joins these two readings under the umbrella term of the medical humanities.

[4] Autobiography works with memory and anticipation, and the autobiographer tries to reconnect the past to the present and both to the future. This extended idea of the self is joined to space, relationships, and private conceptions and ultimately gives way to the conceptual self that situates

Blackwell's autobiography *Pioneer Work* displays this conceptual self, also called "ideological 'I'" by Sidonie Smith and Julia Watson (2010: 76–78), which is pieced together from diary entries, original comments, short medical essays, occasional newspaper clippings, and letters written to her that bring together her private thoughts, her personal relationships, her social alienation, and the need for some communication in written form. This "I" clearly shows that it is "referential"; "it [...] positions itself with reference to the world" (EAKIN 2008: 21). Blackwell enters what Philippe Lejeune has called the "autobiographical pact", telling the truth, as her readers assume. It is this belief in truth-telling that allows us to consider her as an individual, a "'real' or historical 'I'" (SMITH/WATSON 2010: 72), with her own life narrative but also as a representative of women wanting to practice medicine. Blackwell's conceptual self is, therefore, a composite entity of "I", "eye", and "other me", that is, the spiritual/psychological, biological, and the world around her.

Conceptual identity is strongly related to organic and, thus, neurological influences. Drawing on the neurologist Antonio Damasio, Eakin makes "a case for 'the organic basis of everything we are' by arguing not only that self and story emerge from our lives in and as bodies, but that our extended selves, our narrative identities, may contribute to the well-being of our bodily existence" (EAKIN 2008: 59). For Damasio and Eakin, the teller of the narrative and the narrative as such become one so that "'a freestanding observer/teller figure cannot be extrapolated from it [the narrative]'" (DAMASIO, qtd. in EAKIN 2008: 76). As a consequence, identity has to be one with the narrative, that is, the self is not just the character or narrator in the narrative but constitutes the narrative as a whole. While the story is being told, narrator, narratee, and narrative are one. Additionally, this entity is embedded in a cultural context in which it acts, becoming what Eakin calls "Doing Consciousness" (EAKIN 2008: 79). Thus, narrative identity formation unfolds as a cultural act that derives from "the social and somatic 'givens' [...], the factors that temper the illusion of total autonomy inevitably accompanying our acts of self-presentation" (EAKIN 2008: 85).

"Eye" Is for Power

Looking at nineteenth-century medical women's autobiographies implies a number of social, cultural, and professional factors that should be taken into consideration. While for some critics it still seems to come as a surprise that women doctors actively practised medicine in the nineteenth century and even wrote about their experiences, others have by now acknowledged that women made a significant contribution to the nineteenth-century medical profession and that today's access to this knowledge is largely made possible through the recovery and, in some cases, publication of these women's personal

itself in time and space and represents its own version of its own life. Because this continuity through memory is so essential to the sense of who we are, "most people fear memory loss and the death of the extended self that follows from it – witness the widespread anxiety about Alzheimer's disease and aging in the United States today" (EAKIN 2008: 15). One possible result of this fear are life narratives often written at a later point in life; in Elizabeth Blackwell's case in 1895, when she was beyond 70 and living again in England.

testimonies. The fixed gender roles of the time erected significant obstacles for women pursuing a medical career. Some of those who were successful wrote about their visions for the profession and how they developed their own medical gaze as an essential element of their practical work. At the same time, women's use of the medical gaze seems to imply a curious interaction of perceived gendered inferiority and actual medical power.

"The Eye of Power", according to Foucault, facilitates the surveillance of bodies in "a prison, a school or a hospital" (FOUCAULT [1977] 1980: 148) and establishes the opposition between the individual who looks at and observes the other, who, in turn, becomes the one who is governed. Foucault generally emphasizes the correlation between the eye and power.[5] The "act of seeing", for a doctor, is essential for diagnosis, treatment, and potential healing and implies that "all that is *visible* is *expressible*" (FOUCAULT [1963] 1994: 115; emphasis in original), although this may overly simplify the transformation of the visible into the medium of expression. At the same time, of course, in this doctor–patient exchange, vision is literally embodied, with the body as part of a social and somatic contextualization (see HARAWAY 1998). Foucault furthermore argues that the "observing gaze refrains from intervening; it is silent and gestureless" and "leaves things as they are" (FOUCAULT [1963] 1994: 107). The medical gaze of the doctor is, therefore, directed at the patient's body, but, simultaneously, the patient reverses the gaze (CHARON 2005; 2006*b*; 2009). My closer look at Elizabeth Blackwell [Fig. 1], the first U.S.-American woman doctor with a medical degree, is confronted with her autobiography, which returns my gaze as it did her contemporaries'and invites us as readers to follow her identity formation. My observing gaze leaves the text as it is but also appropriates it to satisfy my own and other contemporary readers' desires for knowledge about an extraordinary nineteenth-century U.S.-American woman.

FIG 1. Elizabeth Blackwell (1821–1910).

[5] However, the observed is not without vision. The patient's return gaze or "patient gaze" (FOUCAULT [1963] 1994: xv) can empower or destabilize the doctor's own position.

As the daughter of English immigrants from Bristol, Blackwell spent most of her time as a teacher in the Southern states.[6] All this time, she continued to read medical books and studied medicine and anatomy on her own. Not particularly satisfied with that choice, she one day visited a female friend of the family suffering from cancer, who told her: "'If I could have been treated by a lady doctor, my worst sufferings would have been spared me'" (BLACKWELL [1895] 2005: 74). This statement is vividly illustrated in the image of a male doctor's examination of a woman and reveals its limitations [Fig. 2]. If everything that is visible can be expressed, to pick up Foucault's idea again, it is obvious that the female body is invisible and, therefore, no adequate language exists to describe the invisible. As Susan Wells suggests, "[i]f the female patient were treated by a female physician, she would have had a wider scope for telling her story; it is certain that she faced a less constricted speech situation" (WELLS 2001: 54).

FIG 2. Internal Examination of a Woman, circa 1800.

[6] She was first a governess and teacher in the family of Reverend John Dickson in Asheville, North Carolina, then a music teacher in Charleston, South Carolina, residing with Dr. Samuel H. Dickson, "the most distinguished doctor" (BOYD 2005: 55), as Blackwell's biographer Julia Boyd tells us, and "professor in the Medical College of that town" (BLACKWELL [1895] 2005: 90). Dickson directed Blackwell's medical studies in Charleston. While in North Carolina, Blackwell also taught black slave children but eventually had to stop because this was illegal.

This image of a gynecological examination of a woman by a male doctor and the quotation from Blackwell's autobiography show the obvious grounding of the medical gaze and the doctor-patient relationship in socio-cultural norms and moral codes. The gaze in both cases as well as in other illustrations of the eighteenth and nineteenth centuries is evaded, does not take place, cannot be described as 'looking at' but as 'looking away', and is replaced by the tactile sense of the doctor, the results of which he then translates into words. An illustration of a woman giving birth assisted by a male midwife in the early eighteenth century [Fig. 3] illustrates a slightly different relationship, with the future mother looking up to heaven while the doctor, or, rather, male midwife, has access to the baby being born. All bystanders are focused on the young woman's face. The similarities between the two images are obvious: in both, there is no eye contact between 'patient' and doctor, no visible relationship that might establish a connection and healthy communication between female patient and male doctor. In this image, there is no return gaze on the part of the patient that might question or disrupt the doctor's male and medical gaze.

FIG 3. Obstetrics, Late Seventeenth Century.

The insistence on decency during such an exam is particularly interesting since it seems to ignore the invention of the speculum many centuries before, introduced probably as early as ancient Rome and Greece (EVELETH 2014) and modernized by James Marion Sims (1813–1883), who is "often heralded as the father of American gynecology" (EVELETH 2014). However, in the 1840s, the speculum was not uncritically accepted since even doctors "thought that opening up a woman's body might corrupt those women and turn them into prostitutes or sex-crazed maniacs" (EVELETH 2014). Therefore, a "doctor was specifically instructed to reassure a female patient that he was not looking at her private parts by doing one of two things: gazing off into the distance or maintaining eye contact with her the entire time" (EVELETH 2014). Even this eye contact erases the presence of the woman as a body.

This is precisely the situation that Elizabeth Blackwell wanted to change. Before she began her long and mostly futile line of applications to get into medical school, she needed to put her 'unwomanly' decision, as the nineteenth-century society would see it, into more acceptable words. Her autobiography reveals a second reason for her decision to become a physician, namely a religious one:

> In an agony of mental despair I cried out, "Oh God, help me, support me! Lord Jesus, guide, enlighten me!" My very being went out in this yearning cry for Divine help. Suddenly, overwhelmingly, an answer came. […] All doubt as to the future, all hesitation as to the rightfulness of my purpose, left me, and never in afterlife returned. I knew that, however insignificant my individual effort might be, it was in a right direction, and in accordance with the great providential ordering of our race's progress. (BLACKWELL [1895] 2005: 80–81; emphasis in original)

Religion offered one of the main arguments against women in medicine. The use of the idea of 'unnaturalness' to describe such a desire was justified by the belief that it would go against God's will and violate God-given talents since a woman doctor was believed to violate the God-given duties of giving birth to and raising children and taking care of household and husband. Blackwell used her religious vision to argue that God gave her the talent to become a doctor; thus, she simultaneously used and undermined the religious argument in her favor. Not only did Blackwell intend to become a physician, but she also strove to become a fully licensed doctor with an official degree in order to counteract the work of quacks, who abused "the almost universal willingness of society to be humbugged", as one of Blackwell's contemporaries wrote in 1868 (WAGNER 1868: 774). After about a dozen or so rejection letters, she was finally admitted to Geneva Medical College in Western New York but only because her application had been disclosed to the student body, who believed it to be a hoax by fellow students at a neighboring college. During her studies between 1847 and 1849, vision and gaze were going to play a major role both in her interaction with her fellow students and professors and in the areas of medicine she was going to study.

Blackwell knew that she would be stared at, looked at, and observed constantly and that she had to be good at what she was doing in order to prove that women could be as hard-working and as successful in the medical profession as men. She frequently felt, as Mary Wager points out, "that all eyes were fixed upon her" (WAGNER 1868: 776), that not only her fellow students but also her professors considered her to be in the wrong place, attempting something unnatural and unfeminine. Blackwell simply had to be in the lecture hall, but had many obstacles to overcome. Being stared at was her fate inside and outside of the college. Inside, it was seen as particularly daring of her to attend lectures "of a somewhat delicate nature", which included dissection classes (WAGNER 1868: 776). As we learn from Rosemarie Garland-Thomson, "[w]e stare because we are curious [...]. Staring is an ocular response to what we don't expect to see. Novelty arouses our eyes. [...] We stare when ordinary seeing fails, when we want to know more. So staring is an interrogative gesture that asks what's going on and demands the story" (GARLAND-THOMSON 2009: 3). In this way, staring becomes a starer's quest to know and a staree's opportunity to be known. And Blackwell was such a novelty.[7] Blackwell was objectified through the starers, and their stares were far from being benign or merely curious. They did express society's rejection of a female medical student as unacceptable, breaking social norms, and disrupting social order. "Staring is a form of nonverbal behavior that can be used to enforce social hierarchies and regulate access to resources" (GARLAND-THOMSON 2009: 40). Blackwell's autobiography, therefore, reveals how she needs about fifty years to finally come to terms with those earlier "staring encounters" (GARLAND-THOMSON 2009: 11) and to respond to the starer's desire "to make the unknown known, to render legible something that seems at first glance incomprehensible" (GARLAND-THOMSON 2009: 15).

Medical education consisted of a series of lecture classes held in amphitheaters – like halls, that is, places for viewing in which the audience was seated around and above the performers. While Jeremy Bentham's Panopticon was, in Foucault's analysis, a means to introduce "a system of centralised observation" (FOUCAULT [1977] 1980: 146), the reverse arrangement of the lecture hall reflects the power of the lecturer through centralized knowledge. Susan Wells aptly points out:

> The clinical amphitheater is constructed as a site for the generational transmission of knowledge; the amphitheater forms the physician, who then finally supports the amphitheater. Such a transmission assumes an identity between the surgeons and physicians of the house and those who belong to the same profession. Since the amphitheater replicates the exact knowledge and experience taught in the past, the physician reproduced through its spectacles must be identical to the physician who presents patients: the male doctor demonstrates his craft to the male medical student. (WELLS 2001: 195)

If the dissected body was male, it was especially 'outrageous' for Blackwell to be an observer since she not only saw a naked male body but was also seen by her fellow male students looking at this 'gruesome' sight. She was felt to potentially corrupt the male students who had to endure this sight. The rejection letters that another woman received in Philadelphia from the Philadelphia College of Medicine, the Pennsylvania Medical

[7] For Garland-Thomson, the stare and the gaze are not synonymous. For her, the gaze is "an oppressive act of disciplinary looking that subordinates its victim" (GARLAND-THOMSON 2009: 9). Staring, for her, helps the identity of both the starer and the staree to emerge "through interactive processes" (GARLAND-THOMSON 2009: 10). There are "four interrelated aspects of staring: physical response, cultural phenomenon, social relationship, and knowledge gathering endeavor" (GARLAND-THOMSON 2009: 11). We stare at what is unusual. But what is "unusual is fleeting. [...] Novelty is fragile and staring volatile because the longer we look, the more accustomed a once surprising sight becomes" (GARLAND-THOMSON 2009: 18).

College, and the Jefferson Medical College explain some of the reasons for rejection: "'I think it would be impossible in this country for a lady to mingle with five hundred young men, gentlemen though they be, in the same lecture-room, without experiencing many annoyances'" (qtd. in WAGNER 1868: 781). In the same letter, a nameless female graduate of Geneva College is mentioned who visited Jefferson Medical College to attend a lecture, but it can only be Elizabeth Blackwell as the lone female graduate. Her desire to attend a lecture was granted, but she had to move from total (and from the College's point of view, disruptive) visibility to complete invisibility: "[T]he veteran professor to whom she listened deemed it prudent that she should not appear before the class, but placed her in a small room adjoining, where she could hear the lecture without being observed" (qtd. in WAGNER 1868: 781). Although, as nurses, women had seen many bodies, clothed and unclothed, "they were not", as Susan Wells argues, "themselves to see the body as the object of scientific knowledge. Most of all, they could not be seen as seeing; they could not be authorized witnesses of the scientific rationalization of the body" (WELLS 2001: 199). Women were accused of "'unsex[ing]'" themselves and "'sacrific[ing]'" their modesty (qtd. in WELLS 2001: 200). Women's "strong desires to see, particularly to see the interior of the body", disrupted the "complex economics of medical vision [...]" as male (WELLS 2001: 201).

Outside the college grounds, as Blackwell's contemporary Mary Wager narrates, "the shopkeepers would call to each other to look at [Blackwell], and following the example thus shown, not only the *gamins* and nurse-girls, but fine gentlemen and ladies, would gather in groups to stare at her as she passed, as if she were some monstrous creature fallen among them from some planet" (WAGNER 1868: 776–777). As Blackwell points out in her autobiography: "[A]s I walked backwards and forwards to college the ladies stopped to stare at me, as at a curious animal" (BLACKWELL [1895] 2005: 111). In spite of this alienation, discrimination, and exclusion and in spite of being fixed in this role through all the eyes that were upon her and, at least at first, turned her into an object of ridicule, Blackwell graduated at the top of her class after two semesters lasting from October to January each time and one summer internship in New York City, was highly praised by the president of the college, and "pronounced [...] the *leader* of her class" by a Dr. Lee (cf. her younger brother's letter rpt. in BLACKWELL [1895] 2005: 130; emphasis in original).

A Transnational Vision

Blackwell's subsequent sojourn in Europe, undertaken to complete her education (cf. BIRKLE 2015), can be understood in the light of Emerson's claim that the wider world, the other me, has to be explored in order to understand oneself. Blackwell "felt [...] keenly the need of much wider opportunities for study than were open to women in America" (BLACKWELL [1895] 2005: 133), and teachers and medical friends told her that she "should be able to find unlimited opportunities for study in any branch of the medical art" (BLACKWELL [1895] 2005: 148).[8] In contrast to Emerson, Blackwell was very keen on

[8] Blackwell repeatedly talks about medicine as an art, either as "medical art" (148), "the art of medicine" (201), "'The Art of Healing'" (250), or as "healing art" (275).

visiting the "courtly muses of Europe" (EMERSON [1837] 1957: 79). However, in spite of Blackwell's optimism about studies in Europe, she faced many of the same prejudices she had to and did overcome in the United States. No university offered graduate studies for female medical students at the time. It was not until 1868 that Mary Putnam Jacobi succeeded in being admitted to medical studies in Paris and in getting a medical degree in 1871. Simultaneously, Susan Dimock (1847–1875) studied at the University of Zurich (1868–1871) and went on to Vienna and Paris, where special courses for foreign medical students, women included, were offered at some cost. Women of the respective countries were not yet allowed to study medicine in their own countries (BIRKLE 2015).

The medical profession's transnational vision was hard for women to embrace. While Oliver Wendell Holmes, Sr. (1809–1894), had no problems with spending two and a half years (April 1833–October 1835) studying in Paris with the best physicians the city had to offer, women like Blackwell, Jacobi, and Dimock had to fight assumptions on both sides of the Atlantic about natural inborn drives (KIRCHHOFF 1897) that would deter them from the completion of their studies or about their contribution to American "race suicide", as Theodore Roosevelt (1858–1919) proclaimed (ROOSEVELT [1905] 1998: 209). The American doctors S. Weir Mitchell (1829–1914), (in)famous for his "rest cure", and Edward Hammond Clarke (1820–1877) were joined by German colleagues such as Paul J. Möbius (1853–1907) and others in their attempt at explaining women's inability to study and practice medicine because of the latter's perceived biological inadequacies for such tasks. And yet, women did get a transatlantic education, so that Marie Zakrzewska (1829–1902) could conclude in the early 1870s: "'I am sorry to be forced to say that it is not the Republic of America which has given the proof that 'science has no sex', in so far as that it has furnished the largest number of women students. But it is the Republic of Switzerland which has verified this maxim. Our best women physicians have been educated there as well as in … France'" (qtd. in BONNER 1988: 470).

Blackwell could register at La Maternité in Paris but not as a doctor and was trained together with nurses and midwives. She had a "very grave accident" when she inspected a child's eyes and infected her own eyes (BLACKWELL [1895] 2005: 186). In spite of intensive treatment, Blackwell lost sight in her left eye: "Ah! How dreadful it was to find the daylight gradually fading as my kind doctor bent over me, and removed with an exquisite delicacy of touch the films that had formed over the pupil! I could see him for a moment clearly, but the sight soon vanished, and the eye was left in darkness" (BLACKWELL [1895] 2005: 187–188). Her dream of becoming "*the first lady surgeon in the world*" (BLACKWELL [1895] 2005: 189; emphasis in original) soon vanished after the failure of "hydropathic operations" (BLACKWELL [1895] 2005: 192) in Gräfenberg, Germany, and further treatment in Paris. She would have been the first female surgeon competing with doctors such as Samuel D. Gross (1805–1884) and David Hayes Agnew (1818–1892), who would later be eternalized in Thomas Eakins's famous paintings *The Gross Clinic* (1875) and *The Agnew Clinic* (1889). This side of power was unfortunately denied her.

She herself comments in 1895 on her letters and diary entries of the 1850s and, thus, makes visible the difference in time frame and experience between the narrated self of the 1850s and the narrating self of the 1890s: "The growing perplexity of the conscientious student awakening to the uncertainty of the art of medicine is now apparent in letters written at this time" (BLACKWELL [1895] 2005: 201). She posits her seventy-four-year old self above the younger self in terms of knowledge. What she seems to express here is what Eakin calls the "neurobiological self – this feeling of knowing generated in the body's brain" (EAKIN 2008: 72). The use of the processual term "awakening" suggests Blackwell's awareness of her own mental and physio-biological development. Inspired by Florence Nightingale (1820–1910) and encouraged by the British doctor Elizabeth Garrett Anderson (1836–1917), she returned to the United States, where she was able to establish the New York Infirmary for Women and Children (1857) and later the associated hospital and Women's Medical College of the New York Infirmary (1868). She filled the chair of hygiene, lectured widely on issues such as menstruation and child-bearing and ran both institutions together with her sister Emily Blackwell (1826–1910), who closely followed in her footsteps. She adopted the girl Kitty, who is famously known to have exclaimed after a male doctor's visit: "'Doctor, how very odd it is to hear a *man* called Doctor!'" (BLACKWELL [1895] 2005: 226 emphasis in original), and, thus, easily reveals the constructedness of gender roles. Blackwell returned to London in 1869 to lecture and stay when, as she writes, "the early pioneer work in America was ended" (BLACKWELL [1895] 2005: 265).

Conclusion: The Eye/I of Women in Medicine

The nineteenth-century female medical student and woman doctor perceived the world with different eyes than those of her male colleagues. Seeing herself as a woman doctor was unheard of; considered unnatural, unfeminine, against God's will, destructive to the American nation and any nation on either side of the Atlantic. Envisioning a future in the medical profession needed great strength of imagination, the willingness to challenge traditions and the daring to question authorities. The "true woman" with the requirements of piety, purity, domesticity, and submissiveness would never be able to succeed in this endeavor (WELTER 1966). This social imprint on women's identity had to be shed in many ways. Being stared at was Blackwell's daily experience in Geneva, inside and outside of the college. Her way of countering visual attacks was to lower her eyes, refuse to look back, to deny the return gaze as well as communication, and to simply continue taking notes in class and walking by on the street. But if, as Garland-Thomson argues, "[s]taring bespeaks involvement, and being stared at demands a response", I would suggest that Blackwell's autobiography is such a response, long-delayed, through which she returns the gaze and defends herself against "intrusive overexposure" by exposing her own point of view half a century later (GARLAND-THOMSON 2009: 3; 5). She turns the "hostile glare" of the 1840s into a quest for self-knowledge which she satisfies with her memoir (GARLAND-THOMSON 2009: 17).

Similarly, her transatlantic journey to Europe defied the gender norms at the time. While men could follow what Sidonie Smith has called "the masculine logic of mobility", women were expected to follow the logic of "'sessility'" (SMITH 2001: x). As Smith explains, "[t]o be 'sessile,' in botanical terms, is to be permanently planted, tenaciously fixed, utterly immobile. It is, in a sense, to remain always 'at home,' which has been the traditional locale assigned to women" (SMITH 2001: x). Modes and opportunities of mobility changed in the second half of the nineteenth century, and women medical students certainly took advantage of the improved travel technology to see the world and make it their own as their other me. They undertook the Grand Medical Tour to England, France, Austria, and Germany as means of further education. "As travelers", Sidonie Smith suggests, "women became active agents, learning for themselves about foreign cultures, languages, histories, social organizations, and natural environments, and exercising their independent observational powers" (SMITH 2001: 17).

Very few of the women who traveled wrote about their experiences, and those who did "often masked their curiosity and their agency by muting their narrative 'I'" (SMITH 2001: 18). Blackwell did not follow this path but self-confidently wrote to friends and family, who all supported her ambition. And yet, her autobiography was written in 1895, long after the pioneer years. The narrative includes letters and diary entries of the crucial time from the late 1840s to the 1860s with additional comments of a much later time. The eye that observed at that early early phase was not yet confident enough to publish the story of the "pioneer work"; it needed the mature and experienced "I" of old age to finally make this experience public. It is at this moment that Blackwell's autobiography becomes a "contribution to the evolution of historical processes" and "a cultural act" (HORNUNG 1990: 372).

With an eye on history and a firmly gained self-trust and self-reliance, Blackwell writes herself and her own "I" into history and into the American and English societies from which she had felt excluded when pursuing her pioneer work. *Pioneer Work* does not reveal its genre on the cover; nevertheless, it is a life narrative that "represents a human need for and an expression of the integration into a social system" (HORNUNG 1990: 392). Identification from the outside and self-identification in mid-century were, for Blackwell, at odds with each other. Therefore, she included in *Pioneer Work* letters written by others who would bridge the gap between other- and self-identification.

Ironically, while being clear-sighted about her most fervent wish to become a surgeon, Blackwell literally lost sight of this goal when taking care of children – while in the most domestic space imaginable and being trained in the most feminine duty; as Florence Nightingale writes: "Every woman is a nurse" (NIGHTINGALE [1859] 1969: 3). Ironically, it is the same Nightingale who befriended Blackwell in the 1850s and who writes in 1860 in a letter to John Stuart Mill: "I wish to see as few Doctors, either male or female as possible, for, mark you, the women have made no improvement – they have only tried to be 'men,' and they have only succeeded in being third-rate men'" (qtd. in MONTEIRO 1984: 526). Nightingale seemed to have internalized the oppressive male gaze that Blackwell was often subjected to and that turned her into "crushing objecthood", to use Frantz Fanon's words from a different context of oppression (FANON [1952] 1986: 109). Ironically also, Blackwell's autobiography is not the attempt to record and remember her own work, but is only meant to be part of "some of the first efforts by means of which the medical profession of our day has been opened to women" (BLACKWELL [1895] 2005: 45), as she writes in her preface. She perceives her own contribution as supported by "providential guidance" "in the comparatively trivial incidents of an individual life" (BLACKWELL [1895] 2005: 45). In the tradition of U.S.-American women's autobiography, which may be dated as far back as Mary Rowlandson's (1637–1711) captivity narrative (1682) written upon the request of Increase Mather for the good of all Puritans, Blackwell justifies her life narrative with reference to God's providence and the "request of many friends" with which she complies. Authenticity is assured, according to Blackwell, by "old journals and [...] family correspondence" that give "accuracy to these details of past years" (BLACKWELL [1895] 2005: 45).

The "I" that Blackwell had gained in the medical profession over the years becomes submissive again, at least to some extent. Blackwell's conceptual or ideological self seems to be that of someone who considers her life 'trivial' and subject to providence. Furthermore, she does not fully trust her own "store of memories that constitutes identity and personhood" (EAKIN 2008: 71) but resorts to the support of others.[9] However, these words may simply be her tribute to women's common modesty culture in the nineteenth century. They once more align her with a member of the Transcendentalist movement, this time with the feminist Margaret Fuller (1810–1850), who introduces her own travelogue *Summer on the Lakes, during 1843* (1844) with the following lines addressed to her readers: "Since you are to share with me such foot-notes as may be made on the pages of my life during this summer's wanderings, I should not be quite silent as to this magnificent prologue to the, as yet, unknown drama" (FULLER [1844] 1994: 71). Blackwell, too, overcomes this silence, and her words are neither footnotes nor trivial for women in the nineteenth century. Although we will never be able to meet the real and historical "I" of Blackwell, we can conclude that her biological "eye" and her psychological "I", shaped by the other me of the outside world, merged in narrative and collaborated in the formation of a woman doctor who did pioneer work that opened the medical profession to women.

List of Works Cited

BIRKLE, CARMEN (2009*a*): Traveling and the Discourse of Economy in Nancy Prince's Travel Narrative. In BÉATRICE BIJON and GÉRARD GÂCON (Eds.): *In-Between Two Worlds. Narratives by Female Explorers and Travellers, 1850–1945*. New York: Lang, 17–33.

BIRKLE, CARMEN (2009*b*): Traveling Nurses. Mary Seacole and the Nightingale Encounter. A Transatlantic Story. In CARMEN BIRKLE and NICOLE WALLER (Eds.): *"The Sea Is History": Exploring the Atlantic*. Heidelberg: Universitätsverlag Winter (American Studies – A Monograph Series 177), 99–122.

BIRKLE, CARMEN (2015): Capitals of Medicine. North American Medical Women and Their Encounters with Europe (1850s–1930s). In WALDEMAR ZACHARASIEWICZ and DAVID STAINES (Eds.): *Narratives of Encounters in the North Atlantic Triangle*. Wien: Akademie der Wissenschaften, 85–105.

BLACKWELL, ELIZABETH ([1895] 2005): *Pioneer Work in Opening the Medical Profession to Women*. Introd. AMY SUE BIX. Amherst: Humanity.

BONNER, THOMAS NEVILLE (1988): Pioneering in Women's Medical Education in the Swiss Universities 1864–1914. *Gesnerus – Swiss Journal of the History of Medicine and Sciences* 45.3–4: 461–473.

[9] She does not fully rely on Antonio Damasio's idea of the "'movie-in-the-brain'" (qtd. in EAKIN 2008: 74) and refuses to become one with what she is narrating by giving space to others.

BOYD, JULIA (2005): *The Excellent Doctor Blackwell: The Life of the First Woman Physician.* Phoenix Mill: Sutton.

CHARON, RITA (2005): Bearing Witness: Sontag and the Body. *New England Journal of Medicine* 352.8: 756.

CHARON, RITA (2006*a*; 2008): *Narrative Medicine: Honoring the Stories of Illness*. Oxford/New York: Oxford University Press.

CHARON, RITA (2006*b*): The Self-Telling Body. *Narrative Inquiry* 16.1: 191–200.

CHARON, RITA (2009): Narrative Medicine as Witness for the Self-Telling Body. *Journal of Applied Communication Research* 37.2: 118–131.

CLARKE, EDWARD HAMMOND ([1873] 2009): *Sex in Education, Or, A Fair Chance for Girls*. N. p.: General Books.

DÄWES, BIRGIT et al. (2013): Panel on Life Sciences and Life Writing. In ALFRED HORNUNG (Ed.): *American Lives*. Heidelberg: Universitätsverlag Winter (American Studies – A Monograph Series 234), 537–560.

EAKIN, PAUL JOHN (2008): *Living Autobiographically: How We Create Identity in Narrative.* Ithaca: Cornell University Press.

EMERSON, RALPH WALDO ([1836] 1957): Nature. In STEPHEN E. WHICHER (Ed.). *Selections from Ralph Waldo Emerson*. Boston: Houghton Mifflin, 21–56.

EMERSON, RALPH WALDO ([1837] 1957): The American Scholar. In STEPHEN E. WHICHER (Ed.). *Selections from Ralph Waldo Emerson*. Boston: Houghton Mifflin, 63–80.

EMERSON, RALPH WALDO ([1840] 1957): Self-Reliance. In STEPHEN E. WHICHER (Ed.). *Selections from Ralph Waldo Emerson*. Boston: Houghton Mifflin, 147–168.

EVELETH, ROSE (2014): Why No One Can Design a Better Speculum. *The Atlantic. http://www.theatlantic.com/health/archive/2014/11/why-no-one-can-design-a-better-speculum/382534/* [21 August 2016].

FANON, FRANTZ ([French 1952] 1986): *Black Skin, White Masks*. Trans. by Charles Lam Markmann. London: Pluto.

FOUCAULT, MICHEL ([French 1963] 1994): *The Birth of the Clinic. An Archaeology of Medical Perception.* Trans. by A. M. Sheridan Smith. New York: Vintage.

FOUCAULT, MICHEL ([French 1977] 1980): The Eye of Power. A Conversation with Jean-Pierre Baron and Michelle Perrot. In COLIN GORDON (Ed.), Colin Gordon et al. (Trans.): *Power/Knowledge: Selected Interviews and Other Writings. 1972–1977*. New York: Pantheon / Harvester Press, 146–165.

FULLER, MARGARET ([1844] 1994): Summer on the Lakes, during 1843. In MARY KELLEY (Ed.): *The Portable Margaret Fuller*. New York: Penguin, 69–227.

GARLAND-THOMSON, ROSEMARIE (2009): *Staring. How We Look.* Oxford: Oxford University Press.

GREAVES, DAVID (2001): The Nature and Role of the Medical Humanities. In MARTYN EVANS and ILORA G. FINLAY (Eds.): *Medical Humanities*. London: BMJ Books, 13–22.

HARAWAY, DONNA (1998): The Persistence of Vision. In NICHOLAS MIRZOEFF (Ed.): *The Visual Culture Reader*. London: Routledge, 191–198.

HORNUNG, ALFRED (1990): American Autobiographies and Autobiography Criticism. Review Essay. *Amerikastudien / American Studies* 35.3: 371–407.

HORNUNG, ALFRED (2015): Life Sciences and Life Writing. In HUBERT ZAPF (Ed.): *Literature and Science*. Special Issue of *Anglia* 133.1: 37–52.

KIRCHHOFF, ARTHUR (1897): Vorwort. In ARTHUR KIRCHHOFF (Ed.): *Die akademische Frau: Gutachten hervorragender Universitätsprofessoren, Frauenlehrer und Schriftsteller über die Befähigung der Frau zum wissenschaftlichen Studium und Berufe*. Berlin: Hugo Steinitz, vii–xvi.

LEJEUNE, PHILIPPE (1989): *On Autobiography*. Ed. by PAUL JOHN EAKIN, trans. by Katherine Leary. Minneapolis: University of Minnesota Press.

MITCHELL, S. WEIR ([1871] 2004): *Wear and Tear, Or, Hints for the Overworked*. Introd. MICHAEL S. KIMMEL. Walnut Creek: Altamira.

MÖBIUS, PAUL JULIUS ([1900] 1977): *Über den physiologischen Schwachsinn des Weibes*. München: Matthes & Seitz.

MONTEIRO, LOIS A. (1984): On Separate Roads: Florence Nightingale and Elizabeth Blackwell. *Signs* 9.3: 520–533.

NIGHTINGALE, FLORENCE ([1859] 1969): *Notes on Nursing: What It Is and What It Is Not*. New York: Dover.

ROOSEVELT, THEODORE ([1905] 1998): Address to the National Congress of Mothers, March 13, 1905. In DALE M. BAUER (Ed.): *Charlotte Perkins Gilman: The Yellow Wallpaper*. London: Macmillan, 203–210.

SMITH, SIDONIE (2001): *Moving Lives: 20th-Century Women's Travel Writing*. Minneapolis: University of Minnesota Press.

SMITH, SIDONIE and JULIA WATSON (^{2}2010): *Reading Autobiography: A Guide for Interpreting Life Narratives*. Minneapolis: University of Minnesota Press.

WAGER, MARY E. [1868]: Women as Physicians. *The Galaxy* 6.6: 774–790, Collection *Making of America*. [11 December 2015].

WELLS, SUSAN (2001): *Out of the Dead House: Nineteenth-Century Women Physicians and the Writing of Medicine*. Madison: University of Wisconsin Press.

WELTER, BARBARA (1966): The Cult of True Womanhood: 1820–1860. *American Quarterly* 18.2: 151–174.

ZAPF, HUBERT (2015): Literature and Science. Introduction. In HUBERT ZAPF (Ed.): *Literature and Science*. Special Issue of *Anglia* 133.1: 1–8.

List of Figures

FIG 1

U.S. National Library of Medicine, Bethesda, MD 20894, National Institutes of Health, Health & Human Services. *http://resource.nlm.nih.gov/101448324*.

FIG 2

Jacques Pierre Maygrier (1822): *Nouvelles démonstrations d`accouchemens*. Illustrations drawn by Antoine Chazal, engraved by Forestier and Couche. Frontispiece. Paris: Bechet.

FIG 3

Samuel Janson (1699): Korte en Bondige Verhandeling, van de Voortteeling en 't Kinderbaren met den aankleve van dien: Tot onderrigt der gener, die sig in sulke voorvallen behoorlijk soeken te gedragen. Gedaen door S.I. Med. Doct. Amsterdam: Timotheus ten Hoorn, 106. (Unknown Dutch artist)

Critical Studies of the Nation

Retinal Interfaces and Transparent Eyeballs

The Cultural Imaginary of Surveillance

Birgit Däwes

When Edward Snowden met filmmaker Laura Poitras in Hong Kong in 2013, his disclosures steered public perception toward a phenomenon that has long shaped the relationship between individuals and governmental as well as corporate institutions. While the collection of data as a systematic practice was nothing new, most tacit assumptions about citizens' privacy and individual freedom were shattered by the extent of transnational datamining. "Welcome to the murky new world of surveillance without borders", *Le Monde*'s editorial director Sylvie Kauffmann wrote in response to French legislation on intelligence services after Charlie Hebdo in 2015. "Chancellor Angela Merkel's world", she writes,

> where "friends don't spy on each other" now sounds so 20th-century; in today's world "friends do spy on each other's friends." Citizens have grown so accustomed to giving away big data for private use that governments using metadata to protect them from terrorists may not seem so wrong after all.[1]

Before 2013, institutionalized practices of watching had been predominantly associated with the United States, and specifically with the all-pervasive operations of the National Security Administration (NSA) as an extension of the American government. This semantic reflex was reinforced by representations of surveillance in popular culture, including contemporary Hollywood films such as Tony Scott's *Enemy of the State* (1998), Steven Spielberg's *Minority Report* (2002), Paul Greengrass's film series on Jason Bourne (2002–2016) or Greg Marcks's *The Echelon Conspiracy* (2009), as well as television serials such as *Person of Interest* (2011–2016), *The Americans* (2013) or *Mr Robot* (2015). Even in films that do not center on American surveillance, such as the British production *Freeze Frame* (2004) or the German drama *The Lives of Others* (*Das Leben der Anderen*, 2006), it is mostly governmental institutions that orchestrate, conduct, and abuse the powers of watching others. All of these products feed into the phenomenon that William Staples has called "the culture of surveillance": the contemporary proliferation of visual or digital technologies in the interest of making our lives safer and more convenient, which provide governmental or military agents with significant advantages over organized crime and terrorism.

Given the frequency by which such institutionalized acts of observation have been mediated by cultural products and translated into cultural codes, it is all the more surprising that the emerging field of surveillance studies is still lacking major contributions from cultural and literary studies. Thomas Y. Levin writes that "few analysts of surveillance have recognized the degree to which, parallel with these crucial regulatory disputes,

[1] See also David Lyon, who, as early as 2001, diagnoses transnational surveillance as "an intrinsic aspect of the general economic restructuring of capitalism on a worldwide scale that is commonly referred to as globalization" (LYON 2001: 103).

popular opinion – i.e., general attitudes toward surveillance and its dangers – is also being articulated through, and in important ways also being shaped by, various forms of so-called 'high' and 'low' culture" (LEVIN 2002: 581). Yet so far, the field of surveillance studies has been primarily shaped by disciplines such as sociology, criminology, and political studies, with relatively few recent contributions from the fields of cultural and film studies (LEVIN 2002; LEFAIT 2013; ZIMMER 2015). More recently, David Lyon has given credit to media and cultural studies because of their "analysis of how popular culture interacts with surveillance" (LYON 2007: 22). In his own highly influential analysis, however, as he adds, it is "sociology and communication studies" that "inform the direction" (LYON 2007: 22).

In the following, I would like to challenge the conspicuous absence of research and approach the phenomenon of surveillance from the angle of Transnational American Studies. As a blueprint for my argument, and as a case study to frame it, I would like to use Howard Gordon's and Alex Gansa's *Homeland*, one of the most widely watched television series today (cf. GOFFE 2013).[2] Its sixth season was launched in January 2017, and its network, Showtime, has announced a renewal for two further seasons until 2019 (cf. STOLWORTHY 2016). Through recurrent plot patterns in changing locations – in Washington D.C., Caracas, Tehran (Season 3), Kabul (Season 4), and most recently Berlin (Season 5) – *Homeland* centrally revolves around the politics of surveillance, legitimizing the CIA's tactics as a safeguard for national and global security. My analysis pursues three interrelated goals: First, in an initially structuralist move, to highlight a few exemplary narrative patterns of surveillance culture; second, in the interest of historical groundwork, to trace some of the origins of these patterns into nineteenth-century American literature; and third, to explore their potential to resist and subvert the ways in which we think about surveillance today. In this process, I am particularly interested in the multilateral intersections between surveillance culture and ideology – in Louis Althusser's sense of a "'*representation of the world*' which relates men and women to their conditions of existence, and to each other" (ALTHUSSER [1974] 2011: 25), and which, in order to be functional, has to conceal its traces. Contrary to common assumption, the culture of surveillance does not begin with the late twentieth century; nor is it contingent upon the new digital technologies, such as satellite imaging, biometrics, and facial recognition. Rather, the current proliferation of what William Bogard identifies as "the *imaginary* of surveillant control – a fantastic dream of seeing everything capable of being seen" (BOGARD 1996: 4) distracts us from other sites of ideological power, and from an underlying narrative matrix of a new normative order.

[2] The show is based on the Israeli television drama *Hatufim*, or *Prisoners of War* (2010–2012), which was developed by Gideon Raff, who also served as its director. Whereas this background clearly documents the transnationality of *Homeland*, the unique turn that the American adaptation took (with one prisoner of war instead of the original three; with a CIA agent as a protagonist; and with at least eight seasons compared to Raff's two) justifies an analysis of Gansa and Gordon's serial on its own terms.

"Like a Faceless Gaze": Patterns of Panopticism

According to Michel Foucault, the transformation from states of punishment into surveillance societies took place sometime between 1760 and 1840 (FOUCAULT [1975] 1995: 15) when the state's disciplinary power was gradually relocated from physical violence to psychological control. The emblematic symbol of this new "'anatomy' of power" (FOUCAULT [1975] 1995: 215) is Jeremy Bentham's Panopticon – an architectural model designed in 1791 for prisons, schools, and hospitals, in which individual cells are arranged in a circular structure around a central observatory. Authority is vested in an administrative structure rather than in individual wardens, as power becomes inseparable from the technology of seeing. "Side by side with the major technology of the telescope, the lens and the light beam, which were an integral part of the new physics and cosmology", Foucault writes, "there were the minor techniques of multiple and intersecting observations, of eyes that must see without being seen" (FOUCAULT [1975] 1995: 171). In consequence, the

> perfect disciplinary apparatus would make it possible for a single gaze to see everything constantly. A central point would be both the source of light illuminating everything and a locus of convergence for everything that must be known: a perfect eye that nothing would escape and a center towards which all gazes would be turned. (FOUCAULT [1975] 1995: 173)

Foucault sees this new tactics of power at the heart of modernity: Through panopticism, the state refrains from exercising power physically. Instead, its effect is ensured by a system of anonymous administrators, whose sheer presence would subdue opposition silently, "like a faceless gaze that transformed the whole social body into a field of perception" (FOUCAULT [1975] 1995: 214).

In *Homeland*'s first season, which was first broadcast ten years after 9/11, the panoptic perspective holds a viable promise for national security: A sergeant of the U.S. Marine Corps named Nicholas Brody comes home after eight years of al-Qaeda captivity. While the public celebrates him as a patriotic hero, one CIA agent, Carrie Mathison, suspects that he has been turned into a terrorist. In order to make her case, Mathison illegally sets up a system of audiovisual devices in Brody's home, but even with high-tech, non-stop surveillance, she fails to find the information she is looking for. In addition, her occasional outbreaks of bipolar disorder and her obsession with the case make it difficult for viewers to decide upon credibilities, especially when Brody is increasingly depicted as suspicious, and every character seems to have secrets.

The key to *Homeland*'s success lies in three particular patterns of the show, which allow us to unravel the culture of surveillance by specific structural and narratological features: 1) its multiplicity of visual trajectories, in which – as in Shakespeare's classic technique of the play within the play – we all watch the characters watching each other – and sometimes they watch back. Carrie excessively observes Brody while her supervisor is monitoring her; Brody closely watches his wife for signs of an affair; and the audience is made complicit – yet not omniscient – in these overlapping acts of observation. The show's relativity of perceptual positions also implies a distortion of larger power structures: Instead of the openly visible hierarchy of Foucault's Panopticon, the lines of vision and power are shifting and interchangeable. In consequence, the second distinctive pattern (2) involves an effective dissolution of the line between 'us' and 'them'; a line projected to suggest that the threats to Western society are external and thus containable. Instead of an identifiable Other, the U.S. Marine who possibly works for al-Qaeda marks, in Grant Farred's words, a case of Derridean "autoimmunity" in which the "Self who has taken up the cause of the Other presents [...] an infinitely greater threat to the state precisely because it cannot be identified as Other" (FARRED 2014: 59). This is arguably the most radical spectacle of what post-colonial critics call "anxiety of empire" (cf. LEASK [1992] 2004: 5; SIDDIQI 2008): the preoccupation of Western (or U.S.) hegemony with its own inherent instability. Or, as one critic puts it more simply, Brody "captures a primal American fear: maybe 'we' are not so different from 'them'" (BYASSEE 2013: 42). Third, and most crucially, this show demonstrates a particular narrative pattern of revelation, which not only ensures suspense but also metonymically signifies on epistemological processes as such. As long as Mathison's diegetic surveillance remains ineffective, the story's uncovering requires a heterodiegetic focalizer who makes the audience complicit. In the first official interrogations, when Mathison asks Brody whether he has personally met the terrorist leader Abu Nazir, he denies this, but a flashback reveals to the audience that he is lying. In the final scene of the pilot episode, the focalizer almost imperceptibly shifts the angle of visual direction: The camera watches the protagonist running, then rotates around him and, in a point-of-view shot, adopts his gaze at the U.S. Capitol – with ominous symbolic overtones of menace to American democracy. While thus reinforcing the current climate of fear, and simultaneously suggesting that we have an omniscient perspective, this focalizer operates on poetic principles of ambivalence and distraction.

The narrative politics of *Homeland*, as captured in the first episode of Season 1, describe the central effect of contemporary surveillance culture: In analogy to Carrie Mathison's monitors, the ubiquitous, open display of cameras, and the non-stop media chatter about the NSA draw attention away from the actual sites of power and conflict. As in *Homeland*, they suggest a recognizable antagonist (al-Quaeda, the self-declared 'Islamic State', or the CIA) while our cell phones, tablet computers, and online bank accounts have long been incorporated into a complex, invisible economic matrix in which flows of capital, human bodies, and conversations are continuously tracked. The observatory tower, to speak with Foucault's metaphor, has long been empty. At the same time, this system has rendered its structural agency completely obscure while simultaneously continuing to project a cultural imaginary of identifiable agents operating in the shadows. In consequence, no threat is recognizable: As Iris Radisch wrote in *Die ZEIT* in 2013: "Ohne ein Warnsignal aus der analogen Welt fühlt das alte menschliche Tier, dem so schnell keine Sinnesorgane für die digitale Moderne gewachsen sind, keine Bedrohung. Es schützt sich nicht, duckt sich nicht, kämpft nicht und läuft nicht weg" (RADISCH 2013: 47).

Transparent Eyeballs and Failed Observation: Nineteenth-Century Roots

Surveillance, according to David Lyon, can be defined as "any collection and processing of personal data, whether identifiable or not, for the purposes of influencing or managing those whose data have been garnered" (LYON 2001: 2). At least at first glance, it may seem a daring venture to trace this practice back to the nineteenth century, especially since most critics focus their analyses on the time after 9/11: "The 11 September 2001, attacks on American soil", as Elliot D. Cohen diagnoses, "were a decisive marker in the shift toward a culture of control in America" (COHEN 2010: 7). At a closer look, however, it seems less than coincidental that the term "surveillance" was first used, according to the *OED*, in 1799, eight years after Bentham's panoptic design. Especially in the United States, the obsession with visual modes of control held a firm place within the young nation's cultural imaginary, from the theme of espionage in James Fenimore Cooper's novel *The Spy* (1821) to the systematic office surveillance of Melville's *Bartleby the Scrivener* (1853). Kerry Segrave dates the first reports on tapping telegraph wires to the Civil War (SEGRAVE 2014: 5–6; see also TOWNE 2015), but as Joan Jensen has argued, the political reliance on collecting intelligence even goes back to before the War of Independence (cf. JENSEN 1991: 10). The Great Seal of the United States, designed in 1776, bears on its reverse side the image of the all-seeing eye of Providence, and in the American Revolutionary War, President George Washington employed a group of spies in order to gather intelligence about the British troops. In the nineteenth century, the first private detective agency, established by Allan Pinkerton in 1850, was officially hired by Abraham Lincoln during the Civil War, and later merged into the United States Secret Service after 1865.

Yet even apart from these government-induced processes of observation and control, surveillance holds a firm place in nineteenth-century American culture. Ralph Waldo Emerson's foundational text of American Romanticism describes the relationship between man and nature as essentially panoptical: "Standing on the bare ground", Emerson famously writes, "– my head bathed by the blithe air, and uplifted into infinite space, – all mean egotism vanishes. I become a transparent eye-ball. I am nothing. I see all" (EMERSON [1836] 1983: 10).[3] While this use of seeing is confidently coded as optimistic, other writers of the time approach the issue with more skepticism and satire. As two texts by Edgar Allan Poe and Nathaniel Hawthorne exemplarily demonstrate, the narrative patterns of surveillance culture are much more deeply rooted in American culture than they seem at first glance.

Edgar Allan Poe's "The Tell-Tale Heart", first published in 1843 in the Boston-based magazine *The Pioneer*, is the story of a violent reaction to surveillance – on both a private and a governmental level. From the very beginning, the text is saturated with visual imagery: even the narratee is initially invited to "*observe* […] how calmly I can tell you the whole story" (POE [1843] 1978: 792 [emphasis added]). This "story" turns out to be the

[3] Frank Kelleter was the first to argue that media studies begins with Emerson, even though, "[o]n a purely semantic level, there can be no theory of the media in transcendentalist New England because the term *the media* was not used in its current meaning until 1923, when it first became an umbrella term for newspapers, cinematography, and radio" (KELLETER 2007: 224).

confession of a domestic murder, committed in reaction to a panoptic situation. The unnamed narrator tells us about his (or her) equally anonymous housemate that "I loved the old man" (POE [1843] 1978: 792), but the latter's gaze becomes a motive for homicide:

> I think it was his eye! yes, it was this! He had the eye of a vulture – a pale blue eye, with a film over it. Whenever it fell upon me, my blood ran cold; and so by degrees – very gradually – I made up my mind to take the life of the old man, and thus rid myself of the eye forever. (POE [1843] 1978: 792)

For seven nights, the narrator secretly enters the old man's bedroom and watches him closely by the light of a lantern – which, "with its lid and single ray", can be considered "itself a symbolic eye" (TUCKER 1981: 95). This illuminative device enables the narrator to reverse the order of surveillance, and as he becomes Foucault's "faceless gaze" in turn, the narrator eventually kills the man, dismembers the body, and hides the remains under the floor of his house. Since the murder weapon is the man's bed, the story has been read psychologically as a case of sexual anxiety (BENFEY 1993), or by feminist critics as a revolt against the male gaze: Gita Rajan convincingly argues that the protagonist might as well be female, since there are no gender markings in the text. The eye, accordingly, can be read as "a metaphor of patriarchal scrutiny and social control" (RAJAN [1988] 2009: 46). Yet the story does not end here: Just when the first, private agent of surveillance has thus been successfully eliminated and literally disembodied, the force of state control is at the door: notified by a neighbor, three policemen demand permission to search the premises. Confronted with this further act of surveillance, the narrator preempts the police discovery by exposing the body and confessing the crime.

At a time of westward expansion and Manifest Destiny, "The Tell-Tale Heart" links the dynamics of surveillance to the anxiety of empire: Here, as in *Homeland*, the primary threat comes from the inside, from within the domestic sphere. Jonathan Auerbach sees paranoia itself at the center of the tale (cf. AUERBACH 1989: 47); and James W. Gargano has argued that the old man is, in fact, but an externalized projection of the narrator's own irrational characteristics: "[T]he murderer and the old man appear to be not only related but identical" (GARGANO 1968: 380). If Poe's signature motif of the double is at work here, and – in Arthur Robinson's words – the "Evil Eye" is, in fact, an "evil 'I'" (ROBINSON 1965: 377), the story not only approaches surveillance culture but also shows its inherent epistemological unreliability: Just as Sergeant Brody might or might not be an Islamist terrorist, the murder in Poe's tale might or might not have happened in the first place.

This doubling of layers in combination with a strong narrative resistance to visual control is even more radically employed in Nathaniel Hawthorne's 1835 story "Wakefield", which relates a failed attempt to gather intelligence about a mysterious urban figure. Hawthorne's heterodiegetic narrator introduces us to a character who secretly leaves his family in London in order to spy on them:

> The man, under pretence of going a journey, took lodgings in the next street to his own house, and there, unheard of by his wife or friends [...] dwelt upwards of twenty years. During that period, he beheld his home every day, and frequently the forlorn Mrs. Wakefield. (HAWTHORNE [1835] 1982: 290)

The anonymous narrator invites the reader along to solve this mystery and imagine a surveillance of the protagonist while the latter observes his wife. In his pursuit, the narrator emphasizes both Wakefield's intact diegetic cover and his own panoptic power: "No mortal eye but mine has traced thee" (HAWTHORNE [1835] 1982: 292). In explicitly visual imagery, the story then simulates the pursuit – in classic, spy-like fashion – of the protagonist through the streets of the British capital. "We must hurry after him, along the street", the narrator tells us, "ere he lose his individuality, and melt into the great mass of London life" (HAWTHORNE [1835] 1982: 292). Even before biometrics and facial recognition technologies, however, the object of observation seems to be wary of the invisible gaze: "his eyes, small and lustreless, sometimes wander apprehensively about him, but oftener seem to look inward. He bends his head, and moves with an indescribable obliquity of gait, *as if unwilling to display his full front to the world*. Watch him long enough to see what we have described [...]" (HAWTHORNE [1835] 1982: 295–296 [emphasis added]).

Furthermore, by making readers complicit in an act of spying on the spy, the narrator doubles the position of the observer. This process is less an instance of Foucault's ordered and "spatial 'nesting' of hierarchized surveillance" (FOUCAULT [1975] 1995: 171–172) than a serial and thus temporal multiplication of agents. Instead of producing a result, however, the chase for information or meaning is surprisingly abandoned as the narrator resigns in the end: "We will not follow our friend across the threshold. He has left us much food for thought, a portion of which shall lend its wisdom to a moral; and be shaped into a figure" (HAWTHORNE [1835] 1982: 298). Without a resolution, therefore, the circular displacement of the act of watching points only back to itself in a reflexive gesture, favoring fictional imagery over visual and conclusive exposure.

In a similar gesture, the homodiegetic narrator of Poe's "The Man of the Crowd", first published in 1840, begins with a German book that – like the object of surveillance depicted in the following – does not permit itself to be read. The setting is again London: The first-person narrator relates an experience of two days and one night spent in a fictitiously modified version of what Bill Nichols terms the "observational mode" (NICHOLS 1992: 38) – collecting data on people around him and sorting them into social categories. One old man, however, eludes the visual typology. Even though the narrator follows the man to the outskirts of London and back to the café, making sure that "[a]t no moment did he see that I watched him" (POE [1840] 1978: 513), his surveillant project fails. Realizing that "[i]t will be in vain to follow; for I shall learn no more of him, nor of his deeds" (POE [1840] 1978: 515), he ends, again circularly, on the unreadable book. Critics have widely followed Walter Benjamin in reading this individual as a flâneur, and thus as the prototypical figure of modern urban existence (cf. BENJAMIN [1938–1939] 2006: 79; see also HAYES 2002: 465). In addition, the story also presents a failed surveillance project – not because of a lack of means or because of a faulty strategy (the narrator remains at the subject's heels at all times, and his cover remains intact), but because of an epistemological insufficiency. Here, as in "The Tell-Tale Heart", we find indications of a serialized personality: The narrator, according to Edward H. Davidson, "is so terrified of admitting who or what he is that he projects himself into this desperate and wholly imagined fugitive" (DAVIDSON 1957: 191) and thus follows himself. If thus, again, the observer and the observed are doppelgangers, the promise of identifying and decoding the Other remains unfulfilled once more, turning the biometric attempts at controlling difference into mere shadow play.

Which Homeland? Transnational Rhetorics of Surveillance

Hawthorne's and Poe's stories not only showcase strategies of resistance to panoptic transparency, but they work with the same narratological ambiguities that also propel *Homeland*: The positions of observer and observed are interchangeable; the thin line between self and other is blurred to indistinction; and the narrators, who spend much semiotic energy to establish their authority, eventually turn out to deceive us. In the twenty-first century, as film critics such as Norman Denzin, Thomas Y. Levin, and Catherine Zimmer have argued, this development has taken on a dynamic of its own. According to Levin, the past decades have witnessed a proliferation of what he calls the "rhetorics" of surveillance, in which the process of watching is not merely a theme but a formal and structural condition of many films. From Francis Ford Coppola's *The Conversation* (1974) to Peter Weir's *The Truman Show* (1998), he notices a "surveillant recasting of traditional narrative omniscience" (LEVIN 2002: 590), in which the camera becomes the safeguard of audience control.

Homeland is an apt example of this trend: In its fifth season, the show moved to Berlin in October 2015. Carrie Mathison has left the CIA to work as head of security for a private foundation that helps refugees in the Middle East; her life with her daughter and new boyfriend seems peaceful and balanced, and she has turned towards religion as a dedicated Catholic. As in previous years, the season's central issues are highly topical and merge actual political developments with fictional scenarios. The main title sequence opens with a voice-over of German chancellor Angela Merkel speaking about millions of refugees looking for shelter in Europe, news speakers talking about cyberterrorism and the Islamic State, and John Kerry stating that "Edward Snowden is a coward" (*Homeland* Season 5). As in *Homeland's* first season, the action revolves around national security, international threats, a potential enemy within, and information that is direly needed. The main conflict initially seems to be one between government authorities and hackers, who have managed to break into a CIA server and to download documents that expose an illegal civilian surveillance agreement between the United States and Germany. An American journalist makes a deal with one of the hackers and promises to obtain and publish the files. From an angle of law and civil rights, this seems all the more necessary since we also witness clandestine CIA operations, in which not only terrorists and ISIS recruiters in Germany are assassinated rather than taken to justice, but in which Carrie Mathison's name suddenly appears on the list of targets to be killed. World politics are distilled into conflicts between the show's main characters: just as Carrie seeks to find out who is plotting against her, viewers piece together a conspiracy in which Berlin becomes the target of an Islamist terrorist attack, a CIA plan to have Syrian president Baschar al-Assad replaced by a military officer is sabotaged, and the main villains, ultimately, are the Russians.

Twenty-seven years after the Cold War was declared over, the pervasiveness of what Alan Nadel has famously termed "containment culture" in his book of the same name is evidently still intact: "a national narrative," according to Nadel, "in which insecurity was absorbed by internal security, internationalism by global strategy, apocalypse and utopia by a Christian theological mandate, and xenophobia – the fear of the Other – by courtship" (NADEL 1995: 14). In the fifth season of *Homeland*, the CIA's chief of station in Berlin, Allison Carr, works as a double agent for the KGB; she secretly prevents the change of regime in Syria, strategically seduces senior CIA officer Saul Berenson, the head of European operations, and turns out to have been the one who assigned Carrie's assassination.

In terms of film narratology, *Homeland* stays true to its pattern of blurring the lines between self and other, observer and observed. Again, the dominant threat to the American Empire comes from within, and, as in Poe's and Hawthorne's stories, the lines of surveillance are intermingled in a criss-crossing struggle over gaining information. As Aaron Riccio summarizes, the show's "winning formula" consists of "Carrie and Saul together, looking for evidence that a red-haired American is a traitor". (RICCIO 2015) However, whereas Poe and Hawthorne still vest the authority over the tale in the narrator, contemporary film and television serials benefit from the genre's inherent advantage of the camera eye as a larger, anonymous structure that promises omniscience and closure. In episode four, for instance, after the plane with the Syrian insurgent has exploded, we see Allison Carr walking away from the shocked and unsuspecting senior CIA officers. When she has reached a certain distance, she briefly glances over her shoulder and, making sure no one sees her, shows the trace of a smile. Whereas the ubiquitous surveillance cameras in the diegetic space give us little or no information on what is actually going on, the film camera's extended gaze on Allison's face, revealing her cautious look over her shoulder, exposes her complicity fairly early in the season. Again, a heterodiegetic focalizer provides visual information that is inaccessible to the other characters, exemplifying a process that Catherine Zimmer has noted for contemporary cinema in general, in which "practices of surveillance become representational and representational practices become surveillant, and ultimately the distinctions between the two begin to fade away". (ZIMMER 2015: 2)

The show culminates in a jihadist attack on Germany's capital: A group of ISIS-related terrorists from Syria are about to commit a massacre with sarin gas in Berlin's main station. Having followed her occasionally bipolar intuitions, Carrie single-handedly stops the assassins and averts the threat, but not before we learn that Russia actually knows and approves of the attack and – through Allison – even actively misleads German authorities in order to make it happen. In a crucial scene in episode nine, in which the CIA and the German secret service BND work together in Berlin, we see an orchestrated attempt at surveillance in order to track down Allison and find her allies. As the observers virtually follow her, the extent of operational surveillance tactics becomes obvious: From cell phone wires, GPS tracking and public CCTV cameras to high-resolution satellites and drones, the BND officers can basically access any source of image and sound in real time. However, when Allison's cell phone signal suddenly disappears, the BND officers are entirely clueless, and Saul and Carrie have to educate them on call codes and other techniques of concealment. The political and ideological implications of this scene are telling: While technically skilled, the German operators of the surveillance equipment cannot succeed without American expertise. When it comes to fighting Russia, in other words, the only opponent who can efficiently stand up to continuing Cold War terror is the United

States. The sequence thus perfectly illustrates "the rhetorical strategy" of containment, to use Alan Nadel's words again, "that functioned to foreclose dissent, preempt dialogue, and preclude contradiction. The United States, empowered by the binding energy of the universe", continues to be "the universal container" (NADEL 1995: 14).

As exemplified in this scene, *Homeland* also demonstrates the multiple blurring of boundaries and performs the politics of contemporary surveillance culture in which representation becomes surveillant, and the power of watching achieves poetic justice. In the end, the secret service operations that triggered the season's plot – however they may conflict with civil rights – are legitimized as essential for national and transnational security. The hackers are exposed as either too greedy, too amateurish, or too naïve to be of actual relevance; the investigative journalist is turned into an asset; and while the United States, Germany, and Israel work together as reliable partners, the hierarchy among them remains clear. However transnational *Homeland* may look with regard to setting, language use, or character mobility, it is the ends of American hegemony, ultimately, that continue to justify the means. This message is made even more tangible by the show's incorporation of actual politicians and events: In episode ten, which was aired on 6 December 2015, Allison even refers to the terrorist attacks on France of 13 November, less than three weeks previously, stating that "nobody wants to see another Paris." As viewers follow the all-pervasive camera, they are likely to agree.

Conclusion

When Foucault argues that through the Panopticon, "an obscure art of light and the visible was secretly preparing a new knowledge of man" (FOUCAULT [1975] 1995: 171), he does not mention that this knowledge is not inherent in the structures of seeing. On the contrary, we require techniques of decoding, analyzing, and contextualizing information – in short, of interpretation – in order to make meaning.

In Hawthorne's and Poe's tales, the mysteries accordingly remain unsolved by observation and visual pursuit: Just as readers need to combine textual features into meaningful structures, these narrators' attempts at making sense of their doubles by hermeneutic control prove not to be viable and thus point us to the gaps and fallibilities of data collection. In *Homeland*, on the contrary, we not only see a self-assured thematic recourse to American exceptionalism and Cold War containment, but the show also advertises contemporary surveillance culture as reliable, government-controlled, and mandatory for global security. This is particularly ironic at a time when at least one billion users freely share their data on Facebook, Whatsapp, and Instagram; download mobile apps without reading the forty-nine-page terms of agreement, and feed information into Google's search engines and cloud servers. In the transnational arena, the Foucauldian watchtower has become but an architectural floating signifier, a distracting placeholder for structures that are, in fact, invisible and thus all the more powerful.

If Hawthorne's and Poe's celebrations of fictional ambivalence undermine police force, facial recognition, and observational intelligence in the 1840s, the twenty-first century compels us to find new metaphors for the transnational, post-panoptic scenery of our future. I do not claim to have an answer on what they look like, but in order to have an impact on our camera-saturated "culture of surveillance", these metaphors seem to require realism rather than satire, agency rather than cynicism, and viable alternatives to the naturalized convenience by which we use digital technology. We might have to realize, as Jaron Lanier said in Frankfurt in 2014, that "[i]f we demand free services in the present, we must also learn that we'll actually pay a price for them in the future" and at least admit our complicity in the system. David Lyon writes in his 2015 study, *Surveillance after Snowden*, that what we need is the development of "ethical tools for assessing surveillance, a broadened sense of why privacy matters and ways of translating these into political goals" (LYON 2015: 123). For these purposes, the landscape of transnational transparency holds as much of a pitfall as it may seem promising.

List of Works Cited

ALTHUSSER, LOUIS ([1974] [2]2011): *Philosophy and the Spontaneous Philosophy of the Scientists & Other Essays*. London: Verso.

AUERBACH, JONATHAN (1989): *The Romance of Failure: First-Person Fictions of Poe, Hawthorne, and James*. New York: Oxford University Press.

BENFEY, CHRISTOPHER (1993): Poe and the Unreadable: "The Black Cat" and "The Tell-Tale Heart". In KENNETH SILVERMAN (Ed.): *New Essays on Poe's Major Tales*. Cambridge: Cambridge University Press, 27–44.

BENJAMIN, WALTER ([1938–1939] 2006): *The Writer of Modern Life: Essays on Charles Baudelaire*. Ed. by MICHAEL W. JENNINGS, trans. by HOWARD EILAND. Cambridge, MA: Harvard University Press.

BOGARD, WILLIAM (1996): *The Simulation of Surveillance: Hypercontrol in Telematic Societies*. Cambridge: Cambridge University Press.

BYASSEE, JASON (2013): Spies and Traitors. *The Christian Century* 130.7 (April). Web [22 August 2016].

BYER, ROBERT H. (1986): Mysteries of the City: A Reading of Poe's "The Man of the Crowd". In SACVAN BERCOVITCH and MYRA JEHLEN (Eds.): *Ideology and Classic American Literature*. Cambridge: Cambridge University Press (Cambridge Studies in American Literature and Culture), 221–246.

COHEN, ELLIOT D. (2010): *Mass Surveillance and State Control: The Total Information Awareness Project*. New York: Palgrave Macmillan.

DAVIDSON, EDWARD H. (1957): *POE: A Critical Study*. Cambridge, MA: Harvard University Press.

EMERSON, RALPH WALDO ([1836] 1983): Nature. In *Essays and Lectures*. Ed. by JOEL PORTE. New York: Library of America, 5–49.

FARRED, GRANT (2014): "An American has been turned": Thinking Autoimmunity through *Homeland*. *Derrida Today* 7.1: 59–78.

FINK, STEVEN (2011): Who is Poe's "Man of the Crowd"? *Poe Studies* 44.1: 17–38.

FOUCAULT, MICHEL ([1975] [2]1995): *Discipline and Punish: The Birth of the Prison*. Trans. by Alan Sheridan [1977]. New York: Vintage.

GOFFE, LESLIE (2013): The *Homeland* Phenomenon. *Middle East* 440 (February): 54–56.

GARGANO, JAMES W. (1968): The Theme of Time in 'The Tell-Tale Heart'. *Studies in Short Fiction* 5.4 (Summer): 378–382.

HAWTHORNE, NATHANIEL [1835]: Wakefield. In *Tales and Sketches*. Ed. by ROY HARVEY PEARCE. New York: Library of America, 1982, 290–298.

HAYES, KEVIN J. (2002): Visual Culture and the Word in Edgar Allan Poe's "The Man of the Crowd". *Nineteenth-Century Literature* 56.4 (March): 445–465.

JENSEN, JOAN M. (1991): *Army Surveillance in America, 1775–1980*. New Haven: Yale University Press.

KAUFFMANN, SYLVIE (2015): Surveillance Without Borders. *New York Times*, 17 May. Web [13 January, 2016].

KELLETER, FRANK (2007): "a low degree of the sublime": Ralph Waldo Emerson's Theory of the Media. In ALFRED HORNUNG (Ed.): *Intercultural America*. Heidelberg: Universitätsverlag Winter, 223–238.

LANIER, JARON (2014): *Who Owns the Future?* New York: Simon and Schuster.

LEASK, NIGEL ([1992] 2004): *British Romantic Writers and the East: Anxieties of Empire*. Cambridge: Cambridge University Press.

LEFAIT, SÉBASTIEN (2013): *Surveillance on Screen: Monitoring Contemporary Films and Television Programs*. Lanham/Toronto/Plymouth: Scarecrow Press.

LEVIN, THOMAS Y. (2002): Rhetoric of the Temporal Index: Surveillant Narration and the Cinema of "Real Time." In THOMAS Y. LEVIN, URSULA FROHNE, and PETER WEIBEL (Eds.): *CTRL [SPACE]: Rhetorics of Surveillance from Bentham to Big Brother*. Cambridge/Karlsruhe/London: MIT/ZKM Press, 578–593.

LYON, DAVID (2001): *Surveillance Society: Monitoring Everyday Life*. Buckingham/Philadelphia: Open University Press.

LYON, DAVID (2003): *Surveillance after September 11*. Cambridge: Polity Press.

LYON, DAVID (Ed.) (2006): *Theorizing Surveillance: The Panopticon and Beyond*. Collumption, UK: Willan.

LYON, DAVID (2007): *Surveillance Studies: An Overview*. Cambridge: Polity Press.

LYON, DAVID (2015): *Surveillance After Snowden*. Malden, MA: Polity Press.

LYON, DAVID, KEVIN D. HAGGERTY, and KIRSTIE BALL (2012): Introducing Surveillance Studies. In KIRSTIE BALL, KEVIN D. HAGGERTY, and DAVID LYON (Eds.): *Routledge Handbook of Surveillance Studies*. New York: Routledge, 1–11.

NADEL, ALAN (1995): *Containment Culture: American Narratives, Postmodernism, and the Atomic Age*. Durham/London: Duke University Press.

NICHOLS, BILL (1992): *Representing Reality: Issues and Concepts in Documentary*. Bloomington: University of Indiana Press.

POE, EDGAR ALLAN [1840]: The Man of the Crowd. In *Collected Works of Edgar Allan Poe: Tales and Sketches1831–1842*. Ed. by THOMAS OLLIVE MABBOTT. Cambridge/London: Belknap Press of Harvard University Press, 1978, vol. II, 505–518.

POE, EDGAR ALLAN [1843]: The Tell-Tale Heart. In *Collected Works of Edgar Allan Poe: Tales and Sketches1843–1849*. Ed. by THOMAS OLLIVE MABBOTT. Cambridge, MA: Harvard University Press, 1978, vol. III, 789–798.

RADISCH, IRIS (2013): Angriff auf das digitale Imperium. *Die ZEIT* 51 (12 December): 47.

RAJAN, GITA ([1988] 2009): A Feminist Rereading of Poe's "The Tell-Tale Heart". *Papers on Language & Literature* 24.3 (Summer 1988). Repr. in HAROLD BLOOM (Ed.): *Edgar Allan Poe's "The Tell-Tale Heart" and Other Stories*. New York: Infobase Publishing (Bloom's Modern Critical Interpretations), 39–54.

RICCIO, AARON (2015): *Homeland* Recap: Season 5, Episode 9, "The Litvinov Ruse". *Slant Magazine*, 29 November Web [22 August 2016].

ROBINSON, E. ARTHUR (1965): Poe's "The Tell-Tale Heart". *Nineteenth-Century Fiction* 19.4 (March): 369–378.

SEGRAVE, KERRY (2014): *Wiretapping and Electronic Surveillance in America, 1862–1920*. Jefferson, NC: McFarland.

SIDDIQI, YUMNA (2008): *Anxieties of Empire and the Fiction of Intrigue*. New York: Columbia University Press.

STAPLES, WILLIAM G. (1997): *The Culture of Surveillance: Discipline and Social Control in the United States*. New York: St. Martin's (Contemporary Social Issues).

STOLWORTHY, JACOB (2016): Homeland Season 6 Pushed Back but Renewed for a Further Two Seasons. *The Independent*, 2 June. Web [22 August 2016].

TOWNE, STEPHEN E. (2015): Surveillance and Spies in the Civil War: Exposing Confederate Conspiracies in America's Heartland. Ohio University Press.

TUCKER, B. D. (1981): "The Tell-Tale Heart" and the "Evil Eye". *The Southern Literary Journal* 13.2 (Spring): 92–98.

ZIMMER, CATHERINE (2015): *Surveillance Cinema*. New York/London: New York University Press.

Series, Dictionary Entries, Prize Acceptance Speeches

Homeland. Dir. MICHAEL CUESTA. Created by ALEX GANSA and HOWARD GORDON. Perf. Damian Lewis, Claire Danes, and Mandy Patinkin. Showtime 2011–2016. Television.

LANIER, JARON: "High Tech Peace Will Need a New Kind of Humanism". Peace Prize of the German Book Trade Acceptance Speech. Frankfurt a. M., 12 October 2014. *Web*.

"Surveillance". Oxford English Dictionary (OED). Online. December 2013. Oxford University Press. *Web* [2 January 2014].

"Nonsovereign Histories"

Circumventing the Nation in Spike Lee's *When the Levees Broke*

Nicole Waller

On 29 August 2005, the center of hurricane Katrina passed east of the city of New Orleans, causing major destruction to the city's levee and canal system. It was the failure of these levees that led to the flooding of almost 80 % of New Orleans by 31 August. The levees, poorly designed and built by the US Army Corps of Engineers, were the main cause of death in the city as especially older and impaired residents drowned in the floods.[1] In addition to the neglectful design of the levees by the Corps of Engineers, federal aid to the survivors of the catastrophe was insufficient and often came too late. For five long days, it seemed as though the federal government, the Federal Emergency Management Agency (FEMA), and the nation at large had abandoned New Orleans (WOODS 2009: 1).

Katrina and its aftermath brought back into focus the problematic positioning of New Orleans within the United States. For better or worse, New Orleans has frequently been theorized as an exception to mainstream America, a space which does not quite fit into the conception of US-American nationhood although situated within the nation's territorial boundaries. With its French, Spanish, and African histories and its strategic place as a port of the Atlantic world, New Orleans has long been a case study for theorizing the relationship between the local, the national, and the transnational or global. In the aftermath of hurricane Katrina, this tendency has intensified, and New Orleans serves more than ever as a crucial site for thinking about nationhood and globalization. This article sets out to briefly sketch the history of New Orleans's perceived exceptionality and the way in which critics have developed ever-larger frames for the analysis of the city's political and cultural significance. In the wake of hurricane Katrina, the discussion of these widening frames culminates in Wai Chee Dimock's claim that we need to develop a "nonsovereign history of Katrina" (DIMOCK 2009: 151) which connects local and global scales while circumventing the level of the nation. Building on Dimock's conception, I argue that African American filmmaker Spike Lee's Katrina documentary *When the Levees Broke* of 2006 is just such a "nonsovereign history". While many critics have discussed Lee's work mostly in relation to US-American nationhood, I agree with Anna Hartnell's seminal contention that Lee's documentary points to "the limits of national identity in an increasingly divided and unequal world" (HARTNELL 2012: 17).

In a first step, I will show that Lee's film develops a transnational frame by depicting the nation as a site of exclusion, of the withholding of aid, and thus as a lacuna in the effort to rebuild New Orleans. In Lee's presentation, like in Dimock's conception, local and global levels connect in efforts to rescue and rebuild while federal institutions remain

[1] See CALLENBACH 2006: 7. The overall Katrina-related death toll for the Gulf Coast is estimated at 1,800 people, with an additional 2 million people displaced. See LOWE and SHAW 2009: 803.

aloof. This reading, which critiques the absence of federal support for victims and survivors in New Orleans, would still be compatible with the claims of citizenship, civil rights, and inclusion voiced by many New Orleans residents. Such claims implicitly posit the nation as a coveted space of legitimacy and accountability that must be made to embrace its citizens equally. In a second step, however, Lee's film develops a parallel narrative of the nation as an aggressive structure of governance. Building on the work of Judith Butler, I read this parallel conception of the nation in Lee's film as characterized by new forms of governmentality and older forms of sovereignty that are highly damaging especially for African American and poor populations. With such a conception of the nation, civil rights-based claims of participation must fall short of resolving the problems of racism and systematic exploitation. Lee's film initially portrays the nation as an absence in his construction of survival and activism in the wake of hurricane Katrina. However, in the film's contextualization of the historical, social, and political structures of New Orleans and the larger state of Louisiana, Lee's depiction of federal intervention in the debate about oil ultimately creates an even more critical assessment of the nation-state as a damaging structure of exploitation that can no longer be easily tied to a civil rights agenda. Thus, both Lee's political and his aesthetic choices frequently question and reverse earlier civil rights strategies.

The Nation as Absence: (Dis)Placing New Orleans

Founded in 1718 as a French fortification, New Orleans was ceded to Spain in the 1760s, later ceded back to France, and finally sold to the United States as part of the Louisiana Purchase of 1803. From the moment they had acquired the city, Americans voiced doubt whether New Orleans actually qualified as *American*. Richard W. Bailey has pointed out that Americans who went to see New Orleans after its purchase remarked that they were often called "foreigners" by the city's residents; at the same time, Americans often described the city as "exotic" (BAILEY 2003: 363–364). Part of this exoticism came from the city's position as a global port, but the term was also applied to the city's residents, especially the established French population of Creoles and Cajuns. In addition, as an entrepôt for slaves, New Orleans had a large population of African descent, and the succession of French and Spanish legal codes had also created a large free black population, which was far more influential and outspoken in New Orleans than in many other U.S.-American cities of the time (BAILEY 2003: 364–365). As Barbara Eckstein has argued, even though New Orleans eventually acquired many of the average American municipal structures, this historical otherness never quite vanished from the city's image (ECKSTEIN 2005: 5; THOMPSON 2008: 306).

Many of the city's residents still point to their multinational history and exceptional culture as a source of pride. But the negative effects of this otherness with regard to the larger American nation became obvious in press reports about New Orleans after Katrina, reports which labeled the city's displaced residents as "refugees" (implying their foreignness) and compared the devastated neighborhoods to the "Third World" (O'GRADY 2008; SIMMONS 2009: 478; POWELL 2012: 303; TAYLOR 2012: 495). Coverage focused on post-Katrina crime and looting, suggesting a lawlessness which sprang not from the state of exception's suspension of the law but from the perceived lawlessness of the city's residents (GIROUX 2006: 176–177).

In order to counter the negative effects of such exceptionalist readings, city residents have often claimed and asserted their rights as regular US citizens and as participants in the larger nation. African Americans especially have critiqued the federal government's insufficient intervention in local structures of racism. While federal intervention temporarily ensured African American citizenship rights in the aftermath of the civil war and in the 1960s, many African American residents of New Orleans have argued that this involvement did not go far enough. Residents also interpreted the slow reactions of the government and FEMA after the hurricane as another proof of federal indifference toward the population of New Orleans.

Recent scholarship has underscored New Orleans's exceptional position in the United States by situating the city in transnational frames of analysis, acknowledging both the empowering and the problematic aspects of this approach. Many critics view New Orleans as a Caribbean city, a nexus between North and South America. Clyde Woods reads New Orleans both as a historical center of African diaspora culture and as one of the historical centers of a brutal plantation imperialism stretching from the United States to the Caribbean and to Central and South America (WOODS 2009: 433–434). William Boelhower, Mark Thompson and others have suggested placing New Orleans in the even larger framework of Atlantic studies research.[2] Reviewing historiographic work about New Orleans, Thompson argues that "most accounts of the city are embedded within a national narrative of the US that treats the city as exotic and exceptional—'un-American,' in essence" (THOMPSON 2008: 306). Thompson's project is not to counter this position with a proof of New Orleans's Americanness, but "rather to place the city's history within non-national contexts where the USA is not automatically the object of comparison" (THOMPSON 2008: 306). Most recently, studies of the city after Katrina have situated it in global networks of biopower and biopolitics (MIRZOEFF 2009; GIROUX2006).

It is here that Wai Chee Dimock's work on the environmental causes and results of hurricane Katrina becomes important since Dimock counters the ravages of economic liberalism and globalization with an alternative vision of planetary connections. Her reading of Katrina observes that the concept of national sovereignty and safe, defendable national borders (metaphorically represented by the levees themselves) has failed with respect to storms such as Katrina. Instead of advocating the strengthening of national lines of defense, Dimock traces another approach in the work of a journalist from the local newspaper *New Orleans Times-Picayune*. The newspaper sent its reporter to the Netherlands, where storm surges have proved as devastating and destructive as on the Gulf coast. By tracing the Dutch policy of protecting both the population and the special habitat of the coastal region through flexible floodgates in contrast to the more invasive strategy of warding off storm and water through ever higher levees, the *Times-Picayune*, in Dimock's reading, connected grassroots concerns with a transnational perspective, creating a "nonsovereign history" of "unorthodox paths [which] jump from the micro to the macro, and bypass the default center, going over and under the jurisdiction of the nation. Its scale is both smaller and larger: operating subnationally on the one hand, as a grassroots

[2] See the articles collected in the *Atlantic Studies* special issues 5.2 and 5.3 on *New Orleans in the Atlantic World I* and *II* (2008).

phenomenon, and transnationally on the other hand, as a cross-border phenomenon" (DIMOCK 2009: 146–147). In this way, readers of the *Times-Picayune* were offered not only an alternative technological approach to protecting coastal populations and habitats, but also read about alternative democratic processes of decision-making which included in its considerations the rights of local populations as well as unborn generations and non-human life. Dimock's conclusion is that "[a] nonsovereign history of Katrina shows that, beyond the broken levees, what needs to be mended is the democratic process itself and its need for a reference frame beyond the geography and chronology of the nation" (DIMOCK 2009: 151). Dimock's position circumvents the nation as a political and juridical center by connecting local needs with a global frame in order to provide a new reading of storms and waves which cannot be circumscribed by rigid levees or territorial boundaries.

Spike Lee's film creates just such a "nonsovereign history of Katrina". Lee's film depicts New Orleans as a place of strong local African American community structures, emphasizing the people who live and act as social beings in a very particular place. He also connects these lives and the city's story to a transnational context. But the missing link, in Lee's assessment, is the federal, the national level. To this day, the film suggests, the federal government and federal agencies have refused to truly make room for New Orleans as a US-American city. In turn, Lee's images of the struggle to survive Katrina and rebuild the city create an absence in the space formerly occupied by the American nation.

Until recently, Lee has been discussed as an artist with almost purely national concerns. Paula Massood argues that his films are "textual systems employing quotation, allusion, and homage to explore the shared national trauma of racism and its continuing social, economic, and political affects" (MASSOOD 2008: xxiii). It comes as no surprise, then, that his film, at a first glance, should foreground the question of race and the position of New Orleans in the American nation. Lee describes his initial reaction to the first images of Katrina victims with the following words: "I had a great responsibility [...] to bear witness. Being a black man and seeing my people in that situation, I knew that the stories were going to get misconstrued" (qtd. in CALLENBACH 2006: 6). The concept of witnessing, in Lee's hands, becomes not so much a gesture toward an objective narrative of historical facts, but rather an act of letting the victims speak through the filmmaker and his film. Lee employs witnessing in the sense described by ethnographer Allen Feldman as a strategy of writing trauma, where the witness allows his or her perception to be "reinhabited, expanded, and intermingled" (FELDMAN 1995: 248) with that of the survivors, the missing, and the dead. Consequently, one of Lee's main concerns became opposing both the racism and the pretensions of objectivity which he saw tainting the official version of the events. In contrast to images of black helpless bodies or black criminal looters, both of which were usually presented in the news from a helicopter perspective with an omniscient voice-over, Lee lets the interviewed residents speak for themselves and, as Thomas Doherty has observed, avoids using a "'voice of God' narrator" (DOHERTY 2006: 998). *When the Levees Broke* reconstructs both the events and the city through the voices of its residents, and the film becomes a communal testimony even on a grammatical level: Lee sometimes places cuts in mid-sentence and adds other speaker's phrases so that the various speakers seem to complete each other's utterances.

He thus constructs a joint narrative that works from the bottom up, seemingly "stitched together by the witnesses and commentators" (LEE 2006).

Lee's narrative structure resonates with his overall message: Katrina was not a natural, but a political disaster. Lee emphasizes that local residents are both the victims and the heroes of the catastrophe. It is their rescue efforts that the film foregrounds. In one sequence, eyewitnesses report that federal help came much too late and did not reach large numbers of people, particularly in poor and black neighborhoods. Instead, residents helped each other. Lee shows us footage of people floating on makeshift rafts, paddling with broomsticks, using canoes to rescue neighbors, and carrying children on their shoulders through water that reaches up to their chins. Several eyewitnesses report how they saved loved ones and helped them to get to areas that were not flooded (*Levees* DVD1 00:47:17). Both the spoken words and the images of children and elderly people floating in plastic containers and opened refrigerators emphasize the localized and spontaneous nature of the rescue efforts. The words of three local residents are followed by the words of former New Orleans mayor Marc Morial, who insists that he will never forget the images of suffering among people he loved (*Levees* DVD1 00:48:30). Chief of police Eddie Compass observes that local police helped as quickly as they could, using private boats in order to begin rescue work immediately (*Levees* DVD1 00:49:00). Again, the quality of the rescue mission appears improvised but efficient, semi-private and rooted in local communities and relationships. In the following film sequence, historian Douglas Brinkley points out that these rescue efforts were conducted by citizens of New Orleans and adds that people called them the "Cajun navy" (*Levees* DVD1 00:49:30). In this context, the concept of citizenship explicitly describes not national citizenship, but refers to the older meaning of the term as "inhabitant of a city". The Cajun navy, a makeshift local structure of mutual help, is what sustains New Orleans residents while the rest of the nation is slow to respond. As we move outward and upward from this local involvement, Lee's presentation becomes more and more critical. As Thomas Doherty observes in his review of *When the Levees Broke*, "the apportionment of blame among the three culprits – federal, state, and municipal – will find the buck stopping, in the age of custodial federalism and mass media connectivity, at the desk in Washington, D.C." (DOHERTY 2006: 999). In an interview with Kaleem Aftab, Lee himself states: "What we saw was a complete breakdown on a federal, state, and local level, but I put most of the blame on federal government" (qtd. in the interview with Kaleem Aftab 2007).

Critics have generally agreed on the message implied by such an assignment of blame. Working with theories of displacement, Katrina M. Powell has argued that "Lee's political motivation is to highlight the incompetence of the US government in helping before, during, and after the hurricane. The people interviewed in the film counter narratives told about them, while also constructing a sense of nationhood and of belonging to the city" (POWELL 2012: 303). Powell claims that the people interviewed by Lee "refuse [...] to be counted as outside the space of the United States" (POWELL 2012: 304). For Powell, there is a strong connection between the speakers' self-identification as citizens of New Orleans and as citizens of the United States.

If Lee's speakers are seen as constructing a counter-narrative which serves to (re)insert them into American nationhood, critics have likewise attributed such an agenda to Lee himself and to his use of filmic techniques. Robert Levine has maintained that Lee's camera "forces us to look as closely as possible, often from street and house level, at the day-by-day unfolding of the catastrophe in relation to what could be termed nation-time" (LEVINE 2009: 178). Levine concludes that Lee's film ends up "for the most part ignoring larger planetary and hemispheric contexts, in order to show that national policies based on racial and class hierarchies were ultimately to blame for the suffering that he so powerfully records" (LEVINE 2009: 178). In her analysis of Lee's use of silence and sound, Joyce Irene Middleton observes that "the film encourages rhetorical listening, enabling identification, persuasion, and cross-cultural codes of invention" (MIDDETON 2011: 173) In this way, it works against an "argument culture" to "find a common ground in our public sphere" (MIDDETON 2011: 177–178). Middleton thus likewise links Lee's film with the effort to affirm the American citizenship of New Orleans residents on both literal and symbolic levels: "Spike Lee's jazz film on the levees in New Orleans, a trope for American democracy, shows how acts of listening and silence offer the promise to move us beyond the 'win-rhetoric' of the adversarial, argument culture that limits what rhetoric can be. But, as always, for American citizens to truly achieve this promise, we have to collectively choose it" (MIDDETON 2011: 178). In this reading, the film itself offers us the techniques we could employ to place New Orleans unequivocally within the frame of US-American nationhood.

In contrast to this widespread critical agreement, Anna Hartnell has taken a different stance. In her reading of Lee's treatment of race, she argues that the film gets caught in the traps of double consciousness and ultimately, despite its speakers' efforts, fails to connect the terms "black" and "American" in a potentially liberating or sustaining way. Hartnell acknowledges that the film attempts to counteract the designation of Katrina survivors as refugees by emphasizing African American citizenship and that Lee's speakers often work to contrast the image of African American looters with their own assertions of African Americans as respectable taxpayers and homeowners. But Hartnell remains critical of this gesture, arguing that while such strategies help to insist on African American citizenship rights, they also buy into a discourse of property rights and a work ethic that resonates with ideologies of American nationalism and exceptionalism. She observes:

> [B]y tying the rhetoric of national abandonment to a parallel discourse which privileges traditional individualist notions of American citizenry, we remain within the terms established by the self-reinforcing dualism that has plagued black politics; suspended between the poles of "separation" and "inclusion," this discussion fails to transform the meaning of "America" itself. (HARTNELL 2012: 25)

Hartnell argues that instead of pursuing this non-transformative notion of citizenship, Lee's film eventually "shifts the terrains of American identity to somewhere between the local and the global, and in so doing [...] stretches the limits of national identity to a breaking point" (HARTNELL 2012: 22). In this reading, the film

> gestures to a willingness to explore the possibility of a black American narrative of dispossession, a narrative that points to identifications that reach beyond the national frame and suggests that Lee's intensely "local" depiction of the New Orleans landscape remains intimately linked to the wider global picture. This conjunction of the global and the local

> transcends the oppositions defined by inclusion and separation, insider and outsider, and in so doing questions the very basis of national identity. (HARTNELL 2012: 29)

Hartnell focuses on the way in which Lee's film connects the population of New Orleans with other populations across the globe who are facing US-intervention or occupation. In addition, she claims that the sections in Lee's film on climate change and oil rights further serve to bring into relation poor and dispossessed populations across the world. Such an identification, in Hartnell's reading, is no longer based firmly on the empowering notion of US-American citizenship. Rather, she argues that while Lee's film does articulate claims of African American citizenship rights and an inclusive American national identity, it nevertheless also moves towards highlighting an alternative, global vision:

> *Levees* […] does not rule out the possibility of "a more perfect union," but many currents in the film suggest that this would be a union open to transformation by a world beyond its borders. As *Levees* suggests, New Orleans harbors a complex global legacy that makes it at once unique within America and quintessentially American. African American culture has, of course, long carried the burden of this duality. (HARTNELL 2012: 30)

Hartnell's analysis is crucial for my own project of analyzing more closely the outline of Lee's conceptions of the nation-state. Although Lee does include what one speaker in the film explicitly calls "civil rights moments" in his narrative, the nation nevertheless remains an absence in his depiction of efforts of rescue and rebuilding. Lee's narrative of the Cajun navy poignantly shows how local-level organizing connects with global efforts while federal agencies are consistently denying victims their citizenship rights. In a sequence related to the examples of local rescue, Lee's informants observe that the Canadian Mounties were the first to get to the scene and help the rescue efforts, followed by an offer of assistance from the president of Venezuela. In this very connection of local and global which circumvents the space of the nation, Lee conforms to Dimock's model for a "nonsovereign history of Katrina". This becomes apparent both on a political and an aesthetic level.

Lee's positive presentation of African American political action and local help corresponds to the observations made by Rachel Luft, who has analyzed New Orleans grassroots social justice organizers' political response to Katrina. According to Luft, the "second generation of Katrina social movements" tends to understand disaster as a social construct, a crisis which always hits those hardest who have the highest degree of social vulnerability (LUFT 2009: 500; WEIK VON MOSSNER 2011: 148; 150). As a consequence, many local organizers both provided relief *and* organized resistance to entrenched social hierarchies. Significantly, the organizations which Luft examined use a human rights approach as opposed to a civil rights approach. Instead of appealing to the United States as American citizens, they appeal to international institutions or global networks. As Luft observes, these organizations draw from three specific human rights traditions: transnational theories of the Black Liberation Movement, United Nations principles and declarations, such as the UN Guiding Principles for Internal Displacement, and nongovernmental organizations (LUFT 2009: 500). Although particularly African Americans have a long tradition of claiming civil rights on a national level, there were always parallel, if less popular, traditions striving to create a broader, transnational context for the African American struggle in the United States. In Luft's words, "[a]lthough Black Liberationists and Critical Legal Studies scholars have long questioned the effectiveness of civil rights law for achieving racial justice, movement leaders believed that, finally, after Katrina, the human rights perspective might be more widely attractive to racial justice seekers" (LUFT 2009: 518). Luft sums up: "The post-Katrina human rights orientation was thus a tactic of long-term domestic and global movement building, consistent with the recent turn to human rights by a variety of disenfranchised domestic groups" (LUFT 2009: 518). In this cooperation of local and global, the national level appears as a blank, the site of a failure (see HARTNELL 2012: 24; 28).

This constellation becomes equally obvious in Lee's aesthetic choices. The film's subtitle, "A Requiem in Four Acts", invokes European musical traditions. But from the start, these traditions are blended with non-European music. The film's very first moments present us a musical score of drumming reminiscent of West African musical patterns. The blending of African-derived drumming and European-derived forms of mourning culminates in Lee's frequent use of blues and jazz. In the film's final act, the requiem literally becomes a New Orleans jazz funeral. Here, local coping strategies are set within the context of their larger Atlantic cultural histories.

Lee draws on jazz music's themes and techniques in various ways: through his emphasis on improvisation (the main strategy of the "Cajun navy"), in the emulation of the creative and communal musical structures and performance of jazz musicians (used by Lee in his filmic intertwining of the statements of local residents), and through techniques of refiguration. In his study about the creation of jazz canons, Matthew Alan Thomas observes that Lee's overall technique "emphasizes the participatory and performative modes" (THOMAS 2011: 86). This already becomes clear in the film's opening sequence. Before the action of the film begins, Lee presents us with a montage of images accompanied by Louis Armstrong's performance of the song "Do You Know What It Means to Miss New Orleans". This sequence combines historical footage of New Orleans (storm surges, flooding, busy streets, the Mardi Gras) with images of the aftermath of Katrina. The intercutting of older with more recent images creates historical depth and simultaneously reminds us of the fact that storms and flooding are not new to the area and hence should not take governments by surprise. As Thomas observes, "[t]he scene seeks to create empathy with the contemporary residents of the city by acknowledging that their tribulations have deep historical roots" (THOMAS 2011: 87). Moreover, by presenting these images in a specific manner, Lee lays open the aesthetic and political choices of his narrative technique.

Thomas points out that the opening scene "activates a musical as well as a cinematic code, achieving an ironic balance between the nostalgic tone of the lyrics, images of vibrant Mardi Gras celebrations, and disturbing shots of the devastated city" (THOMAS 2011: 87). The cuts of the sequence are placed to correspond to the rhythm of Armstrong's music, creating a visual score which accompanies the musical one (see CALLENBACH 2006: 6). As Henry Louis Gates has pointed out, such refiguration as a gesture of extension and play is a standard technique in African American jazz. Gates has observed that jazz musicians who take up well-known songs to play them with a twist often engage in what he calls "Signifyin(g)", a refiguration that comments on the original version. Gates writes: "Because the form is self-evident to the musician, both he and his well-trained audience are playing and listening with expectation. Signifyin(g) disappoints these expectations [...]. This form of disappointment creates a dialogue between what the listener expects and what the artist plays" (GATES 1988: 123). Lee creates exactly such a "disappointment" between the music, the lyrics, and the images which grate against them. The musical lightness of the song's beginning is immediately undercut by images of destruction and debris. As the singer evokes his strong feelings, we see images of the damaging storm surge. As he sings that he longs to see the blazing Mississippi, we see historical images of the flooding of the city. As the singer wishes he were there, we see a dilapidated street sign of the Lower Ninth Ward. An image of a flooded street sign with the inscription "Humanity" enforces this irony, as do images of racial segregation and police brutality, footage which is shown at the very moment that the musicians are playing with the most freedom. In the end, Armstrong's music provides the soundtrack for images of a New Orleans jazz funeral, a performance both of mourning and of hope.

The relationship between the footage and the music is complicated even more by the use of layers of sound. While we hear the music, we can also discern the sounds of the images we are shown: we hear the screeching of the streetcar as it pulls up, the rotating helicopter blades as two children are evacuated by air, the thump of a falling man tackled by police officers. These layers of sound not only create yet another dialogue between images and music, but also suggest that the music we hear has a specific history and must be understood in the context of the local sounds of New Orleans. Thomas argues that Lee's technique creates "appreciation and support of a localized African American culture in New Orleans" (THOMAS 2011: 87).

Citing in order to question, trouble, and expand on the borrowed themes, Lee works the music with and against the footage in a specifically African American cultural tradition. Within these aesthetic structures, Lee interviews and features black and white informants alike. In a reversal of the civil rights concern for integrating African Americans within mainstream national structures, Lee blends white voices into African American traditions, traditions which in themselves are suggested to be the result of cultural contact and struggle in the Atlantic world. Lee's New Orleans has never quite been integrated into federal structures, nor have its residents quite received their national citizenship rights. But the film gives little hope that a civil rights agenda can solve this problem and instead employs African American politics and aesthetics to resituate the city within a transnational orientation that connects grassroots with global concerns. What is more, Lee's critique of the nation extends further than pointing to the nation as an absence or a site of exclusion. As I will show in the remainder of this essay, Lee's rendering of the nation also reverberates with theories of biopolitics and governmentality which view the contemporary US-American nation as an aggressive and damaging structure that proves to be particularly threatening for its poor and African American communities.

More Than an Absence: The Nation as Threat

In her essay on Lee's documentary, Anna Hartnell points out that "in spite of many currents in *Levees* that contest black America's positioning as somehow 'outside' the boundaries of the United States, Lee's film nonetheless shows impoverished African Americans as objects of U.S. state power" (HARTNELL 2012: 30). I take this observation as my cue to trace, in Lee's film, an even more damaging role of the nation than conveyed in the withholding of aid and support. I will follow up on this 'other' depiction of the nation via Lee's narrative of oil, which pits the state of Louisiana against the federal government. Given Louisiana's history as a slave state and the fact that slavery was abolished through federal intervention, Lee's situating of the state in this complex constellation of local and global is yet another reversal of traditional civil rights approaches.

It is in his depiction of Louisiana's oil reserves and the environmental and financial effects of oil drilling off the Louisiana coast that Lee's image of the actively damaging potential of the nation becomes clearest. One of the reasons why hurricanes have increased their impact on New Orleans is the erosion of the wetlands which separate the city from the coast and which historically have born the brunt of hurricanes after their landfall. The erosion of these wetlands is mainly caused by the levee and canal system, built in part to facilitate oil drilling and comply with the oil industry's infrastructural needs. In addition, the drilling itself has resulted in immense environmental damages. Louisiana ranks among the top of the nation's oil and gas producing states. Most royalties from the lease agreements with the oil and gas industry, however, go to the federal government, not to the state.

Until 1937, Louisiana and the other Gulf states had uncontested and sole jurisdiction over their coastal waters (MILLER 1997: 205). In a series of Supreme Court cases, the federal government challenged the states' rights to control and profit from these areas. This was at first legitimized by pointing to national security concerns and claiming that coastal waters should be under federal control. In addition, the government (most recently under George W. Bush) emphasized that national security also depended on ensuring federal control over the nation's oil and gas resources. As Gregory Blaine Miller explains, the final outcome of these disputes is that "[w]aters adjacent to the United States coastline are now divided into state and federal jurisdictional zones", with Louisiana controlling the inner portion and the federal government controlling the outer boundaries (MILLER 1997: 204).

In their work on the tidelands controversies, both Gregory Blaine Miller and Patrick Sanders point out that the crucial question, of course, was who would profit from the oil revenues. After the Supreme Court had decided in 1950 that "the marginal sea is a national, not a state concern" (qtd. in MILLER 1997: 208) and denied Louisiana's claims to the territory beyond the low water mark, the Submerged Lands Act of 1953 softened the blow for the Gulf states by declaring that states had control over the territory within three nautical miles from their coastline. The federal government retained control over the submerged lands beyond this line (MILLER 1997: 209). The Gulf states could try to prove that they had a historical right to more of the submerged lands. Texas, for example, succeeded with this claim. But a Supreme Court ruling of 1960 denied Louisiana's claim to such extended boundaries. Louisiana did prove that when the state was admitted to the Union in 1812, Congress had set Louisiana's boundaries to include all islands within not just three nautical miles, but three marine leagues (9 nautical miles) off the coast. But the court agreed with the federal government, which argued that this only meant Louisiana controlled these islands, but not the waters, within this larger zone (see SANDERS 2008: 263; MILLER 1997: 213). Sanders remarks that for Louisiana, the result of the ruling "was financially devastating, considering the vast oil and gas reserves that were contained between the three mile mark and the three league mark" (SANDERS 2008: 263). In addition, the state has to bear the burden of the environmental damage incurred by oil drilling just beyond its control.

These battles resurfaced after Katrina when the federal government wanted to grant an extensive new lease sale in the Gulf of Mexico only weeks after the storm without considering the increased environmental damages. Sanders observes that hurricane Katrina caused a heightened awareness in local citizens and the Louisiana government of the need to protect their environment and preserve the wetlands as a buffer (SANDERS 2008: 256). Spike Lee's film describes the conflict between Louisiana and the US Department of the Interior over the new lease sale and has several local informants state that Louisiana would not depend on federal hurricane relief if the state could either control the revenues of its offshore oil reserves or control how much extraction was permitted in the first place. Earlier in the film, Lee offers us a shot of a map of the United States painted on the wall of a New Orleans playground which was flooded after the storm. Ironically, the flood on the playground seems to have reached exactly the coastal areas of the Gulf states on the painted map, a fact which is still visible in the high-water mark on the wall that bears the map. Lee's camera begins with the national map and then zooms in to show the painted coast of the state of Louisiana, which the high water on the playground has dissolved in the same way that drilling, erosion, and federal control have done in actual life (*Levees* DVD2 00:01:44–47). The image can be read as a highly symbolic rendering of the dispute over and the erosion of the state's seaward boundary. It finds its echo later in the film when David Meeks, city editor of the *Times-Picayune*, remarks that if Louisiana seceded, the state would profit immensely from its oil resources (*Levees* DVD2 01:25:02). In a reversal of the historical connotations of secession, Lee's film invokes the shock of secession, presented in a new context, to point to the disputed positioning of Louisiana in the larger United States. While Lee clearly privileges local and grassroots politics, he thus often portrays the state's political efforts in a sympathetic fashion, while consistently criticizing the federal government and federal agencies. In the debate around oil, moreover, federal institutions take an active role not only in depriving state and local residents of their resources, but also by taking for granted the federal right to endanger and exploit both the population and the landscape. Again, we find here a reversal of the traditional civil rights agenda, which sought to connect local activism with federal intervention against Southern state racism.

Katrina and the flood which hit New Orleans have, of course, inspired various alternative readings and positions among researchers, artists, and politicians, readings which complement and at times contradict the interpretation I ascribe to Lee's film. For example, while she notes the tendency among grassroots movements in New Orleans to connect to transnational networks and organizations, Luft cautions that applying international human rights claims in the context of social movements after Katrina is an unfamiliar strategy both to Americans in general and to many African Americans in particular, given the community's historical investment in the struggle for civil rights. In addition, human rights strategies in the United States are often not clearly focused and cannot easily be employed to make the United States accountable in an internationally binding legal framework (LUFT 2009: 521–522). In her interpretation of *When the Levees Broke*,

Powell likewise points to the problematic dimension of human rights discourses, arguing that "human rights laws set up an exclusionary language, making hierarchical decision-making parameters that deem the dispossessed 'worthy' of saving" (POWELL 2012: 317) or, conversely, can exclude them from such status.

Other critics have questioned the adequacy of singling out federal structures as the most damaging factors. In their work on hierarchies of race and class in the states of the Gulf Coast, Jeffrey Lowe and Todd Shaw locate neoliberal strategies of governance on the local, state, and federal levels as the main reason for the disastrous effects of Katrina. They discuss a study by Paul Frymer et al. which argues that "the very nature of the federal system, with its permissive 'state rights' doctrine, throughout U.S. history has permitted the South (with only a few exceptions, including the Reconstruction and civil rights/antipoverty reform periods) to create its own regimes of inequality" (LOWE/SHAW 2009: 807). In this analysis, federal resources allocated without clear guidelines have served to reinforce state and local-level structures of inequality. Against these structures, "citizen participation with collaborations and alliances that transcended race and class boundaries" has emerged as a "moral center" (LOWE/SHAW 2009: 822). Unlike the connection of grassroots and global networks presented in Lee's film, the authors argue for a combination of grassroots and federal action: "Led by the federal government, the necessary political economic change requires representation from below in order to empower communities" (LOWE/SHAW 2009: 822). In his study on the tidelands controversy and the struggle to control oil revenues, Sanders, on the other hand, advocates cooperation between the state of Louisiana and the federal government to save the wetlands and share oil revenues, a format he calls "cooperative federalism" (SANDERS 2008: 257).

Spike Lee's "nonsovereign history of Katrina" is not only a powerful voice in these political debates. Like Dimock's work, Lee's work also helps us to theorize both the literal and the metaphorical dimensions of the very figures which are most prominent in contemporary conceptions of thinking beyond the nation-state. Nonsovereign histories, after all, often draw on a certain representational repertoire: sound as circulation, water as flow, levees as impossible boundaries. Like Lee and Dimock, many theorists of transnational phenomena have both celebrated images of circulation and fluidity and pointed to their problematic underside. Atlantic scholar Joseph Roach has approached the city of New Orleans through performance, song, and sound in his seminal book *Cities of the Dead* (1996). One of Roach's examples for this approach is the way in which the memory and the bodies of the city's dead are either assigned their separate space or, conversely, allowed to circulate through the city. In this reading, New Orleans's cemeteries, the "Cities of the Dead", are spaces segregating the living from the dead. In contrast, the jazz funeral, in Roach's reading, takes the memory of the dead through the city, involving the community and thus marking the city space with both life and death. Roach states: "Surveying the New Orleans urbanscape, anchored on the landmarks provided by its famous Cities of the Dead, [one] thinks more readily of the city as 'text' […] than as 'speech' […]. Reading the scene as text, the eye takes in a history inscribed by rhetorics of exclusion. […] [But] [h]earing the city as speech (and song), the ear takes in a memory predicated on a rhetoric of inclusion" (ROACH 1996: 277).

At the same time, the circulation of bodies through the city observed and celebrated by Roach clashes jarringly with the post-Katrina images of the bodies of the dead floating through submerged streets, laying bare the contradictions implicit in conceptions of fluidity and flow. Placing the implicit tension of this imagery in a historical perspective, Nicholas Mirzoeff has analyzed the way in which "[a]bsolutism legislated the sea as a zone of both monarchical power and free circulation" (MIRZOEFF 2009: 289). Mirzoeff argues that the Atlantic slave trade in particular served to express this dual gesture of circulation and obstruction, creating a world in which "the spaces of the living and the dead [... were] linked and divided by the sea" (MIRZOEFF 2009: 289). The "central contradiction" of this world "was the use of 'free' oceanic trade to transport people as unfree property, or slaves" (MIRZOEFF 2009: 293). The patterns observed in this historical precedent are still singled out by scholars as formative for the analysis of the present. Henri Giroux claims that the policy of the Bush government has produced a "*new biopolitics of disposability*" (GIROUX 2006: 175) in which the social state and the sort of government which embodied the social contract have already been dismantled. What Giroux calls "negative globalization" is thus a system of circulation and consumption which ultimately proves devastating for those deemed disposable:

> The state no longer protects its own disadvantaged citizens – they are already seen as dead within a transnational economic and political framework. Specific populations now occupy a globalized space of ruthless politics in which the categories of "citizen" and "democratic representation," once integral to national politics, are no longer recognized. (GIROUX 2006: 182.)

In sum, both neoliberalism and the populations resisting it by conceptualizing nonsovereign histories are using the metaphors – and the accompanying theories – of circulation and flow. The task becomes, then, to tell the difference.

Lee's focus on the question of race resonates with such analyses, but his focus on oil seems even more pertinent in this respect. Shortly after the completion of *When the Levee Broke*, the explosion of the *Deepwater Horizon* in the Gulf of Mexico and the oil spill which circulated the oil through the waters with a truly transnational force have pushed us to rethink our analytic frames even further.[3] In a way, oil has come to signify the sinister flipside of conceptions of flow with a striking vehemence through companies like BP and Transocean, which operate internationally and signify globalization's use – or abuse – of the idea of circulation. In contrast to the practices of these companies, the report of the national oil spill commission instituted by President Obama called for stronger *national* regulation and control. Building on Spike Lee's construction of the nation, the question becomes whether highlighting national control can provide a solution. Even though the oil spill seemed to be the result of transnational practices, it was closely linked to federal institutions. The Deepwater Horizon oil rig, although registered as an ocean vessel with the Marshall Islands, was tapping the Macondo oil fields located in US sovereign waters – national, not state waters. The US Minerals Management Service managed the lease and was responsible for enforcing adequate controls. It is thus a national agency which accepted lax security standards in return for national revenues. Posited between the local and the global as an almost invisible agent, the nation-state, far from disappearing, is undergoing a radical shift which we are currently struggling to

[3] Lee himself returned to New Orleans to create a sequel, *If God Is Willing and da Creek Don't Rise* (2010).

assess adequately. In Lee's analysis of Louisiana's struggle over oil, the nation appears not only as an absence, but as an active, damaging presence.

Following Michel Foucault, Judith Butler has argued that forms of national sovereignty based on legitimacy, accountability, and the division of powers are currently being eroded by a governmentality that "operates through policies and departments, through managerial and bureaucratic institutions, through law, when the law is understood as 'a set of tactics,' and through forms of state power, although not exclusively" (BUTLER 2004: 52). Butler's observation is that older forms of sovereignty are currently resurfacing within the structures of governmentality and must be analyzed closely. Thus, merely advocating a return to the structures of the nation-state characterized by legitimacy, accountability, and the division of powers may no longer be a realistic option – and Lee's film, for one, suggests that such a return would be a return to civil rights, a move perhaps no longer adequate for the situation of New Orleans. The absence of the nation in Lee's construction of survival and activism could be read as pointing to the failure of the nation-state characterized by modern principles of sovereignty; Lee's depiction of federal intervention in the debate about Louisiana's oil could be interpreted as tracing the almost invisible, and potentially damaging, workings of the contemporary nation-state characterized by principles of governmentality. In addition, the film's approach to figures of circulation and flow cautions us that theories which reject a return to the nation-state and advocate new, nonsovereign approaches to history, concentrating on fluid processes of border-crossing, must remain alert to the way in which older forms of national sovereignty are re-positioning themselves precisely by making use of globalization and flow.

The solutions suggested by Lee's work, by the work of many New Orleans grassroots organizations, and in the work of scholars like Dimock and Butler point to the necessity of linking local specificity and global connections. In his reading of hurricane Katrina, Giroux argues that "negative globalization" can only be countered by "new forms of resistance that are both more global and differentiated" (GIROUX 2006: 189). *When the Levees Broke* begins to interrogate how exactly this link can be forged. Robert Levine has pointed out that "[t]he local, national, hemispheric, and global-planetary have all come into play in the very best work on Katrina, which has helped to reinvigorate the field of American studies by pushing critics to think anew about geographical and temporal frames [...]" (LEVINE 2009: 178). It is here that Lee's film can inspire us to find ways of rethinking both New Orleans and US-American nationhood.

List of Works Cited

BAILEY, RICHARD W. (2003): The Foundation of English in the Louisiana Purchase. New Orleans, 1800–1850. *American Speech* 78.4: 363–384.

BOELHOWER, WILLIAM (2008): New Orleans in the Atlantic World, I. *Atlantic Studies* 5.2: 151–159.

BUTLER, JUDITH (2004): *Precarious Life. The Powers of Mourning and Violence*. London: Verso.

CALLENBACH, ERNEST (2006): When the Levees Broke. A Requiem in Four Acts. *Film Quarterly* 60.2: 4–10.

DIMOCK, WAI CHEE (2009): World History According to Katrina. In RUSS CASTRONOVO and SUSAN GILLMAN (Eds.): *States of Emergency. The Object of American Studies*. Chapel Hill: The University of North Carolina Press, 143–160.

DOHERTY, THOMAS (2006): Review of *When the Levees Broke: A Requiem in Four Acts* by Spike Lee. *The Journal of American History* 93.3: 997–999.

ECKSTEIN, BARBARA (2005): *Sustaining New Orleans: Literature, Local Memory, and the Fate of a City*. New York: Routledge.

FELDMAN, ALLEN (1995): Epilogue. Ethnographic States of Emergency. In CAROLYN NORDSTROM and ANTONIUS C. G. M. ROBBEN (Eds.): *Fieldwork Under Fire. Contemporary Studies of Violence and Survival*. Berkeley/Los Angeles/London: University of California Press, 224–252.

GATES, HENRY LOUIS (1988): *The Signifying Monkey. A Theory of Afro-American Literary Criticism*. New York: Oxford University Press.

GIROUX, HENRY A. (2006): Reading Hurricane Katrina. Race, Class, and the Biopolitics of Disposability. *College Literature* 33.3: 171–196.

HARTNELL, ANNA (2012): When the Levees Broke. Inconvenient Truths and the Limits of National Identity. *African American Review* 45.1–2: 17–31.

LEE, FELICIA R. (2006): Agony of New Orleans, Through Spike Lee's Eyes. *The New York Times*, 3 August. *http://www.nytimes.com/2006/08/03/arts/television/03leve.html?pagewanted=all.*

LEVINE, ROBERT S. (2009): American Studies in an Age of Extinction. In RUSS CASTRONOVO and SUSAN GILLMAN (Eds.): *States of Emergency. The Object of American Studies*. Chapel Hill: The University of North Carolina Press, 161–182.

LOWE, JEFFREY S., and TODD C. SHAW (2009): After Katrina. Racial Regimes and Human Development Barriers in the Gulf Coast Region. *American Quarterly* 61.3: 803–827.

LUFT, RACHEL E. (2009): Beyond Disaster Exceptionalism: Social Movement Developments in New Orleans after Hurricane Katrina. *American Quarterly* 61.3: 499–527.

MASSOOD, PAULA J. (2008): Introduction. We've Gotta Have It – Spike Lee, African American Film, and Cinema Studies. In PAULA J. MASSOOD (Ed.): *The Spike Lee Reader*. Philadelphia: Temple University Press, xv–xxviii.

MIDDLETON, JOYCE IRENE (2011): Finding Democracy in Our Argument Culture. Listening to Spike Lee's Jazz Funeral on the Levees. In CHERYL GLENN and KRISTA RATCLIFFE (Eds.): *Silence and Listening as Rhetorical Arts*. Carbondale: Southern Illinois University Press, 163–179.

MILLER, GREGORY BLAINE (1997): Louisiana's Tidelands Controversy. *The United States of America v. State of Louisiana* Maritime Boundary Cases. *Louisiana History: The Journal of the Louisiana Historical Association* 38.2: 203–221.

MIRZOEFF, NICHOLAS (2009): The Sea and the Land. Biopower and Visuality from Slavery to Katrina. *Culture, Theory and Critique* 50.2: 289–305.

O'GRADY, DAVID (2008): Low and Behold. Using Fiction/Documentary Hybridity to See the Real Damage of Hurricane Katrina. *Mediascape*, *http://www.tft.ucla.edu/mediascape/Fall08_Ogrady.html*.

POWELL, KATRINA M. (2012): Rhetorics of Displacement. Constructing Identities in Forced Relocations. *College English* 74.4: 299–324.

ROACH, JOSEPH (1996): *Cities of the Dead. Circum-Atlantic Performance*. New York: Columbia University Press.

SANDERS, PATRICK (2008): *Blanco v. Burton*. Louisiana's Struggle for Cooperative Federalism in Offshore Energy Development. *Louisiana Law Review* 69: 255–279.

SIMMONS, LAKISHA MICHELLE (2009): 'Justice Mocked.' Violence and Accountability in New Orleans. *American Quarterly* 61.3: 477–498.

TAYLOR, HELEN (2012): After the Deluge. The Post-Katrina Cultural Revival of New Orleans. *Journal of American Studies* 44.3: 483–501.

THOMAS, MATTHEW ALAN (2011): *Dynamic Canons. How the Pulitzer Prize, Documentary Film, and the U.S. Department of State Are Changing the Way We Think about Jazz.* Dissertation, University of Southern California (Historical Musicology). *http://digitallibrary.usc.edu/cdm/ref/collection/p15799coll127/id/613799* .

THOMPSON, MARK (2008): Locating the Isle of Orleans. Atlantic and American Historiographical Perspectives. *Atlantic Studies* 5.3: 305–333.

WEIK VON MOSSNER, ALEXA (2011): Reframing Katrina. The Color of Disaster in Spike Lee's *When the Levees Broke*. *Environmental Communication* 5.2: 146–165.

WOODS, CLYDE (2009): Introduction: Katrina's World. Blues, Bourbon, and the Return to the Source. *American Quarterly* 61.3: 427–453.

Interview, Film

AFTAB, KALEEM (2007): Interview with Spike Lee. "America's Greatest Disaster". *Sight & Sound* 17.1: 45.

When the Levees Broke: A Requiem in Four Acts. Dir. Spike Lee. HBO Documentary Films, 2006.

A Kaleidoscope of Color or the Agony of Race? Barack Obama's *Dreams from My Father*

Mita Banerjee

Barack Obama's autobiography *Dreams from My Father* reveals, like few other texts, a deep, nuanced and profound awareness of the multiplicity of differences and the interrelatedness of various differences and their context-specificity. What emerges in *Dreams from My Father* is an encyclopedia of difference, a kaleidoscope of differences, none of which can be subsumed by another. In this paper, I would like to read Barack Obama's autobiography *Dreams from My Father* as what I would call a kaleidoscope of difference. Like the colors in a kaleidoscope, each of these differences – race, class, religion, gender, degrees of enfranchisement – blends into another; with each twist in the kaleidoscope, each difference finds itself in the vicinity of another, to which it may previously have seemed unrelated.

The aim of this paper is to argue that it was owing to this kaleidoscopic vision that Obama succeeded in becoming the first black president of the United States, and that his presidency, tragically, turned out to prove United States society's reluctance to view difference as kaleidoscopic. The tragedy of Obama's presidency, especially in his second term in office, was the reluctance of United States social reality to conform to the vision of the kaleidoscope; it was a calamity, tout court, which revolved around the *untranslatability* of difference. In this failure, then, each difference claimed to be absolute, and claimed to be completely independent of, or even superior to, other differences. What had previously seemed or promised to be a kaleidoscope reverted to the stark differences of black and white.

My argument in this paper is structured as follows. First, I suggest that Obama's autobiography *Dreams from My Father* can be read as a kaleidoscopic or encyclopedic vision of the relativity and relationality of difference. Second, I suggest that this vision leads to an 'agony of race' since social reality is pervaded by the antagonism between racial groups, dismissing relationality. Third, I argue that Obama's vision is born out of a shift from an autobiographer's perception to that of a biographer: As a historian of the lives of others, he explores difference through the eyes of others, and is hence forced or enabled to see each person's difference as related to the difference of others. Difference hence becomes not an absolute, but a relative concept. This, of course, may be a contradiction in terms since difference always has to be assessed in relation to another concept; yet, what this means in the context of United States racial history, I would argue, is that each community may tend to elevate its difference over the difference of another community, thus fueling an antagonism of race.

"Amazing Grace" and the "Space Outside the Sentence"

When I started writing this paper in October 2016, little did I know that many of its passages would seem obsolete a mere month later. With Donald Trump as a president elect, Obama's kaleidoscopic vision seems more utopian than ever, but it may also be more important than ever before. At the turn of a new year, 2017, Obama's kaleidoscopic vision has been termed, by the followers of what has been termed a 'whitelash' phenomenon, as what is now said to be the "farce" of political correctness. One of the aspects which this paper sets out to explore against the background of Obama's last days in office and the impending specter of Trump's ascendance to United States presidency, then, are two scenarios with which to convey United States race relations; two scenarios which are mutually exclusive: the color kaleidoscope of a black man whose "color", race, and ethnicity could not ultimately be contained, or the black-and-white vision of a country, half of whose population claims to have been "left behind" by a color kaleidoscope it was at a loss to comprehend (WILSON 2016).

It is in this setting that I would like to return to Obama's eulogy to Reverend Clementa Pinckney. It was in this context, the context of a country reverting to the stark contrasts of black and white, in which Obama was called upon by the African American community to show his colors following the death of Reverend Pinckney, who on 17 June 2015 was shot by a young white man whose aim was nothing short of inciting a race war. As an article in the New York Times states, "Mr. Obama joined with others paying tribute in stressing that the twenty-one-year old white man charged in the killings had failed to achieve his stated goal of inciting racial conflagration" (SACK/HARRIS 2015).

In the eyes of many who watched and witnessed Obama's eulogy to Reverend Pinckney, this was a historical moment. Some argued for Obama to take a stand *not* as a multiethnic, mixed-race president who could be claimed by any community of color, from black to Asian, but as a black man in a country whose race difference could not be contained in the prefabricated categories of United States race relations:

> In one of his presidency's most impassioned reflections on race, President Obama eulogized the Rev. Clementa C. Pinckney on Friday by calling on the nation to emulate the grace that he displayed in his work and that the people of South Carolina demonstrated after the massacre of nine worshipers at Emanuel African Methodist Episcopal Church.
> Before nearly 6,000 mourners and a worldwide television audience, Mr. Obama, who met Mr. Pinckney during his first presidential campaign, placed the shootings in the context of America's long history of violence against African-Americans. (SACK/HARRIS 2015)

It is no coincidence, then, that this was indeed "one of [the] most impassioned reflections on race" (SACK/HARRIS 2015) in Obama's presidency. It was in this context, also, that Obama referred to the nation's impassioned debate over the role of the Confederate flag not only in national self-representation, but also in its collective identity. It is with reference to the Confederate flag that, in light of the presidential election that was to be held in 2016, Obama's words seem dismally prophetic. As he put it in his eulogy,

> "[r]emoving the flag from this state's Capitol would not be an act of political correctness", Mr. Obama said. "It would not be an insult to the valor of Confederate soldiers. It would simply be an acknowledgment that the cause for which they fought – the cause of slavery – was wrong. The imposition of Jim Crow after the Civil War, the resistance to civil rights for all people, was wrong." (SACK/HARRIS 2015)

Pace Trump, then, political correctness emerges here not as a form of discourse terrorism but as an acknowledgment of the violence which can be done by both symbols and speech acts. In her study *Excitable Speech*, Judith Butler writes, "When we claim to have been injured by language, what kind of claim do we make? We ascribe an agency to language, a power to injure, and position ourselves as the objects of its injurious trajectory. We claim that language acts, and acts against us [...]" (BUTLER 1997: 1)

At Reverend Pinckney's funeral, then, it seemed that a suspension of identity politics, the refusal to claim allegiance to one particular ethnic community in the United States, no longer seemed possible. And yet, I would argue here that Obama was able to take a stand as an African American president and as a president who was wary of subscribing to the idea that any identity, racial or otherwise, could ever be fixed. It was in this context where the suspension of the closure of identity politics no longer seemed possible, I would argue, that Obama pledged allegiance in the open-ended manner so significant for his politics both real and literary: At Reverend Pinckney's funeral, Obama burst into song, singing "Amazing Grace" in front of an audience he had taken by complete surprise. Obama's grief over both the Reverend's murder and the racial hatred and bigotry which it symbolized, I argue, could no longer be put into words, but could only be expressed through music or what postcolonial theorist Homi Bhabha has called "the space outside the sentence" (BHABHA 1994: 257). It was a grief which not only encompassed the mourning for the senseless death of Reverend Pinckney, but also for Obama's own faith in a nation which had disproved his belief that it could be multiethnic and multi-differential. As a newspaper report puts it,

> [g]egen Ende seiner Rede stimmt Barack Obama „Amazing Grace“ an, das Volkslied über die „erstaunliche Gnade“ Gottes in schweren Zeiten, das schon den Sklaven in den USA Kraft und Hoffnung gab. Erst zögerlich, dann begleitet von Tausenden Stimmen in der Halle in Charleston singt der erste schwarze US-Präsident die Zeilen, die übersetzt so lauten: „Ich war einst verloren, aber nun bin ich gefunden, war blind, aber nun sehe ich.“ Es ist gut eine Woche nach dem Massaker an neun Afroamerikanern in einer Kirche der Höhepunkt seiner Traueransprache, die mehr wie eine Predigt wirkt. Wie ein Pastor, der sein Land wachrütteln will, zählt er die Lehren der grausamen Bluttat auf, die nun gezogen werden müssen. (SCHMITT-TEGGE/MIERKE 2015)

In his speech, Obama falters on the verge of breaking into song, as if undecided with himself about how to express his grief: His grief over a nation which failed to live up to his hope that the violence which has often been contained in United States race relations could be contained. Surrounded by Methodist clergy at the Emanuel African Methodist Episcopal Church in Charleston, Obama at first only references the song:

> Obama: Amazing Grace! [pauses] Amazing Grace! [hesitates] [starts singing] Amazing Grace, how sweet the sound... [the clergymen and -women surrounding him raise their heads in surprise, then, smile, rising to their feet].

In the paragraphs that follow, I would like to read the vision of the color kaleidoscope, which at the present moment seems more utopian than ever, not only back into the politics of Barack Obama the President, but also of Barack Obama the author and autobiographer. The open-endedness of Obama's singing "Amazing Grace", a spiritual born of African

Americans' fight against slavery and the racial violence which it signified, also marks Obama's autobiography, *Dreams from My Father*, published in 1995, fourteen years before he would be elected president of the United States, the first black president in the history of the nation. The kaleidoscopic vision of race, I will argue in the following passages, can be read on both a national and a transnational level. According to Alfred Hornung,

> Barack Obama's biography encapsulates the principal features of a Transnational American Studies approach. His biracial descent from a white American mother from Kansas and an African father from Kenya, his formative years in the multiethnic environment of the state of Hawai'i, the school experience in the Muslim Indonesian capital of Djakarta, the education in Los Angeles and at Columbia University in New York, and the conscious decision to undertake social work for the African American community in South Side Chicago before entering Harvard Law School represent an academic background and an intercultural network which have prepared him for an unusual political career. (HORNUNG 2016: ix–x)

At the present historical moment, this transnational vision seems more important than ever because it is proof that identity politics can coexist with the awareness that any closure ascribed to social identities can only be imaginary and strategic; and that political correctness, at its best, is a movement which explains to majority communities the violence done to minorities by words and symbols which reference material histories of both violence and oppression. It is hence no wonder that Obama should implicitly have addressed the opponents of political correctness at Reverend Pinckney's funeral: By eliciting empathy for the man killed by racialist violence and for the family he left behind, Obama drove home the message that the Confederate flag, to the victims of the white supremacist logic that the flag symbolized, was much more than a flag.

Obama's vision of race is as prophetic as it is necessary, then, in the idea that he refuses to see any difference as absolute. Rather, each difference is both context-specific and related to other differences. Even as identity politics may be necessary in calling attention to histories of subjugation and oppression, then, this is an identity politics which refuses to capitalize the initial letter of its first word. Obama's is an "identity" politics which refuses to capitalize, both literally and figuratively, the position that it revolves around. As Obama puts it in his foreword to the 2004 edition of *Dreams from My Father*, recalling his initial incentive to write an autobiography,

> I [...] went to work with the belief that the story of my family, and my efforts to understand that story, might speak in some way to the fissures of race that have characterized the American experience, as well as the fluid state of identity – the leaps through time, the collision of cultures – that mark our modern life. (OBAMA [1995] 2007, vii)

This passage is remarkable for a number of reasons. First, because, in assuming the autobiographical mode, Obama inserts himself into an autobiographical tradition which harks back to the work of Benjamin Franklin. In the sense of Franklin's autobiography, the author's life is said to be characteristic of and potentially a model for, the life of the nation (MADSEN 1998). Secondly and even more importantly for my purposes here, Obama positions himself, in this passage, less as a black man than as a man whose identity – both racial and otherwise – can only be seen as "fluid". The nation's multi-ethnic character, by the same token, is implied in this passage to be curiously ungraspable; it is a chimera of identity, the illusion of identity perhaps, which nonetheless has material repercussions on the politics of the nation itself. It is this fluidity which, I have argued above, also marked Obama's song – and the stance of bursting into song – at Reverend Pinckney's funeral. In writing his own life, then, Obama at once sets out to write the life of the nation; yet, he does so less by positioning himself as a role model (in the tradition of Benjamin Franklin), but as someone who sets out to comprehend the race dynamics of the nation by using himself as a 'guinea-pig'. Indeed, Obama's presidential campaign would center on the self-irony of a man describing himself in terms of racial 'mongrelization'. As Alan Fram has noted, Obama's reference to himself as a "mutt" marked not only his investigation of his own racial heritage, but in the curious "off-handedness" of Obama's tone also signaled his insistence that "race" was an issue which had to be addressed, rather than hushed up. As Fram notes,

> [i]t popped out casually, a throwaway line as he talked to reporters about finding the right puppy for his young daughters.
> But with just three offhanded words in his first news conference as president-elect, Barack Obama reminded everyone how thoroughly different his administration – and inevitably, this country – will be.
> "Mutts like me".
> By now, almost everyone knows that Obama's mother was white and father was black, putting him on track to become the nation's first African-American president. But there was something startling, and telling, about hearing his self-description – particularly in how offhandedly he used it.
> The message seemed clear – here is a president who will be quite at ease discussing race, a complex issue as unresolved as it is uncomfortable for many to talk about openly. And at a time when whites in the country are not many years from becoming the minority.
> (FRAM 2008)

Moreover, Barack Obama's kaleidoscopic vision of the interrelatedness of differences not only pertains to an astute perception of the differences within US-American society, but is a transnational vision as well. It is for this reason, then, that I will propose in this paper that, as an encyclopedia of difference, *Dreams from My Father* lends itself to being read through a variety of different methodologies. It can be read through the lens of ethnic studies and whiteness studies, African American studies, class studies, transnational studies of race and transnational whiteness studies (MORETON-ROBINSON/CASEY/NICOLL 2008), transnational religious studies, diaspora studies, and studies of social justice. As this article progresses, I will rehearse some of these readings, but at the same time, I will point to what may in fact be some of the shortcomings of such a rehearsal. For there may be a danger for each of these fields to remain insular, to 'feel' unrelated to other fields. How is our understanding of whiteness studies different, in other words, when we read it not as simply responding to but as being in dialogue with ethnic studies? How, as Matt Wray and Annalee Newitz have asked in studies such as *White Trash*, is our understanding of whiteness also inflected by the meaning of class? They write:

> In a country steeped in the myth of classlessness, in a culture where we are often at a loss to explain or understand poverty, the white trash stereotype serves as a useful way of

> blaming the poor for being poor. The term white trash helps solidify for the middle and upper classes a sense of cultural and intellectual superiority. (WRAY/NEWITZ 1997: 1)

What is so striking about Barack Obama's autobiography *Dreams from My Father*, then, is that it can be said to trigger academic readings of itself in the terms of the fields and methodologies outlined above; yet, it simultaneously points to the *interrelatedness* of these fields. The point made time and again in Barack Obama's autobiography *Dreams from My Father*, is not so much that each difference jostles for space with another, but that each difference may be uncannily close to another. Obama's open-ended notion of difference, or his notion of difference as open-ended, thus constantly translates one difference into another, seeing the interrelatedness, for instance, of both race and class in a transnational dimension. He writes:

> I know, I have seen, the desperation and disorder of the powerless: how it twists the lives of children on the streets of Jakarta or Nairobi in much the same way as it does the lives of children on Chicago's South Side, how narrow the path is for them between humiliation and untrammeled fury, how easily they slip into violence and despair. (OBAMA [1995] 2007: x–xi)

Dreams from My Father may hence constitute a utopia, a vision of each difference that defies closure by pointing to its intersection with others. My point here is that the differences detailed, in an encyclopedic manner, in *Dreams from My Father*, may center on Obama's own position or rather location as a *Grenzgänger* between differences, a shapeshifter who, by his own accord, has never felt completely at home in any community. There is hence, as a complement to what I have termed a kaleidoscopic vision of difference, something which I would call the agony of race: the tendency of 'race' in United States discourse and the history of race relations, to be exclusive, to defy or exclude ambiguity. It is this unbelonging of race which informs, as a form of agonistic labor, Obama's investigation of race in *Dreams from My Father*. This investigation, in turn, is also a self-inspection and a painful, because open-ended, self-introspection. The pain at the heart of Barack Obama's autobiography, I would argue, is precisely the dilemma, as I have tried to suggest above with regard to the expectations brought by many to Obama's eulogy for Reverent Pinckney, of constantly having to show one's colors. These 'colors', what is more, are said to defy the blurring of contours, of shades; they have to be clear-cut, even binary, in a way that Obama (the author) is at a loss to understand. In a sense, then, in his original foreword to *Dreams from My Father*, written in 2004, Obama anticipates the gaze of an African American community wanting him to take a stand at the Charleston Emanuel AME Church: the stand that indeed, 'black lives matter' and that he himself is black. This stance, the expectation that Obama show his colors in an unambiguous kind of way, is captured in his foreword by a curious expression: the notion of being taken "at face value". What Obama's autobiography drives home through the narrator's painful self-searching, then, is that no identity can ever be taken at face value: For any identity to be interpretable "at face value" would be to assume its open-endedness, the state in which it blurs into others and is contiguous to other identities and differences. There is in this passage what I would term an agony of race: the ability to comprehend or impose closure on a concept which can neither be comprehended nor contained, because it is, of course, a fiction, a social construct. Racial identity, as Matthew

Frye Jacobson has written, is made, not given: "Caucasians are made […] not born" (JACOBSON 1999: 4). Obama's agony of race, I would suggest, is hence born both of his knowledge of the chimerical nature of race and the awareness that he lives in a nation which insists on taking race "at face value". Obama writes,

> [those caught up in the binary logic of race] know too much, we have all seen too much, to take my parents' brief union – a black man and a white woman, an African and an American – at face value. As a result, some people have a hard time taking me at face value. When people who don't know me well, black or white, discover my background (and it is usually a discovery, for I ceased to advertise my mother's race at the age of twelve or thirteen, when I began to suspect that by doing so I was ingratiating myself to whites), I see the split-second adjustments they have to make, the searching of my eyes for some telltale sign. They no longer know who I am. Privately, they guess at my troubled heart, I suppose – the mixed blood, the divided soul, the ghostly image of the tragic mulatto trapped between two worlds. And if I were to explain that no, the tragedy is not mine, or at least not mine alone, it is yours, sons and daughters of Plymouth Rock and Ellis Island, it is yours, children of Africa, it is the tragedy of both my wife's six-year-old cousin and his white first grade classmates, so that you need not guess at what troubles me, it's on the nightly news for all to see, and that if we could acknowledge at least that much then the tragic cycle begins to break down … well, I suspect that I sound incurably naive […] (OBAMA [1995] 2007: xv)

This passage can be said to encapsulate, in a nutshell, what I would call the racial politics of Barack Obama's vision. It is a vision, I would argue, that is not so much post-racial as it is differently racialized; that it addresses the material consequences of race without, however, forgetting that race is a construct. This passage encapsulates, moreover, not only Obama's redefinition and suspension of race in its traditional usage but also another facet of what I have called the agony of race. Obama drives home in this passage the idea that the agony of race must not only concern those who inhabit non-white histories and subjectivities, but that the agony of race concerns the nation as a whole. What is especially remarkable in this passage is that in Obama's vision of the multifaceted notion of race as it marks the history and the present of the nation, not only do black and white histories coexist in what should be their common concern with the fact that the material reality of racism continues to persist, but that whiteness itself is seen as multifaceted: In Obama's vision, Plymouth Rock whiteness and Ellis Island whiteness coexist. Not only is whiteness hence as much of a construct as blackness is, but the history of whiteness, as Jacobson has noted, is itself one not only of cultural, but also of racial complexity. The groups, Jacobson writes, who we "see" as white today used to be non-white, a perspective which drives home the arbitrariness of racial definition. Whiteness itself is hence fractured into Plymouth Rock and Ellis Island whiteness; whiteness, too, comes in shades. I would like to argue, then, that this passage exemplifies that Obama's *Dreams from my Father* can be read not only through different methodologies, but that it invites these methodologies. This passage, in drawing attention to the difference between Plymouth Rock and Ellis Island, also draws attention to the history of whiteness as it has been investigated by whiteness studies. Neither whiteness nor blackness, then, are monolithic; they are equally constructed and hark back, to an equal extent, to a multifaceted history of amalgamating heterogeneous elements into a seemingly coherent and monolithic whole.

Obama is African American, then, because his father was Kenyan; his Africanness, he is well aware, differs from his wife's immersion into Chicago's African American community. Not incidentally, it was argued by many during Obama's initial presidential campaign, that his wife Michelle was in fact "blacker" than he was. What this above-quoted passage demonstrates, then, is the extent to which Obama the narrator is aware of the fact that both black and white communities insist on rendering race relations monochrome, and of rendering monochrome the shades within each of these colors. Even as he describes the black-and-white scenario in which he, as a mixed-race man, has been trapped, then, his vision insists on eclipsing both these colors into an infinity of shades of both whiteness and blackness. There is, strikingly enough, a kaleidoscope within whiteness and blackness themselves. It is this vision of the multifold shades of whiteness and blackness that will open up as his autobiography unfolds towards a map of an infinity of colors, where black, white, and Native American communities, among many others, are investigated not in their difference/s, but in their similarities.

Obama is well aware, then, that his refusal to take 'race' or identity at face value will strike many as incurably naïve. It is this naïveté, however, which he is quick to translate into another, and arguably, a quintessentially 'American' quality: his innocence. It is this innocence which, at the outset of his autobiography *Dreams from My Father*, may be his greatest weapon; it is an innocence, and an optimism born of innocence, which may constitute an alternative, even antidote to, what I have termed the 'agony of race'. As Obama goes on to note, "[a]nd yet what strikes me most when I think about the story of my family is a running strain of innocence, an innocence that seems unimaginable even by the measures of childhood" (OBAMA [1995] 2007: xiv). This is an innocence, Obama is quick to admit, which may itself constitute a luxury; it is an innocence which permits Obama the narrator to transcend or at least to dissociate himself from the antagonism of United States race relations. Yet, in a stance so characteristic of his politics, Obama does not elevate his own multiethnic and multiracial vision of what the country could be over others whose perception of color contrasts is much starker than his own. He does not, in other words, judge, let alone look down on those who insist that color differences, *in their material effects*, are much more clear-cut than Obama's deliberately blurry vision would allow. Obama includes in his autobiography, then, not only the history of his own family but that of his wife's family as well:

> My wife's cousin, only six years old, has already lost such innocence: A few weeks ago, he reported to his parents that some of his first grade classmates had refused to play with him because of his dark, unblemished skin. Obviously his parents, born and raised in Chicago and Gary, lost their own innocence long ago, and although they aren't bitter [...], one hears the pain in their voices as they begin to have second thoughts about having moved out of the city into a mostly white suburb, a move they made to protect their son from the possibility of being caught in a gang shooting and the certainty of attending an underfunded school. (OBAMA [1995] 2007: xiv–xv)

Obama's agony of race is defined, then, by his awareness of the discrepancy between his own insight that race is both a fiction and a chimera and his knowledge of the fact that the effects of this chimera are nonetheless both material and 'real'. Obama's agony, and the tragedy not only of his life but also of his politics, is thus the entrapment of having to follow and act upon a concept which one knows is chimerical. In Obama's vision, then, the individual is both caught up in the claustrophobic logic of United States race relations and has the power to transcend this logic. As Michel Foucault has written of the nature of freedom, "[r]ather than speaking of an essential freedom, it would be better to speak of an 'agonism' – of a relationship which is at the same time reciprocal incitation and struggle; less of a face-to-face confrontation which paralyzes both sides than a permanent provocation" (qtd. in McGowan 1991: 141).

It is this same agony of race which, as a young man trying to find his way in a country obsessed with race, racial demarcation, and racial difference, Obama finds in a genealogy of African American men of letters:

> Over the next few months, I looked to corroborate this nightmare vision. I gathered up books from the library – Baldwin, Ellison, Hughes, Wright, DuBois. At night I would close the door to my room, telling my grandparents I had homework to do, and there I would sit and wrestle with words, locked in suddenly desperate argument, trying to reconcile the world as I'd found it with the terms of *my* [emphasis added] birth. But there was no escape to be had. In every page in every book, in Bigger Thomas and invisible men, I kept finding the same anguish, the same doubt: a self-contempt that neither irony nor intellect seemed able to deflect. Even DuBois's learning and Baldwin's love and Langston's humor eventually succumbed to its corrosive force, each man finally forced to doubt art's redemptive power, each man finally forced to withdraw, one to Africa, one to Europe, one deeper into the bowels of Harlem, but all of them in the same weary flight, all of them exhausted, bitter men, the devil at their heels. (Obama[1995] 2007: 85–86)

In its agony of race, an "anguish" born of the awareness that 'race' is both chimerical and nevertheless real in its material effects, Obama's *Dreams of My Father* anticipates the arguments of Critical Race Theory. As Kimberlé Crenshaw et al. write in *Critical Race Theory: The Key Writings that Formed the Movement*,

> [i]t was obvious to many of us that although race was, to use the term, socially constructed (the idea of biological race is "false"), race was nonetheless "real" in the sense that there is a material dimension and weight to the experience of being "raced" in American society [...]. Thus, we understood our project as an effort to construct a race-conscious and at the same time anti-essentialist account of the processes by which law participates in "race–ing" American society. (Crenshaw et al.: xxvi)

Even as Obama's autobiography refuses 'color-blindness' in favor of color-consciousness, it nonetheless highlights what color consciousness, in order to be itself, must obscure, or dismiss: the complexity of race that, in order to be color-conscious, one must deliberately remain unconscious of.

The Life Writing of Race

What is so striking, then, is that this agony of race, for Obama's public perception, has been not a curse but a blessing. If for himself his own journey to self-awareness, which he recalls in painstaking detail in *Dreams from My Father*, is constantly deferred by his awareness of his own racial ambiguity, this very ambiguity may politically have made for his charisma: Because, in a public perception which is so steeped in an unambiguity of racial definition, Obama seems a shape-shifter; forever ambiguous, he can be claimed by many communities at once. It is in this vein that, in a volume edited by Alfred Hornung, he has been claimed not only as the first African American president in the history of the United States, but also as the first Asian American president of the country. Drawing on Toni Morrison's description of Bill Clinton as a "black" president, Greg Robinson makes a similar point about Obama's proximity to metaphors of Asianness. According to Robinson,

> in terms of the kind of cultural signifiers that Toni Morrison identified with respect to Clinton, Barack Obama should more properly be considered our first Asian American president. If you take into account his public persona and life history – and most importantly the transnational nature of his identity – his portrait resonates in fundamental ways with the list of archetypes (or stereotypes) that we might call "tropes of asianness". (ROBINSON 2016: 83)

For those of us trained in 'difference studies' – and inspired by Alfred Hornung's own kaleidoscopic vision, which, not incidentally, led to the founding of the Obama Institute for Transnational American Studies at the University of Mainz in 2017 – *Dreams from My Father* may hence function as an encyclopedia for studying difference in all its multiplicity, but also for reminding us of the interrelatedness of all these different fields. Following the work of Alfred Hornung – a work which was honored with the lifetime achievement award of the American Studies Association in 2013 – the Obama Institute for Transnational American Studies has a number of main emphases, among them life writing, transnational ethnic studies, and the intersection between life writing and life sciences. All of these emphases, arguably, are present in Obama's autobiography *Dreams from My Father*.

Obama's astute awareness of the relativity of difference, its relationality and its contiguity to other differences, is informed by a particular practice of life writing. Obama's book *Dreams from My Father*, then, is not only an autobiography but it is also a biography of the lives of others: of his mother, to whose romance of and fascination with blackness Obama owes his own existence; of his Indonesian stepfather, who was forced to return to Indonesia from the United States and who was left traumatized, hardened and embittered by the experience of torture and the effects of political corruption; of his grandparents, who saw their Hawai'ian dreams constantly deferred and who continued to be amazed by their multiracial grandson whose very presence in their family at times surprised them; and of many others whose lives had intersected with his own during his political campaigning in Chicago. Obama's book *Dreams from My Father* is so unique, then, because it refuses to be only an autobiography of its author, but points instead to the idea that each autobiography is also a biography of others. Mark Twain described this phenomenon in his autobiography, which, published a hundred years after his death in 2010, turned out to have anticipated the emergence of 'life writing' as a field; disappointed with the way in which his own autobiographical project was developing, Twain proceeded to abandon autobiography in favor of biography: As the editors of *Autobiography of Mark Twain* write, "Clemens seems to have become discouraged at least in part over his inability to be completely frank and self-revealing [...]. His solution was, at least temporarily, to recast the autobiography as a series of thumbnail biographies of people he had met over the years" (CLEMENS 2010: 15–16). If in Twain's case, the turning to the writing of biographies of others was born from his belief that no-one would ever be able to tell the unvarnished truth in an autobiography, Barack Obama's autobiography nevertheless implies a similar proximity of the autobiographical to the biographical mode. Obama's biographies of others, moreover, are much more than "thumbnail" biographies; they are fully-fledged life narratives contained in his own autobiography. These biographies, what is more, are at the same time agonistic inquiry into the nature of both 'blackness' and 'whiteness'. What his biographies of both his mother and his grandparents reveal, then, is an inquiry into the nature of white privilege; but because this inquiry is contained in a biography written by a loving son and grandson, it is never tinged with bitterness. It is in this biography of whiteness, then, that Obama's autobiography-cum-biography anticipates and recaptures the logic of whiteness studies. As Aileen Moreton-Robinson et al. have suggested in their introduction to *Transnational Whiteness Matters*,

> [a] key thread that weaves through this book is how notions and claims of virtue operate discursively within transnational whiteness. Virtue, the claiming of a morally superior position that at the same time denies any moral authority to others, functions as a usable property or currency that is deployed to support, defend and perpetuate white dominance. (MORETON-ROBINSON et al. 2008: x)

If Obama's inquiry into the nature of whiteness is also a biography of the lives of his mother and grandparents, then, it also functions as an investigation of the ways in which, *in spite of themselves*, individuals may be implicated in the logic of white privilege.

Thus, the point I would like to make here about *Dreams from My Father* is not only that it is a life writing text par excellence because it so astutely links the autobiography of its author to the biographies of others. Rather, it can be argued that Obama demonstrates his keen awareness of the relativity of difference precisely by engaging with the lives and biographies of others who are differently situated from himself. As an autobiographer turned biographer, Obama can engage with the difference of others and the relationality of their difference to his own because, as their *biographer*, he attempts to see this difference from their perspective. What may be crucial here is to compare the different modes of the autobiographer and the biographer: the biographer arguably is a historian of other people's lives.

Moreover, it is because the differences of others and the difference inhabited by others never remain abstract but are investigated through their position in others' lives that Obama's narrative never passes judgment on the lives of others. It is as a biographer, as an historian of other lives, that he investigates differences other than his own. I believe that this fusion of the autobiographical with the biographical mode could not be more central to Obama's politics: the refusal to privilege one difference over another and hence to engage in a hierarchy of differentiation. It is this refusal, tragically, which would later clash so jarringly with a reality in which the lines between differences would not be blurred, but redrawn, and in which the *antagonism* of racial groups, already present, under erasure (DERRIDA) in Obama's agony of race, would resurge.

The agony of race in Obama's writing is so painful precisely because he is so aware of the antagonism of race which informs the social reality surrounding him. His agony of race, I would suggest, is so painful to witness by us as the readers of his autobiography because once the autobiographer has become another person's *biographer*, having seen the world from their perspective, he can no longer pass judgment, even, at its most extreme, on the racism of this other person. This is especially true of Obama's recollection of his grandmother's fear of an African American man on the bus. The shift from the autobiographical to the biographical mode, then, is at the core of Obama's vision of the relativity and relationality of difference; it is also at the heart of an agony of race born of the knowledge that the social reality around him knows only the antagonism of race. What makes the anguish conveyed by Obama's autobiography even more acute is the fact that the antagonism of race has his own family in its grips; his grandparents, Obama realizes as a youth, are by no means immune to this antagonism, despite their love for him. His grandmother's fear of black men at the bus stop feels to Obama like a form of betrayal:

> [My grandfather] turned around and I saw now that he was shaking. "It *is* a big deal. It's a big deal to me. She's been bothered by men before. You know why she's so scared this time? I'll tell you why. Before you came in, she told me the fella was *black*." He whispered the word. "That's the real reason why she's bothered. And I just don't think that's right." The words were like a fist in my stomach [...] In my steadiest voice, I told him that such an attitude bothered me, too [...]. Gramps slumped into a chair in the living room and said he was sorry he had told me. Before my eyes, he grew small and old and very sad. I put my hand on his shoulder and told him that it was all right, I understood [...]. After they left, I sat on the edge of my bed and thought about my grandparents. They had sacrificed again and again for me. They had poured all their lingering hopes into my success. Never had they given me reason to doubt their love; I doubted if they ever would. And yet I knew that men who might easily have been my brothers could still inspire their rawest fears. (OBAMA [1995] 2007: 88–89)

It is by engaging, as a mixed-race autobiographer, with the biographies of others, that he refuses to privilege identity politics – moored in the lack of the open-endedness of identity as a concept – over the unpredictable turns a life can take. Life writing, in the sense of both autobiography and biography, thus in a way contradicts or at least complements identity politics in *Dreams from My Father*. As I have tried to outline above, Obama is aware that in order to fight racialist structures and structures of social inequality, identity politics may be necessary; but he nonetheless refuses to subscribe to the assertion that identity is not always already open-ended. It is this belief in the open-endedness of identity that may bestow on Obama, the chronicler of his family's life, the gift of being a biographer. For, arguably, a biographer must immerse himself in the lives of others, to be surprised at each turn of the meanders which the lives of these others may take. Nothing in his grandparents' lives, Obama notes, could have predicted the fact that they acquiesced to their daughter's marrying an African man:

> Sure – but would you let your daughter marry one?
> The fact that my grandparents had answered yes to this question, no matter how grudgingly, remains an enduring puzzle to me. There was nothing in their background to predict such a response, no New England transcendentalists or wild-eyed socialists in their family tree. True, Kansas had fought on the Union side of the Civil War; Gramps liked to remind me that various strands of the family contained ardent abolitionists. If asked, Toot would turn

> her head in profile to show off her beaked nose, which, along with a pair of jet-black eyes, was offered as proof of Cherokee blood. (OBAMA [1995] 2007: 12)

Obama is quick to note the ambiguity of this form of 'race treason' in which his white grandmother claims indigenous ancestry; and he is well aware of the debatable romanticism inherent in a contemporary practice in which many white Americans claim to have 'Native' roots. Yet, what about his wonder at his grandparents' acceptance of his mother's marriage to his African father? As a biographer who has to suspend his own expectations of the lives of others, and who must be attuned to the complex and often contradictory turns which these lives may take, Obama has to immerse himself in the lives of his grandparents. As a biographer, he cannot impose his own interpretation and prefabricated categories of 'whiteness' and 'blackness' on these lives, but must instead be attuned to the unexpected turns which these lives may take. His grandparents' life, Obama notes, cannot be contained by the identity categories that their race and ethnicity would jolt them into. Crucially, this is not color-blindness, since Obama's narrative is keenly attuned to the material consequences which racism has on the lives of both black and white Americans; yet, it is the insistence that color-consciousness may come at a price: the price of having to play down or dismiss one's own racial ambiguity in order to be taken, by others, 'at face value'.

In a nation which insists on the antagonism of race rather than subjecting itself to the agony of having to make sense of racial ambiguity, Obama can only be taken at face value, he writes, by taking sides against "white folks". And yet, it is here that the position of the autobiographer may clash with that of the biographer: As a biographer of his mother's and his grandparents' lives, Obama the narrator has realized that 'whiteness' as an identity category fails to capture the complexity and the ambiguity of these lives, the implicit heterogeneity within whiteness; and yet as a an autobiographer, he has to chronicle the ways in which he had to snap out of the biographical mode in order to be able to pronounce the phrase "white folks". To the extent to which he would be able to pronounce this phrase without hesitation, he knows, he will gain acceptance by the African American community; yet, as a biographer, he is simultaneously aware of the ways in which his mother's and grandparents' lives could not be contained by 'whiteness' as both a term and a predication. In his autobiography, Obama recalls his high school years:

> *White folks*. The term itself was uncomfortable in my mouth at first; I felt like a non-native speaker tripping over a difficult phrase. Sometimes I would find myself talking to [my friend] Ray about *white folks* this or *white folks* that, and I would suddenly remember my mother's smile, and the words that I spoke would seem awkward and false. Or I would be helping Gramps dry the dishes after dinner and Toot would come in to say she was going to sleep, and those same words – *white folks* – would flash in my head like a bright neon sign, and I would suddenly grow quiet, as if I had secrets to keep. (OBAMA [1995] 2007: 80–81)

In *Dreams from My Father*, Obama confronts us not only with a kaleidoscope of difference, but also with the things we have invented in order to describe these differences. African American studies, whiteness studies, and Native American studies have emerged as fields which investigate the history and presence of a particular group or group identity.

Yet, the italics in the above-cited passage, the italics inherent in the phrase "white folks", serve as scare quotes in Obama's autobiography, a reminder that each of the names we use to describe a particular category necessarily falls short. These terms, Obama's autobiography reminds us, can only be a form of "shorthand". As he goes on to note, "[t]he term *white* was simply a shorthand for [Ray], I decided, a tag for what my mother would call a bigot" (OBAMA [1995] 2007: 81). Obama's autobiography, by refusing to privilege the autobiographical over the biographical mode, can be read as the longhand version of identity; an account not so much of difference than of the process of differentiation which emphasizes that even though in the political arena we have to resort to identity politics, the clearly delineated boundaries that these categories are defined by are nonetheless both fictional and, ultimately, false.

It is in this sense, then, that Obama's text not only oscillates between different identity categories – thus triggering in our reading the methodologies through which these differences may be and have been defined – but it zooms in not on the lines dividing these differences, but on the spaces which fuse them. What is especially remarkable in this context is that *Dreams from My Father* refuses to separate ethnic studies from indigenous studies. As Sneja Gunew has argued in a Canadian context, the focus on immigrant histories and the subsequent establishment of ethnic studies as an academic discipline may often have led to the marginalization of indigenous lives and histories; ethnic studies and indigenous studies have thus often been seen as being independent of or unrelated to one another. Arguably, this may be true for a United States context as well. *Dreams from My Father*, on the other hand, points precisely to this interrelatedness by stressing, time and again, issues of racial justice as they pertain to Native American communities in the United States:

> *Power*. The word fixed in my mother's mind like a curse. In America, it had generally remained hidden from view until you dug beneath the surface of things; until you visited an Indian reservation or spoke to a black person whose trust you had earned. But here [in Indonesia] power was undisguised, indiscriminate, naked, always fresh in the memory. Power had taken Lolo and yanked him back into line just when he thought he'd escaped, making him feel its weight, letting him know that his life wasn't his own. (OBAMA [1995] 2007: 45)

This passage is remarkable since it encapsulates not only the narrative's kaleidoscopic vision of difference, and of the ways in which different differences spill into one another, but also the sense that differences can be investigated through a transnational vision. Obama's own vision of his life thus superimposes Indonesia and the United States; and once again, it engages in life writing by refusing to judge what might otherwise appear as his stepfather Lolo's harshness towards 'beggars'. Becoming a biographer of Lolo's life, Obama the autobiographer notes that Lolo's spirit was broken by the acts of cruelty and corruption he witnessed in his home country. Powerlessness, the narrative is quick to note, may crisscross and transcend the lines of race, of class, and of nation.

Translated into an academic context, then, what *Dreams from My Father* illustrates is interrelatedness of black and indigenous lives, both of which complicate a model assumed by 'immigrant histories': forced migration and colonization severely contradict the model of the United States solely as a 'nation of immigrants'. It is here that we may return, then, not only to Obama's distinction between Plymouth Rock and Ellis Island, but also to the way in which, as many critics have argued, the emphasis on Ellis Island which turns the history of the nation into that of a 'nation of immigrants', may have marginalized indigenous communities, whose presence is erased anew by a focus on immigration. It must also be said here, however, that this is an instance where Obama the president failed to live up to the potential of Obama the writer and autobiographer. Although he had, in his autobiography, drawn attention to the plight of Native Americans and their continued marginalization by United States politics, he disappointed many when, during his time in office, he did not issue an official apology to Native Americans for an entire history of disenfranchisement. After the governments of both Australia and Canada had officially apologized to Aboriginal communities and First Nations in 2008, Obama's presidency was associated by many with the hope that the United States would follow suit. Even though the Obama government did issue a resolution, then, both the scope and the way in which it was publicized was in no way comparable to the apologies in Australia and Canada. Yet, the resolution, issued in 2009 (a year after apologies had been made to indigenous communities in Australia and Canada) is nevertheless significant:

> President Obama acknowledged the importance of the Apology to Native Peoples and his support for it. Reflecting on the difficult circumstances of Indian nations today, Obama said: "These cases serve as a reminder of the importance of not glossing over the past or ignoring the past, even as we work together to forge a brighter future. That's why, last year, I signed a resolution, passed by both parties in Congress, finally recognizing the sad and painful chapters in our shared history – a history too often marred by broken promises and grave injustices against the First Americans. It's a resolution I fully supported – recognizing that no statement can undo the damage that was done; what it can do is help reaffirm the principles that should guide our future. It's only by heeding the lessons of our history that we can move forward."[1]

Yet, critics have noted that the apology made by Obama was "tucked away" in the Defense Appropriations Act of 2010, and that "President Obama never publicly acknowledged the 'Apology to Native Peoples of the United States'".[2] *Dreams from My Father*, then, remains a vision of the kaleidoscope of difference and of the ways in which different differences are contiguous to and blur into one another. In this as in many other instances, Obama's vision – the vision of the autobiographer – was stopped short by a political reality reluctant to engage in visions.

As the violence against African Americans which seemed to erupt with increasing force under Obama's presidency painfully illustrates, political reality refused to cash the check that a president armed with the innocent belief that the antagonism of race could finally be overcome had presented. As we move into a new presidential era, which has been termed 'post-factual' in its stubborn assurance that populist sentiments are more reliable than historical facts or a knowledge of cultural complexity, such a belief seems more urgent than ever.

[1] *First Peoples Worldwide*: President Obama acknowledges need for Native American Apology. *http://firstpeoples.org/wp/tag/the-apology-to-the-native-peoples-of-the-united-states/.* [17 January 2018]

[2] Robert Longley: Did You Know the US Apologized to Native Americans? 7 July 2016. *http://usgovinfo.about.com/b/2012/12/27/did-you-know-the-us-apologized-to-native-americans.htm.*

List of Works Cited

APPIAH, K. ANTHONY, and AMY GUTMANN (1996): *Color Conscious: The Political Morality of Race*. Princeton: Princeton University Press.

BHABHA, HOMI K. (1994): *The Location of Culture*. London/New York: Routledge.

BUTLER, JUDITH (1997): *Excitable Speech. A Politics of the Performative*. New York: Routledge.

CLEMENS, SAMUEL LANGHORNE ([1924; 1940; 1959] 2010): *Autobiography of Mark Twain*. Vol. I. Ed. by HARRIET ELINOR SMITH. Berkeley: University of California Press.

CRENSHAW, KIMBERLÉ, NEIL GOTANDA, GARY PELLER, and KENDALL THOMAS (Eds.) (1995): *Critical Race Theory: The Key Writings that Formed the Movement*. New York: New Press.

FRAM, ALAN (2008): "Mutts like me" shows Obama's racial comfort. *NBC News*, 8 November, *http://www.nbcnews.com/id/27606637/ns/politics-decision_08/t/mutts-me-shows-obamas-racial-comfort/#.WHDMAaKn3UA*.

HORNUNG, ALFRED (2016): Preface. In ALFRED HORNUNG (Ed.): *Obama and Transnational American Studies*. Heidelberg: Universitätsverlag Winter (American Studies – A Monograph Series 276).

JACOBSON, MATTHEW FRYE (1999): *Whiteness of a Different Color: European Immigrants and the Alchemy of Race*. Cambridge: Harvard University Press.

JACOBSON, MATTHEW FRYE (2006): *Roots, Too: White Ethnic Revival in Post-Civil Rights America*. Cambridge: Harvard University Press.

MADSEN, DEBORAH L. (1998): *American Exceptionalism*. Edinburgh: Edinburgh University Press.

MCGOWAN, JOHN (1991): *Postmodernism and Its Critics*. Ithaca/London: Cornell University Press.

MORETON-ROBINSON, AILEEN, MARYROSE CASEY, and FIONA NICOLL (Eds.) (2008): *Transnational Whiteness Matters*. Lanham, MD: Lexington.

OBAMA, BARACK ([1995] 2007): *Dreams from My Father*. Edinburgh: Canongate.

ROBINSON, GREG (2016): Barack Obama: Our First Asian American President? In ALFRED HORNUNG (Ed.): *Obama and Transnational American Studies*. Heidelberg: Universitätsverlag Winter, 81–92.

SACK, KEVIN, and GARDINER HARRIS (2015): President Obama Eulogizes Charleston Pastor as One Who Understood Grace. *New York Times* online, 26 June.

SCHMITT-TEGGE, JOHANNES, and MARCO MIERKE (2015): Charleston: Obama singt "Amazing Grace" bei Trauerfeier. *Die Welt online*, 26 June. *https://www.welt.de/politik/ausland/article143157079/Obama-singt-Amazing-Grace-bei-Trauerfeier.html*.

WILSON, CHARLES (2016): "Donald Trump's South". Lecture. University of Mainz, 24 November.

WRAY, MATT, and ANNALEE NEWITZ (Eds.) (1997): *White Trash: Race and Class in America*. New York: Routledge.

List of Contributors

MITA BANERJEE is Professor of American Studies and a member of the Executive Board of the Obama Institute for Transnational American Studies at Johannes Gutenberg University Mainz. From 2004 to 2010, she was Professor of American Studies at the University of Siegen, and from 2010 to 2015 Research Fellow at the Gutenberg Research College (GFK) at the University of Mainz. She is speaker of the Center for Comparative Indigenous Studies at the University of Mainz, and the editor of *Comparative Indigenous Studies* (2016). Her research interests include indigenous studies, ethnic American literature and culture (*Race-ing the Century*, 2005), the American Renaissance (*Ethnic Ventriloquism: Literary Minstrelsy in Nineteenth-Century American Literature*, 2008), issues of naturalization and citizenship (*Color Me White: Naturalism/Naturalization in American Literature*, 2013) and medical humanities (*Medical Humanities in American Studies*, 2018). She is co-speaker of the Research Training Group "Life Sciences, Life Writing: Boundary Experiences of Human Life between Biomedical Explanation and Lived Experience," which is funded by the German Research Foundation (DFG).

CARMEN BIRKLE is Professor of North American Literary and Cultural Studies at Philipps University, Marburg. She has taught at the universities of Mainz, Vienna, and at Columbia University in New York City. She was President of the German Association for American Studies from 2014 to 2017. Her research and teaching focus on ethnic and gender studies, literature and medicine, and popular culture. She is the author of *Women's Stories of the Looking Glass* (1996) and *Migration – Miscegenation – Transculturation* (2004), editor of the special issues *Literature and Medicine: Women in the Medical Profession (Parts I* and *II*, 2009) of the journal *gender forum* and co-editor of *(Trans) Formations of Cultural Identity in the English-Speaking World* (1998), *Frauen auf der Spur* (2001), *Sites of Ethnicity* (2004), *Asian American Studies in Europe* (2006), *"The Sea Is History": Exploring the Atlantic* (2009), *Living American Studies* (2010), *Emanzipation und feministische Politiken* (2012), *Communicating Disease: Cultural Representations of American Medicine* (2013), *McLuhan's Global Village Today* (2014) as well as of *Waging Health* (2015) and *Feminismus und Freiheit* (2016). With her current project she investigates the intersection of literature, gender, and medicine in nineteenth-century America.

BIRGIT DÄWES is Professor of American Studies at the University of Flensburg. She received her doctoral and post-doctoral degrees from the University of Würzburg and held previous positions as Professor of American Studies at the Obama Institute of Transnational American Studies at the University of Mainz and at the University of Vienna, and as Visiting Professor at National Sun Yat-sen University in Kaohsiung, Taiwan. She received a number of prestigious awards for her monographs *Native North American Theater in a Global Age* (2007) and *Ground Zero Fiction: History, Memory, and Representation in the American 9/11 Novel* (2011) and is co-editor of the Routledge book series *Transnational Indigenous Perspectives*. Next to Native American and First Nations Studies, her current research focuses on surveillance culture, contemporary American television series, and issues of cultural memory.

SHELLEY FISHER FISHKIN is the Joseph S. Atha Professor of Humanities, Professor of English and Director of American Studies at Stanford University. She holds a Ph.D. in American Studies from Yale University, is Past President of the American Studies Association and is a Founding Editor of the *Journal of Transnational American Studies*. The forty-seven books she has authored, edited or co-edited include *Was Huck Black? Mark Twain and African-American Voices* (1993); *Lighting Out for the Territory: Reflections on Mark Twain and American Culture* (1998); *Is He Dead? A Comedy by Mark Twain* (2003); the twenty-nine volumes of *The Oxford Mark Twain* (2010); *The Mark Twain Anthology* (2010); *Mark Twain's Book of Animals* (2011); and *Writing America: Literary Landmarks from Walden Pond to Wounded Knee* (2015). Her research was featured twice on the front page of the *New York Times,* and twice on the front page of the *New York Times* Arts section. In 2017 at the 8th International Conference on the State of Mark Twain Studies, she was awarded the John S. Tuckey Award for Lifetime Achievement in Mark Twain Studies.

NADJA GERNALZICK is Visiting Professor of English and American Studies at the University of Vienna and teaches as Adjunct Faculty at the Obama Institute for Transnational American Studies at University of Mainz. She studied Comparative Literature and American Studies at the universities of Mainz, San Jose in California and at Columbia University, New York City, and has taught at universities in Canada, Germany and Switzerland. She is founding member of Kulturwissenschaftliche Gesellschaft (KWG) and on the board of reviewers for the Lang series *Literature–Culture–Economy*. Her publications include *Kredit und Kultur: Ökonomie- und Geldbegriff bei Jacques Derrida und in der amerikanischen Literaturtheorie der Postmoderne* (2000) and *Temporality in American Filmic Autobiography: Cinema, Automediality and Grammatology with* Film Portrait *and* Joyce at 34 (2018); she co-edited *Transmediality and Transculturality* (2013) and *The Mediality of Sugar* (forthcoming).

RÜDIGER KUNOW is Professor Emeritus of American Studies at Potsdam University. He taught at the universities of Würzburg, Nürnberg, Freiburg, Hannover, and Magdeburg and was Research Fellow at the University of California, Santa Cruz, as well as Visiting Professor at the University of Texas at Austin, the State University of New Mexico, Albuquerque, and the State University of New York at Albany. From 2005 to 2008 he held the position of President of the German Association for American Studies. He is founding member of ENAS, the European Network in Aging Studies. He served as speaker of the international research project "Transnational American Studies" with U.S. American and German universities and of the European Union research and teaching project "Putting a Human Face on Diversity: The U.S. In/Of Europe." He directed the interdisciplinary research and graduate teaching program "Cultures in/of Mobility" at the School of Humanities at Potsdam University. His major research interests and publications focus on cultural constructions of illness and aging, cultural critique, transnational American studies and the South Asian diaspora in the United States. Among his publications are *Das Klischee: Reproduzierte Wirklichkeiten in der englischen und amerikanischen Literatur* (1994) and, most recently, *Material Bodies: Biology and Culture in the United States* (2018); he co-edited *Age Studies*, special issue of *Amerikastudien/American* Studies (2011) and *Text or Context: Reflections on Literary and Cultural Criticism* (2013).

MANFRED SIEBALD was Professor of American Studies at Johannes Gutenberg University Mainz until his retirement in 2012. He studied at Philipps University, Marburg, and Manchester College, Indiana. He taught at University of Mainz from 1977 until 2012 and occasionally at other colleges and universities, among them Wheaton College, Illinois; Georgia State University in Atlanta; and York University, Toronto. He was assistant editor of the journal *Amerikastudien/American Studies* from 1991 to 2002 and has co-edited *Inklings: Jahrbuch für Literatur und Ästhetik* since 1993. His research areas are the intersections of literature and religion in the U.S.A., American literature and culture of the nineteenth century as well as popular culture, especially detective fiction and music. In these fields, he published several books, including *Der verlorene Sohn in der amerikanischen Literature* (2003), edited and co-edited many volumes as well as contributed numerous articles to periodicals, essay collections and encyclopedia. Currently, he is writing a book on the literary musical in the United States. He continues his lifelong career as a singer-songwriter and in writing fiction.

NICOLE WALLER is Professor of American Studies at the University of Potsdam. She received her Ph.D. from Johannes Gutenberg University in Mainz and has taught at universities in Germany and the United States. She is author of the monographs *Contradictory Violence: Revolution and Subversion in the Caribbean* (2005) and *American Encounters with Islam in the Atlantic World* (2011) and co-editor of *"The Sea is History": Exploring the Atlantic* (2009) and *Politics in Fantasy Media: Essays on Ideology and Gender in Fiction, Film, Television and Games* (2014). Her areas of research and publication include Atlantic Studies, Caribbean Studies, Postcolonial Studies, Arab American literature and culture, and conceptions of Indigeneity. She is currently co-organizing an interdisciplinary research project on American territorialities that critically investigates U.S. colonial and imperialist constructions of nationhood and the way in which people and peoples contesting such national narratives have created and asserted other land- and water-based conceptions of polity.

CHARLES REAGAN WILSON is Professor Emeritus at the University of Mississippi and former Director of the Center for the Study of Southern Culture. He is author of *Flashes of a Southern Spirit: Meanings of the Spirit in the U.S. South* (2007), *Judgment and Grace in Dixie: Southern Faiths from Faulkner to Elvis* (1995), and *Baptized in Blood: The Religion of the Lost Cause, 1865–1920* (1980). He is editor-in-chief of *The New Encyclopedia of Southern Culture* (2004–2012), co-editor of the *Encyclopedia of Southern Culture* (1989), and co-editor of the *Mississippi Encyclopedia* (2017). He taught for three decades at the University of Mississippi, directed over a dozen symposia on the U.S. South, and supervised the doctoral work of twenty-five graduate students. He is currently at work on *The Southern Way of Life: The History of a Concept*.

HUBERT ZAPF is Professor of American Studies and Co-Director of Environmental Humanities at the University of Augsburg. He is an Advisory Board Member of the European Association for the Study of Literature, Culture, and Environment, of the Rowman & Littlefield *Ecocritical Theory and Practice* series, and of the Cambridge University Press *Elements in Environmental Humanities* series. His publications include *Literatur als kulturelle Ökologie* (2002); *Literature as Cultural Ecology: Sustainable Texts* (2016); and "Ecological Thought in Europe and Germany" in *A Global History of Literature and*

Environment (2017); and he edited and co-edited *Amerikanische Literaturgeschichte* (3rd ed. 2010); *American Studies Today: New Research Agendas* (2014); *Literature and Science*, special issue of *Anglia* (2015); *Handbook of Ecocriticism and Cultural Ecology* (2016); and *Ecological Thought in German Literature and Culture* (2017).

ZHANG LONGXI is Professor of Comparative Literature and Translation at the City University of Hong Kong. He holds a Ph.D. in Comparative Literature from Harvard University ('89). He is a Foreign Member of the Royal Swedish Academy of Letters, History and Antiquities and of Academia Europaea, and is the elected President of the International Comparative Literature Association (ICLA) for 2016–2019. He serves as Editor-in-Chief of the *Journal of World Literature* and as Advisory Editor of *New Literary History*. He has published more than twenty books and numerous articles in both English and Chinese, and his English book publications include *The Tao and the Logos: Literary Hermeneutics, East and West* (1992); *Mighty Opposites: From Dichotomies to Differences in the Comparative Study of China* (1998); *Allegoresis: Reading Canonical Literature East and West* (2005); *Unexpected Affinities: Reading across Cultures* (2007); and, most recently, *From Comparison to World Literature* (2015).

Publications of Alfred Hornung

Books and Collections of Essays

Books

(1978): *Narrative Struktur und Textsortendifferenzierung: Die Texte des Muckraking Movement (1902–1912)*. Stuttgart: Metzler.
(1985): *Kulturkrise und ihre literarische Bewältigung: Die Funktion der autobiographischen Struktur in Amerika vom Puritanismus zur Postmoderne*. Habilitationsschrift Universität Würzburg.
(1992): *Lexikon amerikanische Literatur*. Mannheim: Meyers Lexikonverlag.
(2016): *Jack London: Abenteuer des Lebens*. Darmstadt: Lambert Schneider.

Editions

(1990): *Autobiography and Democracy in America*. Thematic Issue of *Amerikastudien / American Studies* 35.3 (Fall 1990).
(1991): *Strained Relations: American Realism and the Domestic Novel*. Thematic Issue of *Amerikastudien / American Studies* 36.1 (Spring 1991) (with HEINZ ICKSTADT).
(1992): *Autobiographie & Avant-garde: Alain Robbe-Grillet, Serge Doubrovsky, Rachid Boudjedra, Maxine Hong Kingston, Raymond Federman, Ronald Sukenick*. Tübingen: Narr 1992 (with ERNSTPETER RUHE).
(1994): *Affirmation and Negation in Contemporary American Culture*. Heidelberg: Universitätsverlag Winter (with GERHARD HOFFMANN).
(1996): *Ethics and Aesthetics: The Moral Turn of Postmodernism*. Heidelberg: Universitätsverlag Winter (with GERHARD HOFFMANN).
(1996): *Democracy and the Arts in the United States*. München: Fink (with REINHARD R. DOERRIES and GERHARD HOFFMANN).
(1997): *Emotion in Postmodernism*. Heidelberg: Universitätsverlag Winter (with GERHARD HOFFMANN).
(1999): *Postcolonialism and Autobiography: Michelle Cliff, David Dabydeen, Opal Palmer Adisa*. Amsterdam: Rodopi (with ERNSTPETER RUHE).
(1999): *Postcolonialisme & Autobiographie: Albert Memmi, Assia Djebar, Daniel Maximin*. Amsterdam: Rodopi (with ERNSTPETER RUHE).
(2000): *Multiculturalism and the American Self*. Heidelberg: Universitätsverlag Winter (with WILLIAM BOELHOWER).
(2001): *Postmodernism and the Fin-de-Siècle*. Heidelberg: Universitätsverlag Winter (with GERHARD HOFFMANN).
(2002): *Global Fictions*. Thematic Issue of *Amerikastudien / American Studies* 47.2 (Summer 2002) (with RÜDIGER KUNOW).
(2004): *Sexualities in American Culture*. Heidelberg: Universitätsverlag Winter.
(2006): *Religion in African-American Culture*. Heidelberg: Universitätsverlag Winter (with WINFRIED HERGET).
(2007): *Intercultural America*. Heidelberg: Universitätsverlag Winter.

(2008/2009): *Arab-American Literature and Culture*. Special Issue of *American Studies Journal* 52 (Winter 2008/09) (with MARTINA KOHL).

(2009): *Representation and Decoration in a Postmodern Age*. Heidelberg: Universitätsverlag Winter (with RÜDIGER KUNOW).

(2009): *Autobiography and Mediation*. Heidelberg: Universitätsverlag Winter.

(2012): *The South in the Age of Obama*. Thematic issue *American Studies Journal* 56.

(2012): *Life Writing Matters in Europe*. Heidelberg: Universitätsverlag Winter (with MARIJKE HUISMAN, ANNEKE RIBBERINK, and MONICA SOETING).

(2012): *Arab American Literature and Culture*. Heidelberg: Universitätsverlag Winter (with MARTINA KOHL).

(2013): *Ecology and Life Writing*. Heidelberg: Universitätsverlag Winter (with ZHAO BAISHENG). Chinese Translation (2016): 生态学与生命写作 [*Shengtaixue Yu Shengming Xiezuo*]. Trans. by LIN JIANG. Beijing: China Social Sciences Press [中国社会科学出版社, Zhongguo Shehui Kexue Chubanshe].

(2013): *American Lives*. Heidelberg: Universitätsverlag Winter.

(2013): *Medialisierungsformen des (Auto-)Biographischen*. Konstanz: Universitätsverlag Konstanz (with CARSTEN HEINZE).

(2016): *Obama and Transnational American Studies*. Heidelberg: Universitätsverlag Winter.

Articles

(1977): “Modern”, “Postmodern” and “Contemporary” as Criteria for the Analysis of 20th Century Literature (with GERHARD HOFFMANN and RÜDIGER KUNOW). *Amerikastudien / American Studies* 22: 19–46; rpt. MANFRED PUTZ and PETER FREESE (Eds.) (1984): *POSTMODERNISM in American Literature: A Critical Anthology*. Darmstadt: Thesen, 12–37; rev. German edition GERHARD HOFFMANN (Ed.) (1988): *Der zeitgenössische amerikanische Roman: Von der Moderne zur Postmoderne*. 3 vols, München: Fink, vol. I, 7–43.

(1981): Sex and Art in Hawkes' Triad: The Pornographic, the Erotic and the Aesthetic Modes. *Amerikastudien / American Studies* 26: 159–179.

(1981): Defusing the Minefield: The Context of Feminist Criticism. In: National Humanities Center (Ed.): *Feminist Literary Criticism*. Working Paper No. 3. NC: Research Triangle Park, 113–122.

(1982): Am Ende der Moderne – Universitäten Würzburg / Norwich / Paris III / Venedig: Ein Kursprojekt (with GERHARD HOFFMANN and RÜDIGER KUNOW). *Deutsche Universitätszeitung* 1 (4 January 1982): 18–19; rpt. Studium in Europa für Europa: Literaturwissenschaft: Beispiel Würzburg. *EG-Magazin* 1 (Januar 1982): 21–22.

(1983): The Political Uses of Popular Fiction in the Muckraking Movement. *Revue Française d'Études Américaines* 17: 333–348.

(1983): Recollection and Imagination in Postmodern Fiction. MAURICE COUTURIER (Ed.): *Representation and Performance in Postmodern Fiction* (Proceedings of the Nice Conference on Postmodern Fiction). Montpellier: Presses de l'Imprimerie de Recherche – Université Paul Valéry, 57–70.

(1984): Amerikanische Dramatiker zur Dramentheorie. GERHARD HOFFMANN (Ed.): *Das Amerikanische Drama*. Bern: Francke, 57–75; 283–287.

(1984): Absent Presence: The Fiction of Raymond Federman and Ronald Sukenick. *Indian Journal of American Studies* 13: 17–31.

(1984): Fantasies of the Autobiographical Self: Thomas Bernhard, Raymond Federman, Samuel Beckett. *Journal of Beckett Studies* 13 (Spring 1984): 91–107.

(1984): USA-Literatur der Gegenwart. *Meyers Enzyklopädisches Lexikon in 25 Bänden*. Mannheim: Bibliographisches Institut, no. 24.

(1984): "Modern", "Postmodern", "Contemporary": A Select Bibliography. MANFRED PUTZ and PETER FREESE (Eds.): *POSTMODERNISM in American Literature: A Critical Anthology* (with RÜDIGER KUNOW). Darmstadt: Thesen, 214–227.

(1985): USA-Literatur. *Meyers Großes Universallexikon*. Mannheim: Bibliographisches Institut, no. 14.

(1985): The Autobiographical Mode in Contemporary American Fiction. *Prose Studies* 8: 69–83.

(1987): Reading One / Self: Samuel Beckett, Thomas Bernhard, Peter Handke, John Barth, Alain Robbe-Grillet. MATEI CALINESCU and DOUWE FOKKEMA (Eds.): *Exploring Postmodernism*. Amsterdam: Benjamins, 175–198.

(1987): German Contributions to Autobiography Studies. *Auto / Biography Studies* 3.1: 12–23.

(1988): USA-Literatur. (All American authors and thematic contributions, total of 750 entries). WERNER HABICHT, WOLF-DIETER LANGE and Brockhaus-Redaktion (Eds.): *Der Literatur-Brockhaus*. 3 vols.

(1989): Art Over Life: Henry James's Autobiography. GERHARD HOFFMANN (Ed.): *Making Sense: The Role of the Reader in Contemporary American Fiction*. München: Fink, 198–219.

(1990): Literary Conventions and the Political Unconscious in Upton Sinclair's Work. DIETER HERMS (Ed.): *Upton Sinclair: Literature and Social Reform*. Frankfurt a.M.: Lang, 24–38.

(1990): Autobiography and Democracy: The Case of Lincoln Steffens and Ida M. Tarbell. GÜNTER H. LENZ, HARTMUT KEIL, and SABINE BROCK-SALLAH (Eds.): *Reconstructing American Literary and Historical Studies*. Frankfurt a.M.: Campus, 238–253.

(1990): Evolution and Expansion in Jack London's Personal Accounts: The Road and John Barleycorn. SERGE RICARD (Ed.): *An American Empire: Expansionist Cultures and Policies, 1881–1917*. Aix-en-Provence: Publications de l'Université de Provence, 197–213.

(1990): Lust und Verlust in den Gedichten von Edgar Allan Poe und Emily Dickinson. *Literaturwissenschaftliches Jahrbuch* 31: 179–197.

(1990): Social Work and Modern Art: The Autobiographies of Jane Addams and Gertrude Stein. RÜDIGER AHRENS (Ed.): *Anglistentag 1989 Würzburg: Proceedings*. Tübingen: Niemeyer, 207–218.

(1990): Norman Mailer, The Executioner's Song. WALTER JENS (Ed.): *Kindlers Neues Literatur Lexikon*. München: Kindler, vol. X, 890 f.

(1990): American Autobiographies and Autobiography Criticism: A Review Essay. *Amerikastudien / American Studies* 35.3: 371–401.

(1991): Philip Roth, Goodbye, Columbus; Zuckerman Trilogy: The Ghost Writer, Zuckerman Unbound, The Anatomy Lesson, The Prague Orgy; The Counterlife. WALTER JENS (Ed.): *Kindlers Neues Literatur Lexikon*. München: Kindler, vol. XIV, 355–358; 359–361.

(1991): "In hoc signo vinces": Religion und Fiktion in Walker Percys postmoderner Welt. BERND ENGLER and FRANZ LINK (Eds.): *Zwischen Dogma und säkularer Welt: Zur Erzählliteratur englischsprachiger katholischer Autoren im 20. Jahrhundert*. Paderborn: Schöningh, 113–123.

(1992): Postmodern Experience and Avant-garde Autobiography: Ronald Sukenick's Life in Fiction. ALFRED HORNUNG and ERNSTPETER RUHE (Eds.): *Autobiographie & Avant-garde*. Tübingen: Narr, 401–412.

(1992): Postmodern – Post Mortem: Death and the Death of the Novel. KRISTIAAN VERSLUYS (Ed.): *Neo-Realism in Contemporary American Fiction*. Amsterdam: Benjamins, 87–102.

(1993): The Making of (Jewish) Americans: Ludwig Lewisohn, Charles Reznikoff, Michael Gold. WOLFGANG BINDER (Ed.): *Ethnic Cultures in the 1920s in North America*. Frankfurt a.M.: Lang, 115–134.

(1993): Autobiographie und Fiktion in der amerikanischen Gegenwartsliteratur. *Chelsea Hotel: A Magazine for the Arts* 3.1: 36–39.

(1993): Autobiographie und literarische Anthropologie in den USA: Gertrude Stein und Maxine Hong Kingston. *Literaturwissenschaftliches Jahrbuch* 34: 259–275.

(1994): The Transgression of Postmodern Fiction: Philip Roth and Cynthia Ozick. GERHARD HOFFMANN and ALFRED HORNUNG (Eds.): *Affirmation and Negation in Contemporary American Culture*. Heidelberg: Universitätsverlag Winter, 229–249.

(1994): Violence in New York City: Hubert Selby's Last Exit to Brooklyn and Bret Easton Ellis's American Psycho. LILIANE KERJAN (Ed.): *L'Amérique urbaine des années soixante / Urban America in the Sixties*. Rennes: Presses Universitaires, 149–159.

(1994): The Re-Vision of America: European Experiences and American Autobiography. DEBORAH L. MADSEN (Ed.): *Visions of America Since 1492*. London: Leicester University Press, 94–110.

(1994): "Make It New": The Concept of Newness in American Studies. GÜNTHER BLAICHER (Ed.): *Anglistentag 1993 Eichstätt*. Tübingen: Niemeyer, 307–319.

(1994): Fremdsprache Englisch in der Lehre. REINGARD M. NISCHIK (Ed.): *Anglistentag 1993 Eichstätt: Forum. Probleme der anglistischen / amerikanistischen Lehre (Proceedings)*. Tübingen: Niemeyer, 4–8.

(1994): Europäische Avantgarde auf amerikanischen Bühnen. Oder: Gibt es ein amerikanisches Avantgarde-Theater? FRANZ NORBERT MENNEMEIER and ERIKA FISCHER-LICHTE (Eds.): *Drama und Theater der europäischen Avantgarde*. Tübingen: Francke, 193–213.

(1995): The Making of Americans: Mary Rowlandson, Benjamin Franklin, Gertrude Stein, Maxine Hong Kingston. GÜNTER LENZ and KLAUS MILICH (Eds.): *American Studies in Germany: European Contexts and Intercultural Relations*. Frankfurt a.M.: Campus, 96–117. Slightly changed German version in WINFRIED HERGET (Ed.): *Amerika: Entdeckung – Eroberung – Erfindung*. Trier: WVT, 241–261.

(1995): The Birth of a Multicultural Nation: Horace M. Kallen's Cultural Pluralism. UDO J. HEBEL and KARL ORTSEIFEN (Eds.): *Transatlantic Encounters: Studies in European-American Relations. Presented to Winfried Herget*. Trier: WVT, 347–358.

(1995): Conference Autobiographies. HANJO BERRESSEM and BERND HERZOGENRATH (Eds.): *Near Encounters: Festschrift for Richard Martin*. Frankfurt a.M.: Lang, 141–145.

(1996): Ethnic Fiction and Survival Ethics: Toni Morrison, Louise Erdrich, David Henry Hwang. GERHARD HOFFMANN and ALFRED HORNUNG (Eds.): *Ethics and Aesthetics: The Moral Turn of Postmodernism*. Heidelberg: Universitätsverlag Winter, 209–220. Shorter version: Moral Questions and Postmodern Fiction. NEIDE DE FARIA (Ed.): *Language and Literature Today: Proceedings of the XIXth Triennial Congress of the International Federation For Modern Languages and Literatures*. 3 vols., Brasilia: Universidade de Brasilia, vol. I, 81–88.

(1996): Postmoderne bis zur Gegenwart. HUBERT ZAPF (Ed.): *Geschichte der amerikanischen Literatur*. Stuttgart: Metzler, 304–375; rev. 2nd ed. (2004), 306–386.

(1997): Autobiography in Postmodern Times. HANS BERTENS and DOUWE FOKKEMA (Eds.): *Postmodernism*. Amsterdam: Benjamins, 221–233.

(1997): The Witchcraft of Fiction / The Fiction of Witchcraft. GERHARD HOFFMANN and ALFRED HORNUNG (Eds.): *Emotion in Postmodernism*. Heidelberg: Universitätsverlag Winter, 309–320.

(1997): Nordamerikanische Literatur im Zeitalter der Postmoderne. ULRIKE LIEDTKE and CLAUDIA SCHURZ (Eds.): *Jeder nach seiner Fasson: Musikalische Neuansätze heute*. Saarbrücken: PFAU, 225–244.

(1998): George Washington Cable's Literary Reconstruction: Creole Civilization and Cultural Change. WOLFGANG BINDER (Ed.): *Creoles and Cajuns: French Louisiana – La Louisiana Française*. Frankfurt a.M.: Lang, 229–246.

(1998): Paradise Lost in the Caribbean. JOCHEN ACHILLES and CARMEN BIRKLE (Eds.): *(Trans)Formations of Cultural Identity in the English-Speaking World, 1997*. Heidelberg: Universitätsverlag Winter, 161–173.

(1998): The Transatlantic Ties of Cultural Pluralism – Germany and the United States: Horace M. Kallen and Daniel Cohn-Bendit. KLAUS J. MILICH and JEFFREY M. PECK (Eds.): *Multiculturalism in Transit: A German-American Exchange*. New York: Berghahn, 213–228.

(1999): The Burning Langscape of Jamaica: Michelle Cliff's Vision of the Caribbean. ALFRED HORNUNG and ERNSTPETER RUHE (Eds.): *Postcolonialism and Autobiography*. Amsterdam: Rodopi, 87–97.

(1999): The Un-American Dream. *Amerikastudien / American Studies* 44.4: 445–453.

(2001): The Gospel according to Norman Mailer: Fictional Evangelists in Postmodern Times. GERHARD HOFFMANN and ALFRED HORNUNG (Eds.): *Postmodernism and the Fin de Siècle*. Heidelberg: Universitätsverlag Winter, 163–173.

(2002): Transculturations: A Transformation of European Civilization into American Culture. *Amerikastudien / American Studies* 47.1: 110–114.

(2003): Hungerkünstler und die jüdisch-amerikanische Literatur: Kafka, Roth, Ozick, Auster. DIETER LAMPING (Ed.): *Identität und Gedächtnis in der jüdischen Literatur nach 1945*. Berlin: Erich Schmidt, 116–126.

(2004): Introduction. ALFRED HORNUNG *Sexualities in American Culture*. Heidelberg: Universitätsverlag Winter, 1–8.

(2004): Flying Planes Can Be Dangerous: Ground Zero Literature. PETER FREESE and CHARLES B. HARRIS (Eds.): *Science, Technology, and the Humanities in Recent American Fiction*. Essen: Die Blaue Eule, 383–403.

(2004): Out of Place: Extraterritorial Existence and Autobiography. *ZAA* 52.4: 367–377.

(2005): Transnational American Studies: Response to the Presidential Address. *American Quarterly* 57.1: 67–73.

(2005): From the Jahrbuch für Amerikastudien to Amerikastudien / American Studies. *Amerikastudien / American Studies* 50.1/2: 11–52.

(2005): Out of Egypt, Out of Place: Humanist Critics at Home in America. KLAUS STIERSTORFER (Ed.): *Return to Postmodernism: Theory-Travel Writing-Autobiography. Festschrift in Honour of Ihab Hassan*. Heidelberg: Universitätsverlag Winter, 339–349.

(2006): Religion and Afro-Modernism: Claude McKay's Transatlantic Syncretism. WINFRIED HERGET and ALFRED HORNUNG (Eds.): *Religion in African-American Culture*. Heidelberg: Universitätsverlag Winter, 111–127.

(2006): Amerikanische Kreuzzüge: Geschichte – Kultur – Politik. PETR ROSEL (Ed.): *English in Space and Time. Englisch in Raum und Zeit: Forschungsbericht zu Ehren von Klaus Faiss*. Trier: WVT, 51–59.

(2006): The Autobiographical Formation of Modern American Theatre: Strindberg and O'Neill. SIGRID RIEUWERTS (Ed.): *History and Drama: Essays in Honour of Bernhard Reitz*. Trier: WVT, 154–163.

(2006): Unstoppable Creolization: The Evolution of the South into a Transnational Cultural Space. *The Global South*. Special Issue of *American Literature* 78.4: 859–867.

(2007): The Personal is the Fictional: Philip Roth's Return to the 1950s in *I Married a Communist* (with ANN MARIE FALLON). ANN MARIE FALLON and GERD HURM (Eds.): *Rebels without a Cause? Renegotiating the American 1950s*. Oxford: Lang, 77–93.

(2007): The History, Culture and Politics of US Crusades [In Chinese]. *Dialogue Transculturel* 20: 189–195.

(2007): The Autobiographical Formation of Modern American Theatre: Strindberg and O'Neill [In Chinese]. *Dialogue Transculturel* 21: 266–276.

(2007): Intercultural America: An Introduction. ALFRED HORNUNG (Ed.): *Intercultural America*. Heidelberg: Universitätsverlag Winter, ix–xix.

(2009): Ground Zero: Cultural Repercussions of 9/11 [in Chinese]. YAN XUNHUA (Ed.): *The United States After September 11: Changes and Continuities*. Beijing, 426–433.

(2009): Transcultural Life Writing. CORAL ANN HOWELLS, and EVA-MARIE KROLLER (Eds.): *The Cambridge History of Canadian Literature*. Cambridge: Cambridge University Press, 536–555.
(2009): European Perspectives of American Studies. MITA BANERJEE (Ed.): *Virtually American? Denationalizing Northern American Studies*. Heidelberg: Universitätsverlag Winter, 55–65
(2009): Die Entstehung der englischen Kurzgeschichte im 19. Jahrhundert. BERNHARD REITZ (Ed.): *"My Age Is As a Lusty Winter": Essays in Honour of Peter Erlebach and Thomas Michael Stein*. Mainz: MUSE, 63–70.
(2010): The Geographical History of Euro-American Lives: Riis, Antin, James, Stein. JELENA ŠESNIĆ (Ed.): *Sighting America / Sighting Modernity: Essays in Honor of Sonia Basic*. Zagreb: FF Press, 93–99.
(2009): Terrorist Violence and Transnational Memory: Jonathan Safran Foer and Don DeLillo. UDO HEBEL (Ed.): *Transnational American Memories*. Berlin: de Gruyter, 171–184.
(2010): Postmoderne bis zur Gegenwart. HUBERT ZAPF (Ed.): *Amerikanische Literaturgeschichte*. 3r ed. Stuttgart: Metzler, 305–392.
(2011): Planetary Citizenship. *The Journal of Transnational American Studies* 3.1: 38–46.
(2011): The Emergence of Transnational American Studies from Ground Zero. ELŻBIETA H. OLEKSY and WIESŁAW OLEKSY (Eds.): *Transatlantic Encounters. Philosophy, Media, Politics*. American Studies and Media, vol. III, Frankfurt a.M.: Lang, 185–199.
(2011): Ground Zero: Cultural Repercussions of 9/11. PRISCILLA ROBERTS, MEI RENYI, and YAN XUNHUA (Eds.): *China Views Nine-Eleven: Essays in Transnational American Studies*. Newcastle upon Tyne: Cambridge Scholars Publishing, 422–433.
(2011): Symposium: Redefinitions of Citizenship and Revisions of Cosmopolitanism–Transnational Perspectives (with GÜNTER H. LENZ, WILLIAM BOELHOWER, ROB KROES, and RÜDIGER KUNOW). *Journal of Transnational American Studies* 3.1: 1–53; 39–46.
(2012): ChinAmerica: Intercultural Relations for a Transnational World. UDO HEBEL (Ed.): *Transnational American Studies*. Heidelberg: Universitätsverlag Winter, 13–30.
(2012): Introduction: The South in the Age of Obama. *American Studies Journal* 56.
(2013): Chinese Garden Culture and Ecological Life Writing. ALFRED HORNUNG and ZHAO BAISHENG (Eds.): *Ecology and Life Writing*. Heidelberg: Universitätsverlag Winter, 299–307.
(2013): The Mediation of Public Lives: The Performance of Barack Obama's Self. CARSTEN HEINZE and ALFRED HORNUNG (Eds.): *Medialisierungsformen des (Auto-)Biographischen*. Konstanz: Universitätsverlag Konstanz, 203–214.
(2013): Therapeutic Intervention of Post-traumatic Stress Disorder by Chinese Medicine: Perspectives for Transdisciplinary Cooperation between Life Sciences and Humanities (with THOMAS EFFERTH and MITA BANERJEE). *Medicine Studies: An International Journal for History, Philosophy, and Ethics of Medicine & Allied Sciences* 3.4 (November 2012): 1–21.
(2014): The Planetary Vision of American Studies. MUSTAFA PULTAR (Ed.): *Kültürötesi Bir Gezgin: Gönül Pultar'a Armağan Kitabı – A Transcultural Wanderer: A Festschrift for Gönül Pultar*. İstanbul: Tetragon Yayınları, 269–276.
(2014): Pacific Triangles and Australasian American Studies. PAUL GILES and JANE PARK (Eds.): Special issue on "Pacific Triangles: Australasia, China and the Reorientation of American Studies" (Roundtable with DONALD PEASE and HEATHER NEILSON). *Australasian Journal of American Studies* 33.2 (December 2014): 162–175.
(2015): Maoism and Postmodernism. *European Review* 23.2: 261–272.
(2015): Life Sciences and Life Writing. *Anglia* 133.1: 37–52.
(2015): Jack London's Journeys of Life. PETER FREESE (Ed.): *The Journey of Life in American Life and Literature*. Heidelberg: Universitätsverlag Winter, 91–100.
(2016): Research Rating *Anglistik / Amerikanistik* of the German Council of Science and Humanities (with VERONICA KHLAVNA and BARBARA KORTE). MICHAEL OCHSNER, SVEN E.

HUG, and HANS-DIETRICH DANIEL (Eds.): *Research Assessment in the Humanities: Towards Criteria and Procedures*. Berlin: Springer, 219–233.

(2016): The Shaking Woman in the Media: Life Writing and Neuroscience. JOHANNA HARTMANN, CHRISTINE MARKS, and HUBERT ZAPF (Eds.): *Zones of Focused Ambiguity in Siri Hustvedt's Works*. Berlin: De Gruyter Mouton, 67–80.

(2016): Ecology and Life Writing. HUBERT ZAPF (Ed.): *Handbook of Ecocriticism and Cultural Ecology*. Berlin: De Gruyter, 334–348.

(2016): Touring Tibetan Villages: Life Writing on the Mountains. FREDERIKE OFFIZIER, MARC PRIEWE, and ARIANE SCHRÖDER (Eds.): *Crossroads in American Studies: Transnational and Biocultural Encounters. Essays in Honor of Rüdiger Kunow*. Heidelberg: Universitätsverlag Winter, 73–84.

(2016): Global Dialogism as an Episteme in the 21 Century. *Exploration & Debate* (ISSN:1004–2229. CN:31–1208 / C. Shanghai), 7 (2015): 69–70.

(2016): America: Global Affairs and Planetary Consciousness. YUAN SHU and DONALD E. PEASE (Eds.): *American Studies as Transnational Practice: Turning Towards the Transpacific*. Lebanon, NH: Dartmouth College Press, 340–364.

(2016): Auma Obama's Intercultural Life Writing. ALFRED HORNUNG (Ed.): *Obama and Transnational American Studies*. Heidelberg: Universitätsverlag Winter, 15–24.

(2017): Life Writing in and beyond the Anglophone World. *a/b: Auto/Biography Studies* 32.2: 179–181.

(2018): Le Pacte Philippe. *European Journal of Life Writing*, vol. VII: 25–31.

Miscellaneous

Contributions to *Abstracts of English Studies*, 1976–1978.

(1980): Rev. of *An Analysis of John Barth's 'Weltanschauung': His Views of Life and Literature*, by EVELYN GLASER-WOHRER. *Amerikastudien / American Studies* 25: 107–108.

(1980): Rev. of *Plot, Story, and the Novel: From Dickens and Poe to the Modern Period*, by ROBERT L. CASERIO. *Studies in the Novel* 12: 390–393.

(1980): Rev. of *Gesellschaftliche Funktionen fiktiver und faktographischer Prosa: Roman und Reportage im amerikanischen Muckraking Movement*, by KLAUS W. VOWE. *Amerikastudien / American Studies* 25: 341–344.

(1985): Rev. of *The Modern American Novel*, by MALCOLM BRADBURY and *Geschichte der amerikanischen Erzählkunst 1900–1950*, by FRANZ LINK. *Amerikastudien / American Studies* 30: 546–547.

(1986): Rev. of *The Metaphysical Novel in England and America: Dickens, Bulwer, Hawthorne, Melville*, by EDWIN M. EIGNER. *Anglia* 104: 254–256.

(1987): Contributions to J. SALZMAN (Ed.): *American Studies: An Annotated Bibliography*. New York: Cambridge University Press.

(1987): Rev. of *Entwicklungen im karibischen Raum 1960–1985*, by WOLFGANG BINDER, ed. *Matatu: Zeitschrift für afrikanische Kultur und Gesellschaft* 2: 128–132.

(1988): Rev. of *Der amerikanische Roman zwischen Naturalismus und Postmoderne 1930–1960*, by DIETER MEINDL. *Anglia*: 552–554.

(1988): The following four contributions in GERHARD HOFFMANN (Ed.): *Der zeitgenössische amerikanische Roman: Von der Moderne zur Postmoderne*. 3 vols., München: Fink:
Zwischen Realismus und Anti-Realismus: Malamud, Roth, Hawkes. Vol. II, 102–145.
Das Prinzip der absenten Präsenz in den Romanen Raymond Federmans und Ronald Sukenicks. Vol. III, 133–156.

Der amerikanische Gegenwartsroman und seine kulturelle Matrix (with RÜDIGER KUNOW). Vol. I, 45–80.

Bibliographie (with RÜDIGER KUNOW). Vol. III, 375–401.

(1990): Rev. of *Satire und Roman: Studien zur Theorie des Genrekonflikts und zur satirischen Erzählliteratur der USA von Brackenridge bis Vonnegut*, by HELMBRECHT BREINIG. *Anglia* 108.3/4: 555–557.

(1995): Mannheim: F.A. Brockhaus, 1988. Revision of entries for paperback edition in 8 vols. Mannheim: B.I.-Taschenbuchverlag.

(1998): PMLA Abroad. *PMLA* 113.5: 1147–1148.

(1999): Preface. ALFRED HORNUNG and ERNSTPETER RUHE (Eds.): *Postcolonialism and Autobiography*. Amsterdam: Rodopi, 1–5.

(2000): Preface. WILLIAM BOELHOWER and ALFRED HORNUNG (Eds.): *Multiculturalism and the American Self.* Heidelberg: Universitätsverlag Winter, VII–X.

(2006): Preface. WINFRIED HERGET and ALFRED HORNUNG *Religion in African-American Culture*. Heidelberg: Universitätsverlag Winter, 7–12.

(2009): Rev. of *Einführung in die Amerikanistik / American Studies*, by UDO J. HEBEL. *Amerikastudien / American Studies* 54.4: 683–685.

(2010): KRUG, INES, et. al. Interview with ALFRED HORNUNG. *As / peers* 3: 55–61.

(2012): Rev. of *In Quest of Nothing: Selected Essays 1998–2008*, by IHAB HASSAN. *Amerikastudien / American Studies* 57.3: 510–511.

(2010): Concluding Panel: Secularization and Its Discontent (with DAVID HALL, ROBERT BOYER, MUQTEDAR KHAN, and GESA MACKENTHUN). KORNELIA FREITAG et al (Eds.): *Religion in the United States*. Heidelberg: Universitätsverlag Winter, 283–303.

(2011): Featured Articles: Three Articles on Transnationalism and American Studies (with JOHN CARLOS ROWE and GREG ROBINSON), *Encyclopedia of American Studies Online*.

(2013): American Lives: Preface. ALFRED HORNUNG (Ed.): *American Lives*. Heidelberg: Universitätsverlag Winter, ix–xvii.

(2013): Editor's Note. *Journal of Transnational American Studies*, 5.1: 1–5.

(2013): Literature. CHRISTOF MAUCH and RÜDIGER B. WERSICH (Eds.): *USA-Lexikon*. 2nd ed. Berlin: Erich Schmidt, 635–647.

(2014): Response to Hubert Zapf. WINFRIED FLUCK, ERIK REDLING, SABINE SIELKE, and HUBERT ZAPF (Eds.): *American Studies Today*. Heidelberg: Universitätsverlag Winter, 253–259.

(2016): Rev. of *Jack London: A Writer's Fight for a Better America,* by CECELIA TICHI. *American Literary History Online Review, Series VI* 1.

(2016): Preface. ALFRED HORNUNG (Ed.): *Obama and Transnational American Studies*. Heidelberg: Universitätsverlag Winter, ix–xv.

(2017): Foreward. RICIA ANNE CHANSKY (Ed.): *Auto / Biography across the Americas: Transnational Themes in Life Writing*. New York: Routledge, xi–xii.